Georgia Milestones Assessment System Test Prep: Grade 4 English Language Arts Literacy (ELA) Practice Workbook and Full-length Online Assessments: GMAS Study Guide

Contributing Author	-	Mary Evans Rumley
Contributing Editor	-	Julie Turner
Contributing Editor	-	George Smith
Contributing Editor	-	Wendy Bundgaard
Executive Producer	-	Mukunda Krishnaswamy
Designer and Illustrator	-	Sowmya R.

First Edition - 2020

NGA Center/CCSSO are the sole owners and developers of the Common Core State Standards, which does not sponsor or endorse this product. © Copyright 2010. National Governors Association Center for Best Practices and Council of Chief State School Officers.

Georgia Department of Education is not affiliated to Lumos Learning. Georgia Department of Education, was not involved in the production of, and does not endorse these products or this site.

ISBN-10: 1-945730-79-X

ISBN-13: 978-1-945730-79-5

Printed in the United States of America

Last updated - July 2022

For permissions and additional information contact us

Lumos Information Services, LLC
PO Box 1575, Piscataway, NJ 08855-1575
http://www.LumosLearning.com

Email: support@lumoslearning.com
Tel: (732) 384-0146
Fax: (866) 283-6471

Lumos Learning
Developed by Expert Teachers

INTRODUCTION

About Lumos tedBook for GMAS Test Practice:
This book is specifically designed to improve student achievement on the GMAS. Students perform at their best on standardized tests when they feel comfortable with the test content as well as the test format. Lumos tedBook for GMAS test ensures this with meticulously designed practice that adheres to the guidelines provided by the GMAS for the number of questions, standards, difficulty level, sessions, question types, and duration.

About Lumos Smart Test Prep:
With more than a decade of experience and expertise in developing practice resources for standardized tests, Lumos Learning has developed the most efficient methodology to help students succeed on the state assessments (See Figure 1).

Lumos Smart Test Prep Mthodology offers students realistic GMAS assessment rehearsal along with providing an efficient pathway to overcome each proficiency gap.

The process starts with students taking the online diagnostic assessment. This online diagnostic test will help assess students' proficiency levels in various standards. With the completion of this diagnostic assessment, Lumos generates a personalized study plan with a standard checklist based on student performance in the online diagnostic test. Parents and educators can use this study plan to remediate the proficiency gaps with targeted standards-based practice available in the workbook.

After student completes the targeted remedial practice, they should attempt the second online GMAS practice test. Upon finishing the second assessment, Lumos will generate another individualized study plan by identifying topics that require more practice. Based on these practice suggestions, further skill building activities can be planned to help students gain comprehensive mastery needed to ensure success on the state assessment.

Lumos Smart Test Prep Methodology

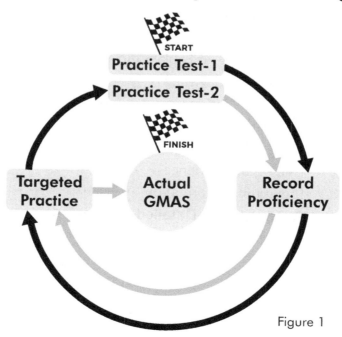

Figure 1

Table of Contents

Chapter 1

Lumos Smart Test Prep Methodology

Step 1: Access Online GMAS Practice Test

The online GMAS practice tests mirror the actual Georgia Milestones Assessment System (GMAS) in the number of questions, item types, test duration, test tools, and more.

After completing the test, your student will receive immediate feedback with detailed reports on standards mastery and a personalized study plan to overcome any learning gaps. With this study plan, use the next section of the workbook to practice.

Use the URL and access code provided below or scan the QR code to access the first GMAS practice test to get started.

URL	QR Code
Visit the URL below and place the book access code **www.lumoslearning.com/a/tedbooks** **Access Code: GMASG4E-91047-P**	

Step 2: Review the Personalized Study Plan Online

After students complete the online Practice Test 1, they can access their individualized study plan from the table of contents (Figure 2) Parents and Teachers can also review the study plan through their Lumos account (parent or teacher) portal.

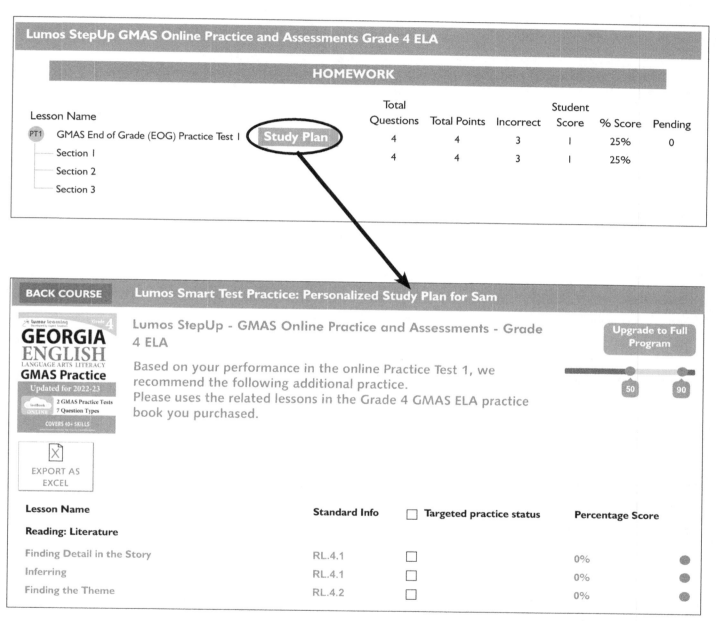

Figure 2

Step 3: Complete Targeted Practice

Using the information provided in the study plan report, complete the targeted practice using the appropriate lessons to overcome proficiency gaps. With lesson names included in the study plan, find the appropriate topics in this workbook and answer the questions provided. Students can refer to the answer key and detailed answers provided for each lesson to gain further understanding of the learning objective. Marking the completed lessons in the study plan after each practice session is recommended.(See Figure 3)

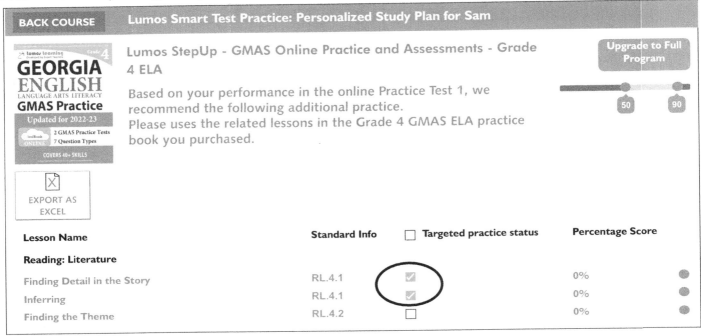

Figure 3

Step 4: Access the Practice Test 2 Online

After completing the targeted practice in this workbook, students should attempt the second GMAS practice test online. Using the student login name and password, login to the Lumos website to complete the second practice test.

Step 5: Repeat Targeted Practice

Repeat the targeted practice as per Step 3 using the second study plan report for Practice test 2 after completion of the second GMAS rehearsal.

Visit www.lumoslearning.com/a/lstp for more information on Lumos Smart Test Prep Methodology or Scan the QR Code

Step 1 → **Visit the URL given below and login to your account**

www.lumoslearning.com

Step 2 → **Click on 'My tedBooks' under the "Account" tab**

Place the Book Access Code and submit.

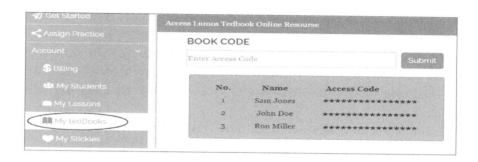

Step 3 → **Add the new book**

To add the new book for a registered student, choose the '**Existing Student**' button, select the student and submit.

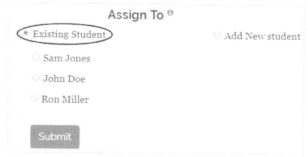

To add the new book for a new student, choose the '**Add New Student**' button and complete the student registration.

Assign To ⁰	
Existing Student	Add New student

Register Your TedBook

Student Name:*   Enter First Name   Enter Last Name

Student Login*

Password*

Submit

Test Taking Tips

1) **The day before the test,** make sure you get a good night's sleep.

2) **On the day of the test,** be sure to eat a good hearty breakfast! Also, be sure to arrive at school on time.

3) **During the test:**

- **Read each question carefully.**

  - Do not spend too much time on any one question. Work steadily through all questions in the section.
  - Attempt all the questions even if you are not sure of some answers.
  - If you run into a difficult question, eliminate as many choices as you can and then pick the best one from the remaining choices. Intelligent guessing will help you increase your score.
  - Also, mark the question so that if you have extra time, you can return to it after you reach the end of the section.
  - Some questions may refer to a graph, chart, or other kind of picture. Carefully review the infographics before answering the question.
  - Be sure to include explanations for your written responses and show all work.

- **While Answering Multiple-choice (EBSR) questions.**

  - Select the bubble corresponding to your answer choice.
  - Read all of the answer choices, even if think you have found the correct answer.

- **While Answering TECR questions.**

  - Read the directions of each question. Some might ask you to drag something, others to select, and still others to highlight. Follow all instructions of the question (or questions if it is in multiple parts)

Chapter 2- Reading: Literature

The objective of the Reading Literature standards is to ensure that the student is able to read and comprehend literature (which includes stories, drama and poetry) related to Grade 4.

To support students master the necessary skills, an example which will help the student understand the concepts related to the standard is given. Along with this, we encourage the student to go through the resources available online on EdSearch to gain an in-depth understanding of these concepts. EdSearch page for each lesson can be accessed with the help of the url or the QR code provided.

A small map is provided after each passage or text in which the student can enter the details as understood from the literary text. Doing this will help the student to refer to key points that help in answering the questions with ease.

Chapter 2

Lesson 1: Finding Detail in the Story

Before answering the questions related to this standard, let us understand the elements of a story (Plot, character and setting)

The Elements (Parts) Of a Story

1. Plot
The plot is the main story of a literary work. There can be more than one plot in a story, and there can be one or more secondary (less important) plots (also called subplots).

2. Character(s)
The actions and thoughts and emotions of the main (major) character(s) have the most influence, are the most important, to the plot. There may be other less important characters (known as minor or secondary characters) in the story, but they will have less influence on the plot.

3. Setting(s)
The setting(s) for a story are the location(s) and/or time period(s) at or in which the story takes place. There can be more than one setting and more than one time period in the same story.

You can scan the QR code given below or use the url to access additional EdSearch resources including videos and mobile apps related to *Finding Detail in the Story*.

Finding Detail in the Story

URL	QR Code
http://www.lumoslearning.com/a/rl41	

Question 1-3 are based on the story below.

After reading the story, enter the details in the map below. This will help you to answer the questions that follow.

"The Elephant Who Saw the World . . .," Mary started speaking. It was Friday, and the students had to share their creative writing stories of the week.

Mary loved writing, and this was her favorite part of the week, when they were able to make up stories for creative writing. She enjoyed it so much that she became really good at it. Even at home on the weekends when she didn't have much homework, she would sit in her room for hours and create stories to share with her friends and family. Her parents always supported her and were her biggest fans.

However, there was one part about every Friday at school that Mary did not enjoy, and that was when she had to share her story in front of the class. The teacher made all of the children share on Friday afternoons, and this made Mary very nervous. She was shy, and although she knew her teacher was right, she didn't like it.

Sitting and listening to the other children, Mary heard her name called. It was her turn to share. She got out of her seat slowly, walked to the front of the room and began.

1. What is the title of Mary's story?

Ⓐ The Elephant Who Liked Candy
Ⓑ The Elephant Who Saw the World
Ⓒ The Elephant Who Wanted to See the World
Ⓓ The Girl who Hated Writing

2. What didn't Mary like doing?

Ⓐ Writing stories
Ⓑ Having her stories corrected by the teacher
Ⓒ Reading her stories in front of the class
Ⓓ Going to school

3. Why was Mary reading her story in front of the class?

Ⓐ It was something she loved to do
Ⓑ Her classmates asked her to
Ⓒ Every Friday the children had to share their creative writing stories
Ⓓ Her parents wanted her to

Question 4 is based on the story below.

After reading the story, enter the details in the map below. This will help you to answer the questions that follow.

This year Jim and I had the most wonderful vacation compared to the one we took last year. We went to Hawaii, which is a much better place to visit than a hunting lodge in Alaska. The hotel we stayed in was a luxury suite. It included a big screen TV with all of the movie channels, a hot tub on the balcony, a small kitchen stocked with local fruits and vegetables, and a huge bed shaped like a pineapple. The weather in Hawaii could not have been any better. We enjoyed many hours on the beach sunbathing and playing volleyball. When we were not on the beach, we were in the ocean swimming or riding the waves on a surf board. Each night we enjoyed eating and dancing with all of our friends at a luau. Our week in Hawaii rushed by, making us wish we had planned a two-week vacation.

Conversely, the hunting lodge in Alaska that we stayed in had no TV, a shower with barely warm water, a small cooler for our food, and cots to sleep on each night. Furthermore, the room wasn't even the worst part of the vacation. The weather was terrible. It rained the entire time we were there. Even with the rain, our guide expected us to go on the all-day fishing trip that was part of our vacation package. All we caught on that fishing trip was a cold from the rain. After the third day in Alaska, we decided to end our nightmare, cut our trip short, and head for home. Without a doubt, we will be going back to Hawaii next year on our vacation.

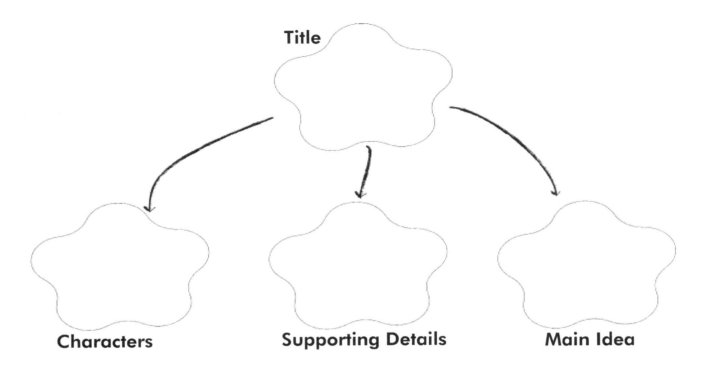

Title

Characters   **Supporting Details**   **Main Idea**

4. Which statement supports the author's opinion that their Alaska vacation was miserable?

Ⓐ Our week in Hawaii rushed by, making us wish we had planned a two-week vacation.
Ⓑ The weather in Hawaii could not have been better.
Ⓒ This year Jim and I had the most wonderful vacation compared to the one we took last year in Alaska.
Ⓓ After the third day in Alaska, we decided to end our nightmare, cut our trip short, and head for home.

Question 5 is based on the story below.

Disneyworld- Here We Come! Part - I

It was a hot summer day in June. My grandmother, Mom, my brother Daniel, my cousin Valerie, and I were headed out for a long vacation. We were, first, going to Mississippi and, then, on to Florida to Disneyworld. Talk about excitement!!! I couldn't contain myself and didn't sleep much at all the night before. Valerie was visiting us because her mom had gotten sick. My wonderful mom had volunteered for her to stay with us the entire summer. It was so cool! Valerie and I were best friends already, much less best cousins. We did everything together all the time, so having her come along was just another treat for me. Of course, I had rather my little snoopy brother, Daniel, didn't come, but oh well! After all, who can complain when you are going to Disneyworld!?

We had to stop in Mississippi to leave my grandmother off at her house before the vacation. That wasn't such a bad idea either, because I loved my grandmother's house, the creek to fish and swim in, and all of her things. The night before we had packed everything we needed. I just couldn't get to sleep. Finally, I must have fallen asleep because the alarm was going off and everyone was hurrying about the house. Dad had made us breakfast. He couldn't go due to his work schedule, but insisted we go and have fun. He even told me to ride the Teacups for him and the Train! Dad is such a laugh.

The car was packed, we had double checked everything and were waving goodbye! Another reason for the stop, in Mississippi, was for rest. It was going to be a long ride to even get that far in one day. Mom turned on the a/c in the car along with the radio, and we settled in. She had it on her favorite country music, so we sang along a few songs of Merle Haggard and Johnny Cash. I must have fallen asleep right after we left the house. The next thing I knew, Mom was waking me up. We had stopped for lunch at a Whataburger restaurant. My favorite, too! She said to eat hearty as we would not stop again until we reached my grandmother's house. I ate a whole Whataburger with fries and an ice tea. Valerie did, too! Daniel had a Jr. Whataburger and so did my grandmother. Mom had a salad with chicken. Back in the car, Valerie and I decided to play, I Spy. It is loads of fun! I was spying all kinds of things from license plates from Washington to blue jays in trees. Daniel tried to join in but would get mad if we guessed his too quickly. So he got out his video game and played it. Mom had to stop for gas, one time, right before we made it to the Mississippi state line. We always honk the horn when we cross over into Mississippi, but she said she was not going to do that since it was now getting dark and it might upset other drivers. I have a very smart mom.

5. What preparations did the author's family make to ensure that the trip was enjoyable? Write your answer in the box below using details from the story as evidence.

Question 6 is based on the story below.

Disneyworld- Here We Come! Part - II

Before we knew it, it was daylight again. Mom was hustling us out of bed and into the kitchen for breakfast. She said to eat hearty as we had many more miles to go before we reached our final destination. So thankful that my grandmother cooked her best oatmeal for us topped with cinnamon, brown sugar, strawberries, and whipped cream! Who could ask for anything more? Yummy!!

Then it was load back into the car and get on the road. This time Mom found an oldies radio station and she was singing along with Patsy Cline, Tennessee Ernie Ford, and Frank Sinatra. Talk about strange music that none of us knew except her! Valerie and I played a game of travel trivia which was sort of fun and of course, Daniel, was back on his video games!

For lunch we stopped at a roadside park and had the sandwiches our grandmother had packed for us along with an apple and sweet iced tea. When we got back on the road, not a sound could be heard. I figured out later that all of us kids had fallen asleep.

A loud bang woke us as Mom clapped her hands and proclaimed our arrival to the Holiday Inn at Disneyworld! I could not tell you who was the most excited as we were all yelling sounds of glee and running around the car to get our luggage out. Mom registered us for our room and we were giggling uncontrollably.

6. How did the author's mom wake the kids once she arrived at the hotel? Write your answer in the box below.

Question 7 is based on the story below.

Disneyworld- Here We Come! Part - III

When we were settled in to our room, Mom explained the sleeping arrangements. Valerie and I would get one of the queen size beds to share, Daniel would get the fold out couch in the living area, and Mom would get the other bed. She said that is night number one, then we will switch on the second night. I love it when my mom thinks of everyone and being fair to all. We were so happy we could have slept on the floor and not minded!! Mom called Dad to let him know we made it safe and sound. Then she called our grandmother, too. She also called Valerie's mom in the hospital so Valerie could talk to her and let her know all was well. Valerie's mom's health was improving daily, too.

Mom ordered pizza for us the first night. We went to bed without any complaining, so excited to be going to Disneyworld the next day!

Mom had picked up a map of the park when she had registered us, so she was busy planning our day while we were falling asleep.

The morning came with a clap and thunder outside of our room. What was going on, we had wondered? Mom explained that it was raining and that we would have breakfast in the hotel lobby and then see what happened. She did tell us that the hotel manager had explained to her that quite often the rains would start and stop during the summers at Kissimmee, Florida. We were not too disappointed after she said that. The hotel offers a free breakfast for everyone. That was definitely a plus in Mom's opinion.

Sure enough after we had eaten the sun came out. The hotel offered a trolley bus to the theme parks, so we opted to take that rather than worrying about parking and walking. Disneyworld stays open all day and late into the evening. Mom said she had mapped out our route to take so we could get to see most everything in our two days along with purchasing us the fast passes to avoid long line delays.

7. They were so happy, they could have slept anywhere and not minded. Write a sentence justifying this using evidence from the passage.

Question 8 is based on the story below.

Disneyworld- Here We Come! Part - V

Again, on the second day, we had the free breakfast and rode the trolley. It wasn't raining this time at all. Mom got out her map, and we began our day. Daniel wanted to go back and ride the Mad Tea Party again, but thankfully Mom said no to that.

We were able to go to Splash Mountain, the Jungle Cruise, the 7 Dwarf's Mine Train and much more. Mom did make a request of her own. She wanted to meet Mickey and Minnie Mouse who were scheduled to appear outside of the Cinderella Castle. She also said she wanted to listen to the Enchanted Tales with Belle and ride the Prince Charming Regal Carrousel. What a crazy silly Mom!

What we didn't know was that she had a plan. It was right after we left the carrousel that we heard fantastic sounds coming down the main street. Yes, parade time right before our eyes. Mom told us to come and sit. There we were on the side of the castle sitting on the ledge in perfect view of the parade. We asked her how she knew to stop there. She said one of the hotel clerks had told her how to find the spot and when to be there. The parade was magnificent to say the least. The characters actually stopped in front of us and performed. Wow! We couldn't have planned it any better.

After the parade, we went to A Pirate's Adventure, Tomorrowland Speedway, and Big Thunder Mountain. Mom said we needed to head toward the front entrance as it was time for fireworks, and we needed to be ready. We got there just in time. The lights lit up the sky behind the Cinderella Castle and throughout Disneyworld. Just picture it!
What a perfect ending to our vacation!

8. **What did not happen on the second day that happened twice on the first day of their visit to Disneyworld? Enter your answer in the box below.**

    It did not _____ on the second day.

    ┌───┐
    │   │
    │   │
    │   │
    └───┘

Question 9 and 10 are based on the story below.

Roses are Red

Everyone knows the poem that goes- Roses are Red, Violets are blue, Sugar is sweet and so are you! But I am not talking poetry right now. I am talking about the roses that Aunt Molly has in her yard. Yeah, you see the pictures of them! Aren't they so beautiful? How does she get them that way?

Notice the two pictures on the page. The white roses come from a huge rose bush. I call it a tree, It is so big! My aunt started that one with a branch cut off of our Great Grandma Witt's rose bush down in Centerville. She brought it home when Great Grandma was still alive. Grandma Witt told her to cut it off, wrap it in wet paper towels, put it in a bucket of red clay dirt from her front yard, and take it home. So my aunt did.

When she got home with it, she dug a deep hole in her backyard. She put the clay dirt in first, then made another hole in the middle of that. Next, she put in rose fertilizer to help it grow. Then, she put in the branch from the rose bush. After that, she pushed the dirt in real tight. When she got ready to water it, she didn't water it straight at the branch. Instead, she watered it slightly to the side of the hole at an angle. She also took a banana peel the next day and wrapped it around where the bottom of the branch was at. An old man had told her to do that whenever she planted rose bushes. I had no idea that you could grow a rose bush just from a branch. You can. The rose bush will start to make new roots under the soil. Bingo, a rose bush!

Now, look at the second red rose picture. This is a rose bush from Tyler, Texas. That town is world famous for growing the best roses. Aunt Molly bought that one about a year ago. It was on sale, she said, or she would never have paid full price for it. She put it on the side of her house near the car-port. She had wanted to grow roses there for a long time. At first, she told me that it was not looking very healthy and she knew why it had been on sale. However, she kept pampering it, adding fresh clay soil around it. Of course, she had to do the banana peel thing to it, too! During the winter, Aunt Molly was afraid it was dead. But to her surprise, it came back bigger than ever. She said it produces cluster roses almost every week.

Well, apparently, she knows how to grow roses. It all seems to work just fine for Aunt Molly.

9. Aunt Molly used a special technique when planting the rose branch from Great Grandma Witt's house. Below are the steps she followed. Enter the correct order sequence in the box given below.

> A. She put a banana peel around the bottom of the branch.
> B. She watered the rose branch at an angle after it was planted.
> C. She added the clay dirt to the hole.
> D. She dug a deep hole.

10. Why did Aunt Molly think that the second rose bush was going to die? Use details in the selection to support your answer.
   Write your answer in the box below.

Question 11 is based on the story below.

THE SECRET GARDEN by Frances Hodgson Burnett - Part 1

CHAPTER I

THERE IS NO ONE LEFT

When Mary Lennox was sent to Misselthwaite Manor to live with her uncle everybody said she was the most disagreeable-looking child ever seen. It was true, too. She had a little thin face and a little thin body, thin light hair and a sour expression. Her hair was yellow, and her face was yellow because she had been born in India and had always been ill in one way or another. Her father had held a position under the English Government and had always been busy and ill himself, and her mother had been a great beauty who cared only to go to parties and amuse herself with gay people. She had not wanted a little girl at all, and when Mary was born she handed her over to the care of an Ayah, who was made to understand that if she wished to please the Mem Sahib she must keep the child out of sight as much as possible. So when she was a sickly, fretful, ugly baby she was kept out of the way, and when she became a sickly, fretful, toddler she was kept out of the way also. She never remembered seeing familiarly anything but the dark faces of her Ayah and the other native servants, and as they always obeyed her and gave her her own way in everything, because the Mem Sahib would be angry if she was disturbed by her crying, by the time she was six years old she was as tyrannical and a selfish little pig as ever lived. The young English governess who came to teach her to read and write disliked her so much that she gave up her place in three months, and when other governesses came to try to fill it they always went away in a shorter time than the first one. So if Mary had not chosen to really want to know how to read books she would never have learned her letters at all.

One frightfully hot morning, when she was about nine years old, she awakened feeling very cross, and she became crosser still when she saw that the servant who stood by her bedside was not her Ayah.

"Why did you come?" she said to the strange woman. "I will not let you stay. Send my Ayah to me." The woman looked frightened, but she only stammered that the Ayah could not come and when Mary threw herself into a passion and beat and kicked her, she looked only more frightened and repeated that it was not possible for the Ayah to come to Missie Sahib.

There was something mysterious in the air that morning. Nothing was done in its regular order and several of the native servants seemed missing, while those whom Mary saw slunk or hurried about with ashy and scared faces. But no one would tell her anything and her Ayah did not come. She was actually left alone as the morning went on, and at last she wandered out into the garden and began to play by herself under a tree near the veranda. She pretended that she was making a flower-bed, and she stuck big scarlet hibiscus blossoms into little heaps of earth, all the time growing more and more angry and muttering to herself the things she would say and the names she would call Saidie when she returned.

"Pig! Pig! Daughter of Pigs!" she said, because to call a native a pig is the worst insult of all. She was grinding her teeth and saying this over and over again when she heard her mother come out on the veranda with some one. She was with a fair young man and they stood talking together in low strange voices. Mary knew the fair young man who looked like a boy. She had heard that he was a very young officer who had just come from England. The child stared at him, but she stared most at her mother. She always did this when she had a chance to see her, because the Mem Sahib— Mary used to call her that oftener than anything else—was such a tall, slim, pretty person and wore such lovely clothes. Her hair was like curly silk and she had a delicate little nose which seemed to be disdaining things, and she had large laughing eyes. All her clothes were thin and floating, and Mary said they were "full of lace." They looked fuller of lace than ever this morning, but her eyes were not laughing at all. They were large and scared and lifted imploringly to the fair boy officer's face. "Is it so very bad? Oh, is it?" Mary heard her say.

"Awfully," the young man answered in a trembling voice. "Awfully, Mrs. Lennox. You ought to have gone to the hills two weeks ago." The Mem Sahib wrung her hands.
"Oh, I know I ought!" she cried. "I only stayed to go to that silly dinner party. What a fool I was!" At that very moment such a loud sound of wailing broke out from the servants' quarters that she clutched the young man's arm, and Mary stood shivering from head to foot. The wailing grew wilder and wilder. "What is it? What is it?" Mrs. Lennox gasped.

"Some one has died," answered the boy officer. "You did not say it had broken out among your servants."

"I did not know!" the Mem Sahib cried. "Come with me! Come with me!" and she turned and ran into the house.

11. **Why did Mary get upset when she woke up that morning? Write your answer in the box below using details from the passage for support of your answer.**

Question 12 is based on the story below.

Sandy's Soccer

Sandy Thomas enrolled in soccer when she was in first grade. She had loved to watch the soccer games on TV with her dad. Sandy's dad was a high school soccer coach. It was his passion, as well as hers. Sandy was elated when she convinced her parents to let her play soccer rather than take ballet. Her friends were astonished as they had all signed up for ballet and expected her to, as well.

The team she was on this year was called, The Blue Jets. She was playing her favorite position, goalie. She practices at home with a goal her dad made for her. He tries to make the goal and she blocks it almost every time.

12. Which of the following shows details from the story? Select all that apply.

    Ⓐ Sandy and her dad loved soccer.
    Ⓑ Sandy plays goalie.
    Ⓒ She and her dad practice a lot.
    Ⓓ None of the above

Question 13 is based on the passage below.

John F. Kennedy

John Fitzgerald "Jack" Kennedy (May 29, 1917 – November 22, 1963)

President John F. Kennedy, our 35th President of the United States, has often been referred to as simply JFK. He was President from January 1961 until he was assassinated in November 1963. He is known for his famous quote, "Ask not what your country can do for you. Ask what you can do for your country." He was the youngest US President elected and the only Roman Catholic to serve office. He is also the only US President to win the famed Pulitzer's Prize.

He is well known for his advancements in aiding the Civil Rights Movement. During his term, the Peace Corps was established, the "New Frontier" domestic program, and the Cuban Missile Crisis also occurred.

He was killed by Lee Harvey Oswald in Dallas, Texas. It is thought that there was a conspiracy to commit the murder. Jack Ruby then killed Oswald in a jail corridor. The majority of Americans alive during the time believed that it was not done simply by just one man.

13. Which of the following apply to President Kennedy? Select all that are found as facts in the article.

    Ⓐ President Kennedy was the youngest man to be elected President to the US.
    Ⓑ He did not win the Pulitzer's Prize.
    Ⓒ He supported the Civil Rights Movement.
    Ⓓ All of the above.

Question 14 is based on the story below.

THE THREE GOLDEN APPLES - By Nathaniel Hawthorne

Part 1

Did you ever hear of the golden apples, that grew in the garden of the Hesperides? Ah, those were such apples as would bring a great price, by the bushel, if any of them could be found growing in the orchards of nowadays! But there is not, I suppose, a graft of that wonderful fruit on a single tree in the wide world. Not so much as a seed of those apples exists any longer.

And, even in the old, old, half-forgotten times, before the garden of the Hesperides was overrun with weeds, a great many people doubted whether there could be real trees that bore apples of solid gold upon their branches. All had heard of them, but nobody remembered to have seen any. Children, nevertheless, used to listen, open-mouthed, to stories of the golden apple-tree, and resolved to discover it, when they should be big enough. Adventurous young men, who desired to do a braver thing than any of their fellows, set out in quest of this fruit. Many of them returned no more; none of them brought back the apples. No wonder that they found it impossible to gather them! It is said that there was a dragon beneath the tree, with a hundred terrible heads, fifty of which were always on the watch, while the other fifty slept.

In my opinion, it was hardly worth running so much risk for the sake of a solid golden apple. Had the apples been sweet, mellow, and juicy, indeed that would be another matter. There might then have been some sense in trying to get at them, in spite of the hundred-headed dragon.

But, as I have already told you, it was quite a common thing with young persons, when tired of too much peace and rest, to go in search of the garden of the Hesperides. And once the adventure was undertaken by a hero who had enjoyed very little peace or rest since he came into the world. At the time of which I am going to speak, he was wandering through the pleasant land of Italy, with a mighty club in his hand, and a bow and quiver slung across his shoulders. He was wrapt in the skin of the biggest and fiercest lion that ever had been seen, and which he himself had killed; and though, on the whole, he was kind, and generous, and noble, there was a good deal of the lion's fierceness in his heart. As he went on his way, he continually inquired whether that was the right road to the famous garden. But none of the country people knew anything about the matter, and many looked as if they would have laughed at the question, if the stranger had not carried so very big a club.

14. Part A

Fill in the blanks with vocabulary from Part 1.

The golden apples grew in the garden of _____.

Part B

Children listened _____ to the stories of the golden apples.

Part C

_____ young men set on a quest to find the apples.

Part D

He was _____ in the skin of a fierce lion.

Chapter 2

Lesson 2: Inferring

You can scan the QR code given below or use the url to access additional EdSearch resources including videos and mobile apps related to *Inferring*.

ed Search	*Inferring*	
URL		**QR Code**
http://www.lumoslearning.com/a/rl41		

Question 1 is based on the poem below.

> I found a shell, a curly one;
> Lying on the sand.
> I picked it up and took it home,
> Held tightly in my hand.
> Mommy looked at it and then,
> She held it to my ear,
> And from the shell there came a song
> Soft and sweet and clear.
> I was surprised, I listened hard,
> And it was really true:
> If you can find a nice big shell,
> You'll hear the singing too.
> --Unknown

1. Why was the poet surprised?

   Ⓐ She found a curly shell on the beach.
   Ⓑ Her mother put it to her ear.
   Ⓒ She didn't expect to hear a song from the shell.
   Ⓓ She was frightened of the shell.

Question 2 is based on the story below.

After reading the story, enter the details in the map below. This will help you to answer the questions that follow.

Alexander the Great

Nearly two thousand five hundred years ago, there lived a king called Alexander the Great. He was the son of Philip II of Macedonia. When prince Alexander was a boy, a magnificent horse that was for sale was brought to the court of his father. The animal was to be sold for thirteen talents. Talents are ancient coins. Many were eager to buy the horse, but no one could get close enough to saddle the restless animal. He was wild and impossible to ride.

Alexander pleaded with his father to let him try. Realizing that the horse was terrified of its own shadow, he turned the horse towards the sun, so that its shadow fell behind it. This calmed the horse, and the prince proudly rode away. Observing this, his father said, "My son, look for a kingdom worthy of your greatness. Macedonia is too small for you."

That is exactly what Alexander tried to do when he grew up. He fought many battles and always rode Bucephalus (that was the horse's name.) Friendship and trust grew between the man and his horse.

When Bucephalus died of wounds received in battle, Alexander was heartbroken and deeply mourned the loss of his horse.

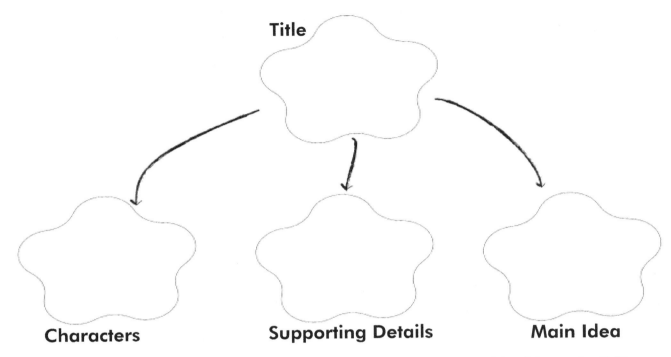

2. According to the passage, why do you think the horse was unrideable and wild?

    Ⓐ because it was angry
    Ⓑ because it was hungry
    Ⓒ because it was scared
    Ⓓ because it was good at riding

3. From the passage below. What can you infer from Cindy's actions?

Cindy's mom called her to supper. When Cindy arrived in the kitchen, she looked at the food on the stove and made a face. She looked in the freezer and saw a frozen pizza and asked her mom if she could cook it instead.

    Ⓐ That she was excited about what her mother had cooked
    Ⓑ She was not very hungry for dinner.
    Ⓒ She didn't think the meal was ready.
    Ⓓ She didn't like what her mother cooked for dinner.

Question 4 and 5 are based on the story below.

After reading the story, enter the details in the map below. This will help you to answer the questions that follow.

Mary loves writing stories

"The Elephant Who Saw the World," Mary started speaking. It was Friday, and the students had to share their creative writing stories of the week.

Mary loved writing, and this part of the week, when they were able to make up stories for creative writing, was her favorite part. She enjoyed it so much that she became really good at it. When she was home on the weekends and she didn't have much homework, she would sit in her room for hours and create stories to share with her friends and family. Her parents always supported her and were her biggest fans.

However, there was one part about every Friday at school that Mary did not enjoy, and that was when she had to share her story in front of the class. The teacher made all of the children share on Friday afternoons, and this made Mary very nervous. She was shy, and although she knew her teacher was right, she didn't like it.

After sitting and listening to the other children's share, Mary finally heard her name called. She knew it was her turn to share. She got out of her seat slowly, walked to the front of the room and began.

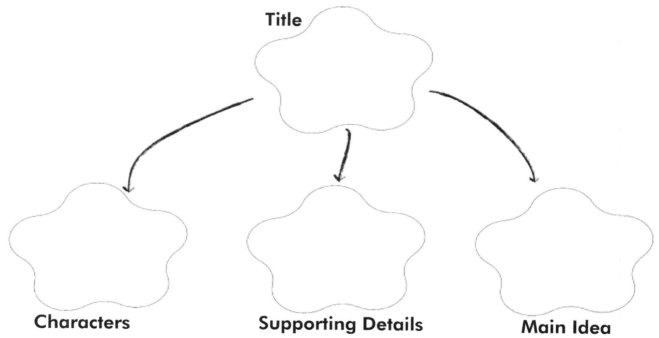

4. **What do you think Mary did next?**

Ⓐ Mary began running out of the classroom.
Ⓑ Mary began reading her story in front of the class.
Ⓒ Mary began to cry because she was scared.
Ⓓ Mary began to tell the teacher she didn't write a story.

5. Why did Mary's parents support her love for writing stories?

Ⓐ so she wouldn't sit in front of the TV all day
Ⓑ to make sure she stayed busy
Ⓒ because she liked to write and was good at it
Ⓓ to make sure she kept her writing skills better than everyone else's

6. From the passage below, where do you think Ben and his dad were going?

As Ben woke up on Sunday, he was thinking that it would be great to do something special with his dad that day, as he didn't see him very often. When he looked outside the window, he noticed that the sun was out, but a new blanket of snow had fallen during the night. He was getting dressed thinking of what they could do when all of a sudden he heard his dad say, "It is a sunny day. Grab your skis on the way down!" Ben ran to get his skis and they left.

Ⓐ to the zoo
Ⓑ to the mall
Ⓒ to the mountain
Ⓓ to school

Question 7 and 8 are based on the passage below.

Thelma lay on the windowsill. She heard a loud noise, so she lifted her head and looked outside. The noise woke her up, and now she wasn't happy. The color of the sky was changing from dark to a light pinkish yellow,and she could hear the birds starting to chirp. Her back arched high as she stretched a deep stretch. She decided it was time to go and find some food because she was starting to get hungry.

7. From the passage below, at what time of day do you think this is happening?

Ⓐ in the evening at sunset
Ⓑ in the early afternoon
Ⓒ in the early morning at sunrise
Ⓓ in the middle of the day

8. What kind of animal is Thelma?

Ⓐ a horse
Ⓑ a cricket
Ⓒ a mouse
Ⓓ a cat

Question 9 and 10 are based on the passage below.

Before going to bed on Friday night, Susie's parents told her that they had a surprise planned for the weekend and that she would have to wake up really early on Saturday morning. When she woke up, they left the house quickly and started driving. While in the car, Susie looked outside to see if she could figure out where they were going. She noticed that it was getting really hot out and the sun was shining brightly. Then she noticed that the surfboards were in the car. Finally, they stopped, and Susie said, "I know where we are going!"

9. From the passage below, what season is it?

Ⓐ summer
Ⓑ spring
Ⓒ winter
Ⓓ fall

10. Where do Susie and her family probably live?

Ⓐ in Alaska
Ⓑ close to the beach
Ⓒ in the mountains
Ⓓ in Arkansas

Question 11 is based on the story below.

DISNEYWORLD- HERE WE COME! PART - V

Again on the second day, we had the free breakfast and rode the trolley. It wasn't raining this time at all. Mom got out her map and we began our day. Daniel wanted to go back and ride the Mad Tea Party again, but thankfully Mom said no to that.
We were able to go to Splash Mountain, the Jungle Cruise, the 7 Dwarf's Mine Train and much more. Mom did make a request of her own. She wanted to meet Mickey and Minnie Mouse who were scheduled to appear outside of the Cinderella Castle. She also said she wanted to listen to the Enchanted Tales with Belle and ride the Prince Charming Regal Carrousel. What a crazy silly Mom!
What we didn't know was that she had a plan. It was right after we left the carrousel that we heard fantastic sounds coming down the main street. Yes, parade time right before our eyes. Mom told us to come and sit. There we were on the side of the castle sitting on the ledge in perfect view of the parade. We asked her how she knew to stop there. She said one of the hotel clerks had told her how to find the spot and when to be there. The parade was magnificent to say the least. The characters actually stopped in front of us and performed. Wow! We couldn't have planned it any better.
After the parade we went to A Pirate's Adventure and Tomorrowland Speedway, and Big Thunder Mountain. Mom said we needed to head toward the front entrance as it was time for fireworks and we needed to be ready. We got there just in time. The lights lit up the sky behind the Cinderella Castle and throughout Disneyworld. Just picture it! What a perfect ending to our vacation

11. What did the author describe and ask you as a reader to visualize near the end of the story? Write your answer below.

Question 12 and 13 are based on the story below.

Celia Cruz

She was born in Havana, Cuba in 1925. She was told by her grandmother that she could sing before she could talk. Her grandmother used to laugh and tell the family that she practiced her singing at night. (She was thought to have cried most of the night.) Cruz' work in radio during the 1940's in Cuba led to her fame and she traveled throughout Latin America with a female band. She won her first award singing on an amateur hour TV show. Cruz sang a version of a tango song that was very popular in Cuba.

In the 1950's Celia Cruz joined the Sonora Mantancera as a lead female singer. Then she was able to go to the Tropicana, the best establishment for Cuban music. If you performed at the Tropicana, you had made it in the singing world of Cubans.

She then went to Mexico for a one year contract right before Fidel Castro took over Cuba. She and her band never returned. Cruz moved to New York in 1961. By this time she was a well- known Cuban singer and independent from her band. She became known as the "Salsa Queen" due to her style of music. During the 1990's she gained great popularity among the younger generations, as her music reappeared. Cruz has been honored by five Presidents of the United States. She died of brain cancer in 2003, but her music and legend continue to thrive throughout the world.

12. Use vocabulary from the passage to complete the sentence.

She was known as the _____.

13. She did or did not return to Cuba? Write your answer in the box below as "yes" or "no"

Question 14 is based on the story below.

The Wolf and the Lamb

A Wolf, meeting with a Lamb astray from the fold, resolved not to lay violent hands on him, but to find some plea, which should justify to the Lamb himself his right to eat him. He then addressed him: "Sirrah, last year you grossly insulted me." "Indeed," bleated the Lamb in a mournful tone of voice, "I was not then born." Then said the Wolf: "You feed in my pasture." "No, good sir," replied the Lamb, "I have not yet tasted grass." Again said the Wolf: "You drink from my well." "No," exclaimed the Lamb, "I never yet drank water, for as yet my mother's milk is both food and drink to me." On which the Wolf seized him, and ate him up, saying: "Well! I won't remain supperless, even though you refute every one of my imputations." The tyrant will always find a pretext for his tyranny, and it is useless for the innocent to try by reasoning to get justice, when the oppressor intends to be unjust.

14. What was the wolf trying to do when he wanted to eat the lamb? Circle the correct answer choice

Ⓐ Justify his pleasure.
Ⓑ Prove he was stronger.
Ⓒ Not eat the lamb.
Ⓓ All of the above.

Question 15 is based on the story below.

The Dog, the Rooster and the Fox

A Dog and a Rooster, traveling together, took shelter at night in a thick wood. The Rooster perched himself on a high branch, while the Dog found a bed at the foot of the tree. When morning dawned, the Rooster, as usual, crowed very loudly. A Fox, hearing the sound, and wishing to make a breakfast on him, came and stood under the branches, saying how earnestly he desired to make the acquaintance of the owner of so sweet voice."If you will admit me," said he, "I should very much like to spend the day with you."The Rooster said: "Sir, do me the favor to go round and wake up my porter, that he may open the door, and let you in." On the Fox approaching the tree, the Dog sprang out and caught him and quickly tore him in pieces.Those who try to entrap others are often caught by their own schemes.

15. **What was the fox's intent? Write a sentence in the box below to explain your answer using evidence found in the fable.**

Chapter 2

Lesson 3: Finding the Theme

Let us understand the concept with an example.

Fred Goes to the Dentist

Fred had never been to the dentist. All of his life he had heard horror stories about the buzzing drills, the huge needles, and the scary tools the dentist used to torture his patients. Since none of his teeth were hurting, Fred just couldn't understand why his mom was insisting on taking him to see one. She told him that it was important to visit the dentist each year and to get your teeth cleaned. That was just silly to Fred since he cleaned his teeth everyday by brushing and flossing them. But nothing would change his mother's mind. He found it hard to believe that she would think it was a good idea to take him somewhere to be tortured. However, he had no choice but to go.

On the way to the dentist, Fred's imagination went wild. He pictured walking into a room with a huge chair that the dentist would strap him to. He could just see the dentist pulling out a huge drill and drilling his tooth while his mother and several others held him in the chair. By the time he got to the dentist's office, he was shaking all over. To his surprise, the office was nothing like he expected. The dentist was nice and the chair was comfortable and didn't have any straps with which to tie him to it. He looked around the room and didn't see any huge drills or torture devices. All the dentist did was look in his mouth, show him how to properly brush and floss his teeth, and give him a balloon. His mom made an appointment to have his teeth cleaned. Maybe this wouldn't be as bad as he had thought it would be.

Determine the theme from details in the text.

The title is very good because it tells the reader what the subject (or main idea or theme) of the text is: Fred's visit to the dentist. More details about the theme are: Fred's imagination about what a visit to a dentist would be like ("All of his life he had heard horror stories... dentist used to torture his patients.";"... hard to believe that she would think it was a good idea to take him somewhere to be tortured."; "...huge chair that the dentist would strap him to."; "...dentist pulling out a huge drill and drilling his tooth while his mother and several others held him in the chair.")

But there is another theme here too: about how Fred's attitude changed during the visit, from fear to calm, from negative to positive.

Summarize the text.

Summarizing the text means restating the most important ideas or events in as few words as possible, without leaving out any important details. Here are some examples of questions you can use to help you summarize a text.

1. Who is the main character? Fred.
2. What did the character want? To avoid going to the dentist.
3. What was the problem? He was very frightened.
4. How did the character try to solve the problem? He didn't. His mom forced him to go.
5. What was the resolution? After being there for his appointment, he realized that his fears were not realistic.

Here is an example of what you might write to summarize the text:

Fred's mom was taking him for his first visit to the dentist. He was frightened because he had heard horror stories about other people's visits to dentists. He also did not see why he had to go for a cleaning since he flossed and brushed his teeth every day. But once he got there, he realized that all of his fears were not realistic. His attitude changed from being fearful to being more relaxed, so he was no longer afraid of going back for another visit.

You can scan the QR code given below or use the url to access additional EdSearch resources including videos and mobile apps related to *Finding the Theme*.

ed Search

Finding the Theme

URL	QR Code
http://www.lumoslearning.com/a/rl42	

Question 1 is based on the story below.

After reading the story, enter the details in the map below. This will help you to answer the questions that follow.

Fred Goes to the Dentist

Fred had never been to the dentist. All of his life he had heard horror stories about the buzzing drills, the huge needles, and the scary tools that the dentist used to torture his patients. Since none of his teeth were hurting, Fred just couldn't understand why his mom was insisting on taking him to the dentist. She told him that it was important to visit the dentist each year to have his teeth checked and cleaned. This seemed silly to Fred because he cleaned his teeth everyday by brushing and flossing them, but nothing would change his mother's mind. He found it hard to believe that she would think it was a good idea to take him somewhere to be tortured. However, he had no choice but to go.

On the way to the dentist, Fred's imagination went wild. He pictured walking into a room with a huge chair that the dentist would strap him to. He could just see the dentist pulling out a huge drill and drilling his tooth while his mother and several others held him in the chair. By the time he got to the dentist's office, he was shaking all over.

Surprisingly, the office was nothing like he expected. The dentist was friendly, and the chair was comfortable. It didn't have any straps. He looked around the room and didn't see any huge drills or torture devices. He was relieved when all the dentist did was look in his mouth, show him how to properly brush and floss his teeth, and give him a balloon. His mom made another appointment to have his teeth cleaned in six months. Maybe this wouldn't be as bad as he had thought it would be.

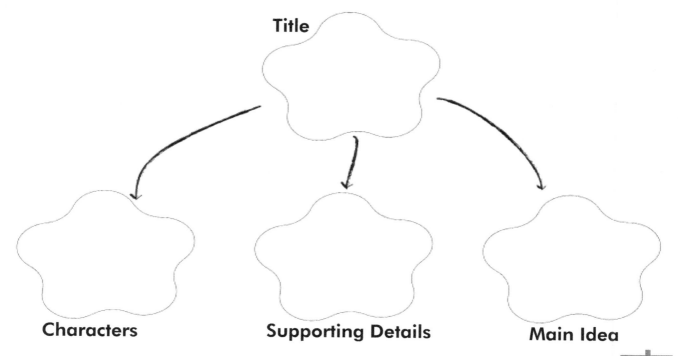

Title

Characters   **Supporting Details**   **Main Idea**

1. What is the theme of the passage?

Ⓐ Dentists are good people so don't worry about visiting them.
Ⓑ Moms usually know best so trust them.
Ⓒ Things are usually not as bad as you think they will be.
Ⓓ An imagination is good but it can make things seem scary sometimes.

2. What is the theme of the below passage?

Opal walked into the store not wanting to do what she had planned. She knew when she took the makeup without paying for it that it was wrong. She felt so guilty. She knew she couldn't keep the makeup. So, gathering up all of her courage, she walked over to the security officer and confessed what she had done. He admonished her for shoplifting but let her off with a warning because she had been honest. She felt very relieved.

Ⓐ The unknown can be scary
Ⓑ It is best to be honest
Ⓒ Don't cry over spilled milk
Ⓓ Mom knows best

3. What is the theme of the below passage?

Libby's grandmother didn't have much money, so she couldn't buy Libby an expensive present for Christmas like her other grandmother could. She didn't want to buy her a cheap toy that wouldn't last long, but she just couldn't afford the things that were on Libby's wish list. She decided to make Libby a quilt. She was concerned that her granddaughter wouldn't like the gift, but it was the best that she could do.

When Christmas day arrived, Grandmother went to Libby's house. She saw all of the nice gifts that her granddaughter had received. She was worried as Libby began to open her present. Libby squealed with delight when she saw the handmade quilt. She ran and hugged her grandmother and thanked her. She ran and put the new quilt on her bed. The rest of the day she talked about how much she loved the quilt, especially since her grandmother had made it all by hand.

Ⓐ It is not the cost of the gift that matters but the thought and love put into it.
Ⓑ Expensive gifts are better than hand-made ones.
Ⓒ Hand-made gifts are as good as expensive toys.
Ⓓ Good manners have positive results.

4. Which of the following is NOT the theme of this passage?

Ⓐ It's not the cost of the gift that matters.
Ⓑ Expensive gifts are better than homemade ones.
Ⓒ A gift from the heart is valuable.
Ⓓ A gift made with love is the best gift of all.

5. What is the theme of the below passage?

Today was Rhonda's first day at her new school. She was very nervous and wished that she was going back to her old school; but, that was impossible since her family had moved. Although she didn't have many friends at her old school, she would still prefer being back there because she knew the teachers, the routines, and the rules.

The first day, Rhonda met three girls that she really liked. They had all of their classes together, so she spent much of the day with them. But Rhonda's favorite discovery was that this school offered art and music classes; her old school had neither. Rhonda and her new friends had a great time in art that first day. She couldn't wait to go to music tomorrow. Maybe this new school would work out well after all.

Ⓐ Friends help each other
Ⓑ Bullying hurts everyone
Ⓒ Change can be good
Ⓓ It's OK to be different

6. What can you learn from the below passage?

Polly's little brother begged her to read him a story. She told him to go away, that she didn't have time to bother with him. But, a few minutes later, he came back and asked her again. This time, she yelled at him to go away, and she heard him crying as he ran down the hallway. Later, when she went to the family room, her mother told her that she had hurt her brother's feelings. Polly looked over at him and told him that she was sorry. Although she apologized, her little brother's feelings were still hurt; he felt like Polly didn't like to spend time with him. Polly's mom told her that sometimes words were not enough. So, when Polly got his favorite book and asked him to read with her, her little brother smiled and ran to sit by Polly. He hugged her and told her that she was the best big sister a brother could have.

Ⓐ Knowledge is power
Ⓑ Never give up
Ⓒ Face your fears
Ⓓ Actions speak louder than words

Question 7 is based on the story below.

After reading the story, enter the details in the map below. This will help you to answer the questions that follow.

Karen and Steve were both in Ms. Taylor's math class. Ms. Taylor wasn't very strict about when they had to turn their work in, and Steve took full advantage of that. He always did his homework for his other classes, but he would put off the math assignments thinking he could do them later. However, Karen finished each assignment that Ms. Taylor assigned right away. She had to work a little longer each night, but she didn't want to get marked down for turning in her math homework late. At the end of the semester, Karen and Steve both wanted to go to the amusement park. Ms. Taylor called Steve's mother to let her know about Steve not turning the work in on time, and Steve's mother put Steve on restriction until all of his work was turned in. What a horrible weekend for Steve! Even though he stayed up really late each night, he still couldn't finish everything. The whole time Steve was working, Karen had a great time eating hot dogs at the amusement park, watching movies, and having a great weekend. When they got their report cards, Steve was lucky to get by with a "C" minus in math while Karen got an "A."

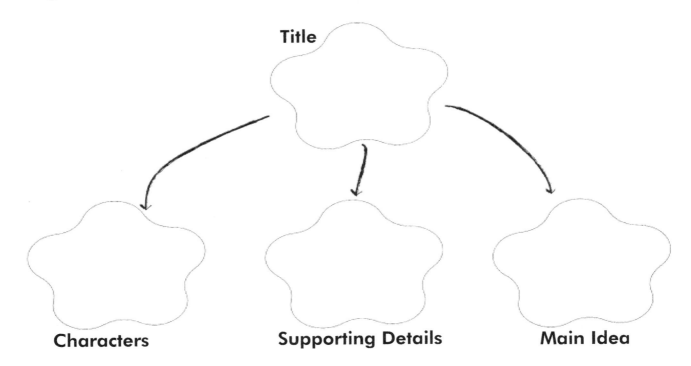

7. What did Karen and Steve learn from this?

Ⓐ It doesn't matter when you do it as long as it gets done.
Ⓑ Lazy people are sometimes rewarded with good things.
Ⓒ It's better to do things on time instead of putting them off for later.
Ⓓ Doing things early doesn't help you earn rewards in life.

Question 8 is based on the story below.

Mr. Toad and Mr. Rabbit were eating at the food court in the shopping mall. Mr. Toad was eating many slices of pizza and drinking a huge soda, and Mr. Rabbit was watching him.

"Hey, Mr. Toad. If you give me some of your pizza, I'll let you have the next fly I find," called out Mr. Rabbit.

Mr. Toad said no, even though he was very full. "I'm sorry, Mr. Rabbit," Mr. Toad said, "but this pizza cost a lot of more so I won't be able to share."

Mr. Rabbit was sad and waited for Mr. Toad to finish. Then they left the mall together. On their way out the door, a hunter saw them and started to chase them. Mr. Toad normally could have escaped, but since he had eaten so much, he was moving quite slowly. The hunter caught Mr. Toad. Mr. Rabbit was able to escape easily.

8. What is the theme of the story?

Ⓐ It's better to share.
Ⓑ If you paid for it, it's all yours.
Ⓒ Better late than never
Ⓓ Racing can be difficult.

Question 9 is based on the story below.

Frank studied all of the time, and felt that he was very smart. One day at school, a student from Frank's class asked him if he wanted to play baseball, but Frank said, "I've read all about baseball in books, and it sounds boring. No, thanks."

Another day, a different student asked Frank if he wanted to go for a burger after school. Frank responded, "I've read that burgers are made with beef heart and organ meat. No, thank you."

Frank's classmates were hesitant to ask Frank to hang out. As a result, Frank decided to study about the importance of having friends.

9. What would be an appropriate theme for the above passage?

Ⓐ It's not nice to be mean to your friends.
Ⓑ Friends are always getting in the way.
Ⓒ Learning from books is no substitute for real life experience.
Ⓓ Friendship gets in the way of learning important things.

10. What would be an appropriate theme for the below passage?

A monkey put his hand into a jar of cookies and grasped as many as he could possibly hold. But, when he tried to pull out, his hand wouldn't fit! Unwilling to lose the cookies, and yet unable to pull out his hand, he burst into tears and cried about his situation.

    Ⓐ The grass is always greener on the other side.
    Ⓑ Always ask before taking.
    Ⓒ Don't be greedy.
    Ⓓ Work now and play later.

Question 11 is based on the poem below.

YOUNG NIGHT THOUGHT

All night long and every night,
When my mama puts out the light
I see the people marching by,
As plain as day, before my eye.
Armies and emperors and kings,
All carrying different kinds of things,
And marching in so grand a way,
You never saw the like by day.
So fine a show was never seen
At the great circus on the green;
For every kind of beast and man
Is marching in that caravan.
At first they move a little slow,
But still the faster on they go,
And still beside them close I keep
Until we reach the Town of Sleep.

By Robert Louis Stevenson

11. What is the poet trying to do with his visions? Write your answer in the box below.

```
┌─────────────────────────────────────────────────────────┐
│                                                         │
│                                                         │
│                                                         │
│                                                         │
│                                                         │
│                                                         │
└─────────────────────────────────────────────────────────┘
```

Question 12 is based on the poem below.

I found a shell, a curly one;
Lying on the sand.
I picked it up and took it home,
Held tightly in my hand.

Mommy looked at it and then,
She held it to my ear,
And from the shell there came a song
Soft and sweet and clear.

I was surprised, I listened hard,
And it was really true:
If you can find a nice big shell,
You'll hear the singing too.

--Unknown

12. Choose the most appropriate title for this poem.
   Circle the correct answer choice

   Ⓐ The Singing Shell
   Ⓑ The Song
   Ⓒ Sea Shells
   Ⓓ Sea Shell Song

Chapter 2

Lesson 4: Summarizing the Text

You can scan the QR code given below or use the url to access additional EdSearch resources including videos and mobile apps related to *Summarizing the Text*.

ed Search

Summarizing the Text

URL	QR Code
http://www.lumoslearning.com/a/rl42	

1. Choose the best summary of the below text.

Mary walked quietly through the house so that she would not wake her parents. Before entering the kitchen, she stood and listened. She wanted to make sure that no one had heard her and woken up. She slowly opened the cabinet door, trying to make sure that it didn't squeak. As Mary reached into the cabinet, something warm and furry touched her hand. Mary ran from the kitchen screaming loudly. Her father ran in to see what had happened. He started laughing when he saw their cat Purr Purr sitting quietly in the kitchen cabinet wagging her tail.

Ⓐ Mary went to the kitchen. She stopped and listened. She opened the cabinet. She screamed. Her dad laughed.

Ⓑ Mary snuck quietly into the kitchen. When she opened the cabinet, something touched her hand and made her scream. Her dad came to help and discovered it was their cat in the cabinet.

Ⓒ The cat hid in the cabinet and scared Mary when she reached into it.

Ⓓ Mary walked into the kitchen after listening to make sure that no one body heard her. She opened the cabinet slowly and felt something touch her. She ran away screaming. She didn't know that it was her cat Purr Purr.

2. Choose the best summary of the below text.

I was so scared when I first learned that I would be having my tooth pulled. I didn't sleep at all the night before the procedure. I was terrified that it would hurt more than I could tolerate. I was shaking when I sat in the dentist's chair. He promised me that it would not hurt, but I certainly had my doubts. The dentist gave me some medicine. When I awoke, my tooth was gone, and I didn't remember a thing.

Ⓐ The writer was scared about having to have a tooth pulled and thought it would hurt. The dentist gave her medicine, and she didn't feel it when her tooth was pulled.

Ⓑ The writer was scared. She got her tooth pulled. The dentist gave her medicine.

Ⓒ The dentist gave the writer some medicine so that it wouldn't hurt when her tooth was pulled.

Ⓓ The writer was scared about having her tooth pulled. She didn't sleep the night before. She was terrified. She was shaking. The dentist gave her medicine. She didn't feel a thing when he pulled her tooth.

3. Choose the best summary of the below text.

Huckleberry Hound ran through the yard and into the field next to his house. Suddenly, he put his nose to the ground and started sniffing as he walked. Yep, he definitely smelled a rabbit. He raised his head and howled loudly to let the other dogs know what he had found. Then, he shot after the rabbit like a bolt of lightning. He chased the rabbit for what seemed like hours, but he never caught it. He returned to his yard with his head hanging and his tail tucked between his legs.

Ⓐ Huckleberry Hound smelled a rabbit. He chased it for a long time, but never caught it.

Ⓑ Huckleberry Hound smelled a rabbit. He ran across the yard to the field. He howled so the other dogs would know he found a rabbit. He shot after the rabbit and chased it for a long time. He didn't catch the rabbit. He went home with his head hung down.

Ⓒ Huckleberry Hound chased a rabbit.

Ⓓ Huckleberry Hound smelled a rabbit. He put his nose to the ground and followed its trail. He definitely smelled a rabbit. He chased it for a long time. He let the other dogs know he had found a rabbit. He didn't catch the rabbit.

4. Summarize the below text using one sentence.

I had been craving chocolate ice cream all day. Finally, the school was over and I could get a huge chocolate ice cream cone. The line was long, but it was worth the wait. The first taste of my ice cream cone was delicious. Then, the worst thing imaginable happened. I bumped into the person behind me and dropped my ice cream cone and it fell on the floor.

Ⓐ I craved ice cream all day, but when I finally got a cone I dropped it and it fell on the floor.

Ⓑ I craved ice cream all day, but I dropped it.

Ⓒ I bought chocolate ice cream, and I bumped into someone and dropped it.

Ⓓ The first taste of ice cream was great because I had been craving it all day.

5. Summarize the below text using only one sentence.

Opal walked into the store not wanting to do what she had planned. She knew when she took the makeup without paying for it that it was wrong. She felt so guilty. She knew she couldn't keep the makeup. So, gathering up all her courage, she walked over to the security officer and confessed what she had done.

Ⓐ Opal was ashamed of what she did, so she returned it.

Ⓑ Opal stole some makeup; however, she returned it because she felt guilty.

Ⓒ Opal walked to the store, and she returned the make-up.

Ⓓ Opal walked to the store, and gathered up her courage because she had stolen some makeup.

Question 6-8 are based on the story below.

Mary loves writing stories

"The Elephant Who Saw the World," Mary started speaking. It was Friday, and the students had to share their creative writing stories of the week.

Mary loved writing, and this part of the week, when they were able to make up stories for creative writing, was her favorite part. She enjoyed it so much that she became really good at it. When she was home on the weekends and she didn't have much homework, she would sit in her room for hours and create stories to share with her friends and family. Her parents always supported her and were her biggest fans.

However, there was one part about every Friday at school that Mary did not enjoy, and that was when she had to share her story in front of the class. The teacher made all of the children share on Friday afternoons, and this made Mary very nervous. She was shy, and although she knew her teacher was right, she didn't like it.

After sitting and listening to the other children's share, Mary finally heard her name called. She knew it was her turn to share. She got out of her seat slowly, walked to the front of the room and began.

6. Choose the sentence that best summarizes the passage.

Ⓐ The teacher required each student to read their story out loud.
Ⓑ They were presenting creative short stories as part of their Friday share time.
Ⓒ Although Mary loved creative writing, she did not enjoy reading her stories out loud.
Ⓓ Mary agreed that it would be good experience, but she still didn't like it.

7. Which information is NOT necessary for the summary?

Ⓐ Mary enjoyed creating the stories, but when it came to presenting them, she got really nervous.
Ⓑ She enjoyed writing.
Ⓒ Writing was a strong point of Mary's.
Ⓓ Mary wrote at home during her free time.

8. What would be the best summary for the passage above?

Ⓐ Mary wrote a story about an elephant who traveled the world. She loved writing stories and was excited when they had to do one for class. The teacher always asked the students to present their stories to the class during Friday share time. This was the part that Mary didn't like. She got really nervous speaking in front of the class although she knew it would be a good experience. When it was her turn, she took a deep breath and started sharing her story.

Ⓑ Mary wrote a story called "The Elephant Who Saw the World." Her family supported her passion for writing stories because she was so good at it. She was excited when the teacher assigned this for class one day.

Ⓒ "The Elephant Who Saw the World," Mary started speaking. It was Friday, and the students had to share their creative writing stories of the week. Mary loved writing, and this part of the week, when they were able to make up stories for creative writing, was her favorite part. She enjoyed it so much that she became really good at it. When she was home on the weekends and she didn't have much homework, she would sit in her room for hours and create stories to share with her friends and family. Her parents always supported her and were her biggest fans. However, there was one part about every Friday at school that Mary did not enjoy, and that was when she had to share her story in front of the class. The teacher made all of the children share on Friday afternoons, and this made Mary very nervous. She was shy, and although she knew her teacher was right, she didn't like it. After sitting and listening to the other children's share, Mary finally heard her name called. She knew it was her turn to share. She got out of her seat slowly, walked to the front of the room and began.

Ⓓ Mary loved writing stories. She wrote one about a donkey traveling the world and had to present it in front of the class. She was nervous about this.

Question 9 and 10 are based on the passage below.

It was a beautiful day outside. A group of children were playing in the yard. They noticed a bees' nest on the roof, so they started throwing rocks, sticks, and other items to try to knock it down. The nest moved a little, but it didn't fall to the ground. Instead, hundreds of bees flew out going in many directions.

Robert turned and ran away as fast as he could while yelling, "Get down! Get down!" He could hear Louise screaming. Robert dove to the ground as many bees flew over him. He could hear all of the other kids responding in the same way.

The bees' nest was still hanging. John looked around the yard for something really long to use. He noticed his dad's rake sitting by the porch, so he took the rake and ran over to the porch. He swung it as hard as he could, hitting the nest. The nest was dislodged, went flying through the air, and landed near Robert. With a shriek, Robert jumped to his feet and ran to the other side of the yard. The others were also yelping and trying to run away.

9. What is the best summary for the above passage?

Ⓐ   John continued throwing things at the nest even after his friends were lying on the ground.

Ⓑ   John wanted to destroy a bees' nest with his friends. They destroyed it and had to try and escape when the bees came flying out of it. Everyone was scared.

Ⓒ   John and his friends were planning to destroy a bees' nest. They started throwing rocks and sticks at the nest. The bees swarmed from the nest, the kids started to run to escape the bees. The nest was still hanging so John knocked it off with a rake. It landed near Robert who jumped up and ran to the other side of the yard.

Ⓓ   John and his friends prepared to destroy a bees' nest. They threw sticks and stones at the nest to knock it off the porch. It didn't work, so John had to do it again. The nest went flying towards Robert who got scared and ran to the other side of the yard.

10. Which sentence is NOT necessary for the summary?

Ⓐ   It was a beautiful day outside.
Ⓑ   The kids wanted to destroy a bees' nest.
Ⓒ   John and his friends tried to run from the bees that came flying out of their nest when the kids hit it.
Ⓓ   Robert yelled, "Get down! Get down!"

Question 11 is based on the passage below.

The United States National Parks System

George Catlin, an artist who traveled throughout North America in the 1800's, was one of the first people to be concerned about the westward expansion impact on the beauty of the land being destroyed. He felt that only the government could protect the land and Native Americans by creating a national park.

The popularity of this belief gained national recognition and in 1872 Congress established Yellowstone National Park. This designated public lands to be authorized by the federal government for all to enjoy. The foundation of the system began with President Woodrow Wilson creating the National Parks Service in 1916.

In 1933 by Executive Order, the National Park Service was established to maintain the lands. This transferred the 63 national monuments and military sites from the Forest Service and the War Department to the new service that included areas of beautification, historical, scientific and cultural importance.

Finally in 1970, under the General Authorities Act, Congress made known that all units have legal standing in the national system.

"though distinct in character, are united through their inter-related purposes and resources into one national park system as cumulative expressions of a single national heritage; that, individually and collectively, these areas derive increased national dignity and recognition of their superb environmental quality through their inclusion jointly with each other in one national park system preserved and managed for the benefit and inspiration of all people of the United States..."

Congress now generally makes additions to the National Parks System to add any national parks. Currently there are 376 areas covered by the National Parks System throughout the United States and its holdings. All areas are protected in accordance with the acts of Congress.

11. Explain in your own words why the artist, George Catlin wanted to preserve the land. Write your answer in the box below.

Question 12 is based on the passage below.

Sam Walton

Sam Walton (1918-1992) founded Walmart and Sam's Club. He opened the first Wal-Mart Discount City in 1962 after having several franchise Ben Franklin stores. His main effort was to market American made products. Although after his death, this practice was not continued. He placed his stores close to distribution centers, thereby having stores in multiple areas, not just in major cities.

He was listed as the richest man in the US from 1982 to 1988. Walmart and Sam's Club stores operate in the US and in 15 other countries including, Canada, Japan, Mexico, and the UK.

12. Sam Walton tried to do which of the following with his stores? Circle the correct answer choice.

Ⓐ   He tried to offer US made products in his chain of stores to help promote US made products and to help the country thrive.

Ⓑ   Walton tried to have more stores than any other chain of discount stores.

Ⓒ   Sam Walton offered his employees many days off and was never open on a holiday.

Ⓓ   Sam Walton made sure that all of his stores were in major cities.

Question 13 is based on the poem below.

I think that I shall never see

I think that I shall never see
A poem lovely as a tree.

A tree whose hungry mouth is prest
Against the earth's sweet flowing breast;

A tree that looks at God all day,
And lifts her leafy arms to pray;

A tree that may in summer wear
A nest of robins in her hair;

Upon whose bosom snow has lain;
Who intimately lives with rain.

Poems are made by fools like me,
But only God can make a tree.

Joyce Kilmer

Public domain

13. Who do you think that the poet is comparing a tree to in this poem? Write your answer in the box below.

Question 14 is based on the story below.

THE THREE GOLDEN APPLES, Part - 2

So he journeyed on and on, still making the same inquiry, until, at last, he came to the brink of a river where some beautiful young women sat twining wreaths of flowers.

"Can you tell me, pretty maidens," asked the stranger, "whether this is the right way to the garden of the Hesperides?"

The young women had been having a fine time together, weaving the flowers into wreaths, and crowning one another's heads. And there seemed to be a kind of magic in the touch of their fingers that made the flowers more fresh and dewy, and of brighter lines, and sweeter fragrance while they played with them than even when they had been growing on their native stems. But, on hearing the stranger's question, they dropped all their flowers on the grass, and gazed at him with astonishment.

"The garden of the Hesperides!" cried one. "We thought mortals had been weary of seeking it, after so many disappointments. And pray, adventurous traveler, what do you want there?"

"A certain king, who is my cousin," replied he, "has ordered me to get him three of the golden apples.

"Most of the young men who go in quest of these apples," observed another of the damsels, "desire to obtain them for themselves, or to present them to some fair maiden whom they love. Do you, then, love this king, your cousin, so very much?"

"Perhaps not," replied the stranger, sighing. "He has often been severe and cruel to me. But it is my destiny to obey him."

"And do you know," asked the damsel who had first spoken, "that a terrible dragon, with a hundred heads, keeps watch under the golden apple-tree?"

"I know it well," answered the stranger, calmly. "But, from my cradle upwards, it has been my business, and almost my pastime, to deal with serpents and dragons."

The young women looked at his massive club, and at the shaggy lion's skin which he wore, and likewise at his heroic limbs and figure; and they whispered to each other that the stranger appeared to be one who might reasonably expect to perform deeds far beyond the might of other men. But, then, the dragon with a hundred heads! What mortal, even if he possessed a hundred lives, could hope to escape the fangs of such a monster? So kind-hearted were the maidens, that they could not bear to see this brave and, handsome traveler attempt what was so very dangerous, and devote himself, most probably, to become a meal for the dragon's hundred ravenous mouths.

"Go back," cried they all,—"go back to your own home! Your mother, beholding you safe and sound, will shed tears of joy; and what can she do more, should you win ever so great a victory? No matter for the golden apples! No matter for the king, your cruel cousin! We do not wish the dragon with the hundred heads to eat you up!"

The stranger seemed to grow impatient at these remonstrances. He carelessly lifted his mighty club, and let it fall upon a rock that lay half buried in the earth, near by. With the force of that idle blow, the great rock was shattered all to pieces. It cost the stranger no more effort to achieve this feat of a giant's strength than for one of the young maidens to touch her sister's rosy cheek with a flower.

14. Why did the young women want him to go back home?

Question 15 is based on the story below.

THE THREE GOLDEN APPLES, Part - 11
THE THREE GOLDEN APPLES, By Nathaniel Hawthorne

Part 11

I know not how long it was before, to his unspeakable joy, he beheld the huge shape of the giant, like a cloud, on the far-off edge of the sea. At his nearer approach, Atlas held up his hand, in which Hercules could perceive three magnificent golden apples, as big as pumpkins, all banging from one branch.

"I am glad to see you again," shouted Hercules, when the giant was within hearing. "So you have got the golden apples?"

"Certainly, certainly," answered Atlas; "and very fair apples they are. I took the finest that grew on the tree, I assure you. Ah! it is a beautiful spot, that garden of the Hesperides. Yes; and the dragon with a hundred heads is a sight worth any man's seeing. After all, you had better have gone for the apples yourself."

"No matter," replied Hercules. "You have had a pleasant ramble, and have done the business as well as I could. I heartily thank you for your trouble. And now, as I have a long way to go, and am rather in haste,—and as the king, my cousin, is anxious to receive the golden apples,—will you be kind enough to take the sky off my shoulders again?"

"Why, as to that," said the giant, chucking the golden apples into the air, twenty miles high, or there-abouts, and catching them as they came down,—"as to that, my good friend, I consider you a little unreasonable. Cannot I carry the golden apples to the king, your cousin, much quicker than you could? As his majesty is in such a hurry to get them, I promise you to take my longest strides. And, besides, I have no fancy for burdening myself with the sky, just now."

Here Hercules grew impatient, and gave a great shrug of his shoulders. It being now twilight, you might have seen two or three stars tumble out of their places. Everybody on earth looked upward in affright, thinking that the sky might be going to fall next.

"O, that will never do!" cried Giant Atlas, with a great roar of laughter. "I have not let fall so many stars within the last five centuries. By the time you have stood there as long as I did, you will begin to learn patience!"

"What!" shouted Hercules, very wrathfully, "do you intend to make me bear this burden forever?"

"We will see about that, one of these days," answered the giant. "At all events, you ought not to complain, if you have to bear it the next hundred years, or perhaps the next thousand. I bore it a good while longer, in spite of the back-ache. Well, then, after a thousand years, if I happen to feel in the mood, we may possibly shift about again. You are certainly a very strong man, and can never have a better opportunity to prove it. Posterity will talk of you, I warrant it!"

"Pish! a fig for its talk!" cried Hercules, with another hitch of his shoulders. "Just take the sky upon your head one instant, will you? I want to make a cushion of my lion's skin, for the weight to rest upon. It really chafes me, and will cause unnecessary inconvenience in so many centuries as I am to stand here."

"That's no more than fair, and I'll do it!" quoth the giant; for he had no unkind feeling towards Hercules, and was merely acting with a too selfish consideration of his own ease. "For just five minutes, then, I'll take back the sky. Only for five minutes, recollect! I have no idea of spending another thousand years as I spent the last. Variety is the spice of life, say I."

Ah, the thick-witted old rogue of a giant! He threw down the golden apples, and received back the sky, from the head and shoulders of Hercules, upon his own, where it rightly belonged. And Hercules picked up the three golden apples, that were as big or bigger than pumpkins, and straightway set out on his journey homeward, without paying the slightest heed to the thundering tones of the giant, who bellowed after him to come back. Another forest sprang up around his feet, and grew ancient there; and again might be seen oak-trees, of six or seven centuries old, that had waxed thus again betwixt his enormous toes.

And there stands the giant, to this day; or, at any rate, there stands a mountain as tall as he, and which bears his name; and when the thunder rumbles about its summit, we may imagine it to be the voice of Giant Atlas, bellowing after Hercules!

15. How does the myth end? Mark all that apply.

Ⓐ Hercules held the sky up until Atlas returned.
Ⓑ Atlas agreed to take back the sky for a while.
Ⓒ Hercules was able to get the golden apples that Atlas brought and take them back to the king.
Ⓓ Atlas tricked Hercules and did not return with the golden apples.

Chapter 2

Lesson 5: Describing Characters

Character(s)

The actions and thoughts and emotions of the main (major) character(s) have the most influence, are the most important, to the plot. There may be other less important characters (known as minor or secondary characters) in the story, but they will have less influence on the plot.

Let us understand the concept with an example.

The Servant's Escape
By Vivek Krishnaswamy

Late at night when there are people walking around the streets of the city, I lie in my bed hoping that one day I will have the freedom to go out when I want and to get a job outside of the house that I live and work in, with a salary higher than what I am making now.

Today was a typical day around here. It was one o'clock in the afternoon and I was washing the lunch dishes when the mistress of the house walked into the kitchen and said angrily: "Marcos! What is this? What is this? My clothes have been washed but they have not been IRONED!! Do it now or you will be punished!!" So I stopped washing dishes and walked to her room with her dress in my hand, ironed it quickly, then went back to washing dishes. She and the master were always complaining about my work, and rarely complimented me, even though I tried to never disobey them. But there were times when I did not do exactly what they wanted me to do in the exact manner they wanted, and I would get punished with beatings from the gardener. And, I was not allowed to leave the house – I was, in reality, a prisoner.

One night an idea struck me! I looked at the back door and thought: why couldn't I escape from the house through the back door when the family was out, and then come back in before the family returned? I always knew their schedules. While I was out I could look for another job, and if I found one, I would tell the family, and I could leave if they agreed. If they said no, I was doomed; I could just escape but their friends in the police department would track me down and arrest me!

For several weeks I struggled to find a proper job that would give me some time for myself, that also had a place for me to live, and paid a better salary. I finally found what I was looking for. It was a small grocery store where I would help the owner run the store. On the second floor was a small room in which I could live. And the salary was higher.

The next day I went to my master's office. I was very nervous; I wanted so badly to leave. I asked him very politely, "Master?" "Humph?" he replied. "Master I wish to leave this house and find a new job for myself." "WHAT? Why would you want to do that? Have we mistreated you, have we not provided everything that is necessary for your survival?" he asked. "Yes master, but I would like to change my occupation as it has been five years of my service, and if it is alright with you, then I will take my leave sir." I said. "Have you found a job?" he asked. "No sir" I lied. "I am not allowed to leave the house." "So then how will you survive when you are looking for a job?" he asked. Marcos said: "There are times during the day when I have finished my work, and I could go out looking for a job then." "If you can find another boy or girl who is as efficient as you then you will be allowed to leave your service. I will send one guard with you and give you two hours a day to look for someone to replace you, but once your two hours are up, you will return to this house and finish the rest of your chores. Do you understand?" he said in a very serious tone of voice." "Yes sir, as you wish." I left the room in a very happy mood.

For the next three weeks I looked for a replacement. During this time not any insult or beating could depress me. I was so happy. At last I found someone to take my place. Then I was free, and my new life was paradise. I had enough money to spend on things I wanted, and all of the food that I wanted for free. My room was a bit smaller but all the freedom that I enjoyed during my free time more than made up for the smaller living space. This was the life that I was waiting for. This is what I had worked for those five years.

Describe in depth a character. Here are the words and phrases you might use to describe Marcos, the main character, using specific details from the text.

Marcos had the courage to hope for a better life than the one he was living: "I lie in my bed **hoping** that one day I will be able to have the freedom to go out when I want and to get a job outside of the house that I live and work in, with a salary higher than what I am making now." And he had the courage to do things to make his hope come true: "One night **an idea struck me!**"; "**For several weeks I struggled** to find a proper job…"; "The next day I went to my master's office. I was **very nervous**; I wanted so badly to leave;" "**For the next three weeks** I looked for a replacement."

Even though he hated his job and living in that house, he was smart enough to not let his anger show; he always tried to satisfy the master and mistress: "So I **stopped** washing dishes and walked to her room with her dress in my hand, **ironed it quickly**, then **went back to washing dishes**."

Marcos was also very clever. He knew how to reply to the master when the master asked "Have you found a job?" "No sir" **I lied**. "I am not allowed to leave the house." He lied because if he had said yes, the master would know that Marcos had sneaked out of the house, which would probably make the master angry and not let Marcos leave.

Publisher's Note: I pretended that I was a student who was assigned to read this story and then describe in depth a character, setting, or event. I chose to describe the main character, because the author had Marcos, the main character, tell the story and the story was mostly about what Marcos felt and what he did. The setting was not important; it could have been any house in any place. I could have chosen an event, but by having Marcos tell the story, he told about all the important events.

You can scan the QR code given below or use the url to access additional EdSearch resources including videos and mobile apps related to *Describing Characters*.

ed Search

Describing Characters

URL	QR Code
http://www.lumoslearning.com/a/rl43	

Question 1 and 2 are based on the story below.

Timothy

Timothy is a student at my school. He is well-liked by all of the teachers and students. We all know that we can count on Timothy to keep our secrets, to help us if we ask, and to always be on time. We know that he is always honest and expects others to be honest as well.

Last summer, Timothy got a job walking dogs each morning. When school started this year, everyone encouraged him to quit his job, but he decided to keep it. He knew it would be hard to get up every morning at 5 a.m. in order to get all of the dogs walked and then go to school all day. Additionally, he planned to sing in the chorus, play basketball, and be a mentor in the tutoring program this year. He knows it will not be easy, but he thinks his hard work will be worth it. He is trying to save enough money to go to a youth camp next summer.

1. **According to the above passage, which set of adjectives would you choose to describe Timothy?**

   Ⓐ responsible and depressed
   Ⓑ trustworthy and thoughtless
   Ⓒ responsible and ambitious
   Ⓓ arrogant and unfriendly

2. **Based on the above passage, what do you think Timothy would do if someone asked him to help them cheat on a test?**

   Ⓐ He would help them cheat but ask them not to tell anyone.
   Ⓑ He would tell them that cheating is dishonest and encourage them not to do it.
   Ⓒ He might help them cheat because he doesn't want them to make a bad grade.
   Ⓓ He might tell them to ask someone else to help them cheat.

Question 3 and 4 are based on the story below.

Fred Goes to the Dentist

Fred had never been to the dentist. All of his life he had heard horror stories about the buzzing drills, the huge needles, and the scary tools that the dentist used to torture his patients. Since none of his teeth were hurting, Fred just couldn't understand why his mom was insisting on taking him to the dentist. She told him that it was important to visit the dentist each year to have his teeth checked and cleaned. This seemed silly to Fred because he cleaned his teeth everyday by brushing and flossing them, but nothing would change his mother's mind. He found it hard to believe that she would think it was a good idea to take him somewhere to be tortured. However, he had no choice but to go.

On the way to the dentist, Fred's imagination went wild. He pictured walking into a room with a huge

 LumosLearning.com

chair that the dentist would strap him to. He could just see the dentist pulling out a huge drill and drilling his tooth while his mother and several others held him in the chair. By the time he got to the dentist's office, he was shaking all over.

Surprisingly, the office was nothing like he expected. The dentist was friendly, and the chair was comfortable. It didn't have any straps. He looked around the room and didn't see any huge drills or torture devices. He was relieved when all the dentist did was look in his mouth, show him how to properly brush and floss his teeth, and give him a balloon. His mom made another appointment to have his teeth cleaned in six months. Maybe this wouldn't be as bad as he had thought it would be.

3. Based on the passage, how do you think Fred felt about going to his first visit to the dentist?

Ⓐ He was excited and looked forward to it.
Ⓑ He was afraid and didn't understand the reason he had to go.
Ⓒ He was afraid but wanted to go and see the drills.
Ⓓ He felt shy about meeting the dentist.

4. How do you think Fred felt after seeing the dentist office and meeting the dentist?

Ⓐ scared
Ⓑ intimidated
Ⓒ relieved
Ⓓ joyful

Question 5-7 are based on the story below.

Adam lives with his dad and his older brother Stanley. Adam and Stanley share a room. Most of the time Adam enjoys sharing a room with his brother, but there are times that he wishes he had his own room. Being brothers, they have a lot in common; however, they are different in many ways.

Adam likes to spend time with his friends. If he is not with them, he is texting them or playing games with them online. Adam is always busy. He cannot stand to sit around and do nothing. In fact, the only time he is still is when he is sleeping. Adam plays football, basketball, soccer, and baseball. He loves to be involved in school activities or at the town's youth volunteering center. He spends a lot of his time encouraging people to recycle. Although he loves spending time with his friends, he is willing to give up time with them to help others.

Stanley, on the other hand, loves to stay at home. He enjoys activities that can be done alone such as reading, drawing, and spending time with his dogs. Most days after school he can be found at home enjoying one of his favorite activities. He thinks recycling is important and makes sure his family does it. Although he likes being alone, he enjoys volunteering at the youth center with his brother. He thinks it is important to make a difference in the lives of others, which is the reason that he thinks he would like to be a doctor. Adam and Stanley have some differences, but they do join together to make an impact in their community.

5. Choose the set of words that best describes Stanley.

Ⓐ solitary and caring
Ⓑ rude and outgoing
Ⓒ selfish and quiet
Ⓓ solitary and rude

6. Based on the passage, how do you think Adam and Stanley feel about one another?

Ⓐ They like and respect one another.
Ⓑ They do not like to spend time together.
Ⓒ They do not enjoy one another's company.
Ⓓ They are jealous of each other.

7. Choose the set of words that best describes Adam.

Ⓐ friendly and greedy
Ⓑ thoughtful and outgoing
Ⓒ unhappy and mean
Ⓓ outgoing and greedy

8. Which adjective describes how Beau was feeling?

It was the last round of the school spelling bee and only two students were left. Beau's heart was pounding and he was sweating. He began fidgeting with the button on one of his shirt sleeves.

Ⓐ anxious
Ⓑ proud
Ⓒ depressed
Ⓓ envious

Question 9 and 10 are based on the story below.

Libby's grandmother didn't have much money, so she couldn't buy Libby an expensive present for Christmas like her other grandmother could. She didn't want to buy her a cheap toy that wouldn't last long, but she just couldn't afford the things that were on Libby's wish list. She decided to make Libby a quilt. She was concerned that her granddaughter wouldn't like the gift, but it was the best that she could do.

When Christmas day arrived, Grandmother went to Libby's house. She saw all of the nice gifts that her granddaughter had received. She was worried as Libby began to open her present. Libby squealed with delight when she saw the handmade quilt. She ran and hugged her grandmother and thanked her. She ran and put the new quilt on her bed. The rest of the day she talked about how much she loved the quilt, especially since her grandmother had made it all by hand.

9. How would you describe the way Libby's grandmother felt before Libby opened her gift?

(A) nervous
(B) kind
(C) lazy
(D) angry

10. How do you think Libby's grandmother felt after Libby opened the gift?

(A) sad
(B) hungry
(C) angry
(D) happy

Question 11 is based on the story below.

A Chosen Child

Mary Ann Woods was a bright and happy 10 year old. She loved playing with her friends outside and working on arts and craft projects with her mother. Mary Ann even helped her dad out in the yard with the garden, weed eating, mowing, and clipping hedges. Mary Ann was an only child and often longed to have a baby brother or sister. She truly envied her neighborhood friends that had many siblings.

Her house was just as large as most of the other houses, but several bedrooms were empty. Not that they didn't have furniture in them, it was that no one lived or slept in the rooms unless guests came for a visit. Mary Ann liked to go in the rooms and pretend that her make-believe sister lived there. She would sit on the bed and pretend to be talking to her, smiling and even laughing out loud at times.

While she was doing just that one day, her mom walked down the hall. She heard talking and laughing, but it wasn't coming from Mary Ann's bedroom. Puzzled, her mom peered around the corner to one of the guest bedrooms and spotted Mary Ann on the bed looking up to the ceiling.

"Child, what on Earth are you doing?" questioned her mother.

"Oh, sorry, Mom, didn't mean to scare you or mess up the bed." She replied.

"I was talking to Josephine."

"And WHO is Josephine, might I ask?"

"My imaginary sister!" And with that reply, Mary Ann hopped off the bed and scurried out of the room.

Her mother was in a quandary, as she wondered why Mary Ann would need an imaginary sister, when she had friends galore. That evening after dinner, Mary Ann's mother told her dad about what had occurred earlier in the day. "Sam, I am quite concerned about her behaving in this manner. What do you think we should do?"

"Do? Why do anything, Sheila? It is normal for kiddos to have pretend friends." Replied Sam, Mary Ann's dad.

"Do you think we need to tell her now? You know we said we would when she got old enough to understand."

Mary Ann's dad breathed a deep sigh and agreed it was time for the dreaded talk. You see Sheila and Sam couldn't have children and they had adopted Mary Ann when she was only a few days old. The adoption had cost them quite a bit of money. In fact, it was all of their savings at the time. They were so thrilled to be able to have Mary Ann as their baby, they did not care about the expense. It was only later as Mary Ann grew up when they wanted to adopt another child that they realized it was not feasible with the costs. They had moved into the large house so that Mary Ann could be in a neighborhood full of other children to be her playmates.

How to break the news was on both of their minds as they tried to prepare for bed. As always, Mary Ann had helped with the dishes and was about to make her way upstairs. Her dad asked her to come sit in the living room with him and her mom. Thinking nothing of it, Mary Ann skipped into the room.

"What's up, Dad?"

Her dad began to tell the story of her adoption. Mary Ann sat quietly, face wrinkled, and listened intently to every word. Her mom held one hand and her dad the other. They were both in tears as they explained that due to health reasons, they could not have children of their own. They grinned as they told of how excited they were to be able to adopt her. Words of love and commitment flowed from their mouths. When they had finished, they looked Mary Ann in the eyes and said, "You are our chosen child!"

Mary Ann hugged them both fiercely and exclaimed with her own sigh of relief, "No wonder I do not have brown eyes like either of you! I love being chosen! My turn to choose! So now I choose you, too, forever to be my chosen parents!"

11. Part A

After reading the passage, what type of characteristic traits do you think Mary Ann has? Select all that apply.

Ⓐ She is a helpful child.
Ⓑ She is a troubled child.
Ⓒ She is a loving child.
Ⓓ She bullies everyone.
Ⓔ She is bright and helpful.

Part B

Write a sentence that supports your answer based on the evidence in the story. Write your answer in the box below.

Question 12 is based on the story below.

THE SECRET GARDEN by Frances Hodgson Burnett - Part 1

CHAPTER I

THERE IS NO ONE LEFT

When Mary Lennox was sent to Misselthwaite Manor to live with her uncle everybody said she was the most disagreeable-looking child ever seen. It was true, too. She had a little thin face and a little thin body, thin light hair and a sour expression. Her hair was yellow, and her face was yellow because she had been born in India and had always been ill in one way or another. Her father had held a position under the English Government and had always been busy and ill himself, and her mother had been a great beauty who cared only to go to parties and amuse herself with gay people.

She had not wanted a little girl at all, and when Mary was born she handed her over to the care of an Ayah, who was made to understand that if she wished to please the Mem Sahib she must keep the child out of sight as much as possible. So when she was a sickly, fretful, ugly baby she was kept out of the way, and when she became a sickly, fretful, toddler she was kept out of the way also. She never remembered seeing familiarly anything but the dark faces of her Ayah and the other native servants, and as they always obeyed her and gave her her own way in everything, because the Mem Sahib would be angry if she was disturbed by her crying, by the time she was six years old she was as tyrannical and a selfish little pig as ever lived. The young English governess who came to teach her to read and write disliked her so much that she gave up her place in three months, and when other governesses came to try to fill it they always went away in a shorter time than the first one. So if Mary had not chosen to really want to know how to read books she would never have learned her letters at all.

One frightfully hot morning, when she was about nine years old, she awakened feeling very cross, and she became crosser still when she saw that the servant who stood by her bedside was not her Ayah.

"Why did you come?" she said to the strange woman. "I will not let you stay. Send my Ayah to me." The woman looked frightened, but she only stammered that the Ayah could not come and when Mary threw herself into a passion and beat and kicked her, she looked only more frightened and repeated that it was not possible for the Ayah to come to Missie Sahib.

There was something mysterious in the air that morning. Nothing was done in its regular order and several of the native servants seemed missing, while those whom Mary saw slunk or hurried about with ashy and scared faces. But no one would tell her anything and her Ayah did not come. She was actually left alone as the morning went on, and at last she wandered out into the garden and began to play by herself under a tree near the veranda. She pretended that she was making a flower-bed, and she stuck big scarlet hibiscus blossoms into little heaps of earth, all the time growing more and more angry and muttering to herself the things she would say and the names she would call Saidie when she returned.

"Pig! Pig! Daughter of Pigs!" she said, because to call a native a pig is the worst insult of all.

She was grinding her teeth and saying this over and over again when she heard her mother come out on the veranda with some one. She was with a fair young man and they stood talking together in low strange voices. Mary knew the fair young man who looked like a boy. She had heard that he was a very young officer who had just come from England. The child stared at him, but she stared most at her mother. She always did this when she had a chance to see her, because the Mem Sahib— Mary used to call her that oftener than anything else—was such a tall, slim, pretty person and wore such lovely clothes. Her hair was like curly silk and she had a delicate little nose which seemed to be disdaining things, and she had large laughing eyes. All her clothes were thin and floating, and Mary said they were "full of lace." They looked fuller of lace than ever this morning, but her eyes were not laughing at all. They were large and scared and lifted imploringly to the fair boy officer's face.

"Is it so very bad? Oh, is it?" Mary heard her say. "Awfully," the young man answered in a trembling voice. "Awfully, Mrs. Lennox. You ought to have gone to the hills two weeks ago."

The Mem Sahib wrung her hands.

"Oh, I know I ought!" she cried. "I only stayed to go to that silly dinner party. What a fool I was!" At that very moment such a loud sound of wailing broke out from the servants' quarters that she clutched the young man's arm, and Mary stood shivering from head to foot. The wailing grew wilder and wilder. "What is it? What is it?" Mrs. Lennox gasped.

"Some one has died," answered the boy officer. "You did not say it had broken out among your servants."

"I did not know!" the Mem Sahib cried. "Come with me! Come with me!" and she turned and ran into the house.

12. The passage describes Mary's characteristics and behavior. Mark all that apply.

Ⓐ Mary was a sweet quiet child and quite agreeable.
Ⓑ Mary was very spoiled by the servants and selfish.
Ⓒ Mary was ill-tempered and tyrannical.
Ⓓ All of the above.

Question 13 is based on the fables below.

The Stag, The Wolf and The Dog
The Stag at the Pool

A stag saw his shadow reflected in the water, and greatly admired the size of his horns, but felt angry with himself for having such weak feet. While he was thus contemplating himself, a Lion appeared at the pool. The Stag betook himself to flight, and kept himself with ease at a safe distance from the Lion, until he entered a wood and became entangled with his horns. The Lion quickly came up with him and caught him. When too late he thus reproached himself: "Woe is me! How have I deceived myself! These feet which would have saved me I despised, and I gloried in these antlers which have proved my destruction."

What is most truly valuable is often underrated.

The Wolf and the Lamb

A Wolf, meeting with a Lamb astray from the fold, resolved not to lay violent hands on him, but to find some plea, which should justify to the Lamb himself his right to eat him. He then addressed him: "Sirrah, last year you grossly insulted me." "Indeed," bleated the Lamb in a mournful tone of voice, "I was not then born." Then said the Wolf: "You feed in my pasture." "No, good sir," replied the Lamb,

"I have not yet tasted grass." Again said the Wolf: "You drink of my well." "No," exclaimed the Lamb, "I never yet drank water, for as yet my mother's milk is both food and drink to me." On which the Wolf seized him, and ate him up, saying: "Well! I won't remain supperless, even though you refute every one of my imputations."

The tyrant will always find a pretext for his tyranny, and it is useless for the innocent to try by reasoning to get justice, when the oppressor intends to be unjust.

The Dog, the Rooster and the Fox

A Dog and a Rooster, traveling together, took shelter at night in a thick wood. The Rooster perched himself on a high branch, while the Dog found a bed at the foot of the tree. When morning dawned, the Rooster, as usual, crowed very loudly. A Fox, hearing the sound, and wishing to make a breakfast on him, came and stood under the branches, saying how earnestly he desired to make the acquaintance of the owner of so sweet voice.

"If you will admit me," said he, "I should very much like to spend the day with you."

The Rooster said: "Sir, do me the favor to go round and wake up my porter, that he may open the door, and let you in." On the Fox approaching the tree, the Dog sprang out and caught him and quickly tore him in pieces.

Those who try to entrap others are often caught by their own schemes.

13. Now compare all three fables and analyze each character and give an adjective or two to describe them. Write your answer in the box below.

| 1. The Stag | 2. The Lion | 3. The Wolf | 4. The Lamb |
| 5. The Rooster | 6. The Dog | 7. The Fox | |

14. Who are the main characters in the below story? Circle the names.

The Haunted House on Rio Vista Drive

The neighborhood of Rio Vista Drive had two parts to it. On one side of Riverside Avenue were about 14 houses. Each house had approximately three bedrooms, two baths, an extremely grand living area, kitchen, washroom, and most often a small office area. The backyards were all chain linked hurricane fences of around 1.2 acres with a covered garage, back driveway and security locked gate. Most of the front yards were unique to themselves and had a theme which was painted on a plaque on the outside of the house itself. The realtors said that the architect had named each house as he had built it and decorated the fronts to match the names.

However, on the other side of Rio Vista Drive at the end of the block- a dead end, stood a rickety two story house assumed to be about 50-75 years old. This was dubbed the Haunted House. There was an old woman, Widow Crankston, who lived there. The kids say she would come out in the evening and sit on her porch. Several thought they saw her carrying a black cat and presumed she was a witch of sorts. Briars grew up along the fence line and sidewalks. The windows were covered in cobwebs and the like. It had been years and years since the house had been painted or anything in the yard taken care of either. Many a dare had been made among the neighborhood kids to go and ring the doorbell or knock on the door. Most dares were made on Halloween or around that time.

So it was on the night before Halloween that Howard, Ernie and Edward were riding their bikes down Rio Vista Drive. Up one side and down the other, quickly turning around before they reached Widow Crankston's Haunted House! Suddenly, Howard came to a screeching stop right in front of the house.

"Ok, dare ya' to do it!" He hollered at Ernie.
"No, dare you!" Ernie screamed back.
"Scaredy Cats!" Laughed Edward!! "I will do it!"

So off he went, straight up to the front door. He rang the doorbell, but no one answered. Hurriedly he turned around and was running down the steps when he heard a tiny voice behind him.

"Yes, young man, may I help you?" Inquired , as she peeped out the massive door. "Is today Halloween, I thought it was tomorrow. Let me get you some chocolate brownies and a caramel apple. Do your friends want some, too? Haven't had young- ins come here in ages. Please sit on the porch while I get y'all treats and some cold milk."

Edward stopped in his tracks. She wasn't an old witch, but just a kind hearted little old lady. He motioned for Howard and Ernie. Both came running up the sidewalk just in time to eat the goodies!

Now the other kids in the neighborhood aren't sure yet what to think. There are no more briars, no more cobwebs, and the fresh paint on the house looks wonderful. The boys have a part-time job cleaning and painting while enjoying good company and great snacks!

Question 15 is based on the story below.

THE THREE GOLDEN APPLES, Part - 5
THE THREE GOLDEN APPLES, By Nathaniel Hawthorne

Meanwhile, Hercules travelled constantly onward, over hill and dale, and through the solitary woods. Sometimes he swung his club aloft, and splintered a mighty oak with a downright blow. His mind was so full of the giants and monsters with whom it was the business of his life to fight, that perhaps he mistook the great tree for a giant or a monster. And so eager was Hercules to achieve what he had undertaken, that he almost regretted to have spent so much time with the damsels, wasting idle breath upon the story of his adventures. But thus it always is with persons who are destined to perform great things. What they have already done seems less than nothing. What they have taken in hand to do seems worth toil, danger, and life itself.

Persons who happened to be passing through the forest must have been affrighted to see him smite the trees with his great club. With but a single blow, the trunk was riven as by the stroke of lightning, and the broad boughs came rustling and crashing down.

Hastening forward, without ever pausing or looking behind, he by and by heard the sea roaring at a distance. At this sound, he increased his speed, and soon came to a beach, where the great surf-waves tumbled themselves upon the hard sand, in a long line of snowy foam. At one end of the beach, however, there was a pleasant spot, where some green shrubbery clambered up a cliff, making its rocky face look soft and beautiful. A carpet of verdant grass, largely intermixed with sweet-smelling clover, covered the narrow space between the bottom of the cliff and the sea. And what should Hercules espy there, but an old man, fast asleep!

But was it really and truly an old man? Certainly, at first sight, it looked very like one; but, on closer inspection, it rather seemed to be some kind of a creature that lived in the sea. For, on his legs and arms there were scales, such as fishes have; he was web-footed and web-fingered, after the fashion of a duck; and his long beard, being of a greenish tinge, had more the appearance of a tuft of sea-weed than of an ordinary beard. Have you never seen a stick of timber, that has been long tossed about by the waves, and has got all overgrown with barnacles, and, at last drifting ashore, seems to have been thrown up from the very deepest bottom of the sea? Well, the old man would have put you in mind of just such a wave-tost spar! But Hercules, the instant he set eyes on this strange figure, was convinced that it could be no other than the Old One, who was to direct him on his way.

15. Hercules was a very strong man. Choose from the list below all the details that help support this characteristic.

Ⓐ He was destined to perform great things.
Ⓑ With a single blow he could down trees.
Ⓒ He should not have wasted his time talking to the maidens.
Ⓓ All of the above.

Chapter 2

Lesson 6: Describing the Setting

You can scan the QR code given below or use the url to access additional EdSearch resources including videos and mobile apps related to *Describing the Setting.*

Describing the Setting

URL	QR Code
http://www.lumoslearning.com/a/rl43	

Question 1 is based on the story below.

Alexander the Great

Nearly two thousand five hundred years ago, there lived a king called Alexander the Great. He was the son of Philip II of Macedonia. When Prince Alexander was a boy, a magnificent horse that was for sale was brought to the court of his father. The animal was to be sold for thirteen talents. Talents are ancient coins. Many were eager to buy the horse, but no one could get close enough to saddle the restless animal. He was wild and impossible to ride.

Alexander pleaded with his father to let him try. Realizing that the horse was terrified of its own shadow, he turned the horse towards the sun, so that its shadow fell behind it. This calmed the horse, and the prince proudly rode away. Observing this, his father said, "My son, look for a kingdom worthy of your greatness. Macedonia is too small for you."

That is exactly what Alexander tried to do when he grew up. He fought many battles and always rode Bucephalus (that was the horse's name.) Friendship and trust grew between the man and his horse. When Bucephalus died of wounds received in battle, Alexander was heartbroken and deeply mourned the loss of his horse.

1. When did this story take place?

Ⓐ two thousand five hundred years ago
Ⓑ two hundred and fifty years ago
Ⓒ twenty five hundred years ago
Ⓓ It is happening now

Question 2 is based on the story below.

Fred Goes to the Dentist

Fred had never been to the dentist. All of his life he had heard horror stories about the buzzing drills, the huge needles, and the scary tools that the dentist used to torture his patients. Since none of his teeth were hurting, Fred just couldn't understand why his mom was insisting on taking him to the dentist. She told him that it was important to visit the dentist each year to have his teeth checked and cleaned. This seemed silly to Fred because he cleaned his teeth everyday by brushing and flossing them, but nothing would change his mother's mind. He found it hard to believe that she would think it was a good idea to take him somewhere to be tortured. However, he had no choice but to go.

On the way to the dentist, Fred's imagination went wild. He pictured walking into a room with a huge chair that the dentist would strap him to. He could just see the dentist pulling out a huge drill and drilling his tooth while his mother and several others held him in the chair. By the time he got to the dentist's office, he was shaking all over.

Surprisingly, the office was nothing like he expected. The dentist was friendly, and the chair was comfortable. It didn't have any straps. He looked around the room and didn't see any huge drills or torture devices. He was relieved when all the dentist did was look in his mouth, show him how to properly brush and floss his teeth, and give him a balloon. His mom made another appointment to have his teeth cleaned in six months. Maybe this wouldn't be as bad as he had thought it would be.

2. The setting for the second paragraph of the above passage is probably:

Ⓐ the dentist's office
Ⓑ an automobile
Ⓒ Fred's home
Ⓓ school

Question 3-5 are based on the story below.

Huckleberry Hound ran through the yard and into the field next to his house. Suddenly, he put his nose to the ground and started sniffing as he walked. Yep, he definitely smelled a rabbit. He raised his head and howled loudly to let the other dogs know what he had found. Then, he shot after the rabbit like a bolt of lightning. He chased the rabbit for what seemed like hours, but he never caught it. He returned to his yard with his head hanging and his tail tucked between his legs.

3. At the beginning of the story, where was Huckleberry Hound?

Ⓐ in the yard
Ⓑ in a field
Ⓒ on the porch
Ⓓ in his kennel

4. Where did Huckleberry Hound chase the rabbit?

Ⓐ in the yard
Ⓑ in a field
Ⓒ on the porch
Ⓓ in his kennel

5. Where was Huckleberry Hound at the end of the story?

Ⓐ in the yard
Ⓑ in a field
Ⓒ on the porch
Ⓓ in his kennel

Question 6 and 7 are based on the story below.

I had been craving chocolate ice cream all day. Finally, the school was over and I could get a huge chocolate ice cream cone. The line was long, but it was worth the wait. The first taste of my ice cream cone was delicious. Then, the worst thing imaginable happened. I bumped into the person behind me and dropped my ice cream cone and it fell on the floor.

6. Where was the writer of the above passage while she was craving chocolate ice cream?

    Ⓐ at home
    Ⓑ at school
    Ⓒ at work
    Ⓓ at the mall

7. Where was the writer when she dropped her ice cream on the floor?

    Ⓐ at the ice cream shop
    Ⓑ in the park
    Ⓒ in her car
    Ⓓ at home

Question 8 is based on the story below.

"Dad and I need to go out of town this weekend," said Mom. "We'll be back on Monday, so the three of you are going to spend the weekend with your two aunts. "

Lindsay, Scarlet, and Austin loved their aunts and were really excited. They ran upstairs and started getting their things together to take with them. They put everything in one bag that they would need for school. They were going to stay with Aunt Margaret for two nights and the last night with their Auntie Josephine.

At the end of the school day, the children came running out of classroom doors from all different directions. Aunt Margaret was waiting for her nieces and nephew at the entrance of the school. She was wearing a bright red suit with a sparkly cat pin on it. She also had on a proper wool hat to match. She noticed a scuff on her shoes when her nieces and nephew ran up to her.

She cried, "Oh, my goodness! I am so happy you are here. The children at your school are just a bunch of toughies. I was nearly trampled while I was standing here! Let's get into the car." Aunt Margaret pointed to a large, green, four-door station wagon that was parked in the lot.

The next day, a funny-sounding honk came from the front of the house. The children ran outside and saw Auntie Jo sitting in her convertible. She was wearing a big cowboy hat. She wore a pair of polka dot shorts with a too large shirt.

8. Where does the end of the story take place?

   Ⓐ outside in the yard
   Ⓑ in the children's bedroom
   Ⓒ at the children's school
   Ⓓ at Aunt Margaret's house

Question 9 is based on the story below.

Mary loves writing stories

"The Elephant Who Saw the World," Mary started speaking. It was Friday, and the students had to share their creative writing stories of the week.

Mary loved writing, and this part of the week, when they were able to make up stories for creative writing, was her favorite part. She enjoyed it so much that she became really good at it. When she was home on the weekends and she didn't have much homework, she would sit in her room for hours and create stories to share with her friends and family. Her parents always supported her and were her biggest fans.

However, there was one part about every Friday at school that Mary did not enjoy, and that was when she had to share her story in front of the class. The teacher made all of the children share on Friday afternoons, and this made Mary very nervous. She was shy, and although she knew her teacher was right, she didn't like it.

After sitting and listening to the other children's share, Mary finally heard her name called. She knew it was her turn to share. She got out of her seat slowly, walked to the front of the room and began.

9. Where does the story take place?

   Ⓐ Mary's house
   Ⓑ Mary's school playground
   Ⓒ Mary's classroom
   Ⓓ Mary's neighborhood library

Question 10 is based on the story below.

It was a beautiful day outside. A group of children were playing in the yard. They noticed a bees' nest on the roof, so they started throwing rocks, sticks, and other items to try to knock it down. The nest moved a little, but it didn't fall to the ground. Instead, hundreds of bees flew out going in many directions.

Robert turned and ran away as fast as he could while yelling, "Get down! Get down!" He could hear Louise screaming. Robert dove to the ground as many bees flew over him. He could hear all of the other kids responding in the same way.

The bees' nest was still hanging. John looked around the yard for something really long to use. He noticed his dad's rake sitting by the porch, so he took the rake and ran over to the porch. He swung it as hard as he could, hitting the nest. The nest was dislodged, went flying through the air, and landed near Robert. With a shriek, Robert jumped to his feet and ran to the other side of the yard. The others were also yelping and trying to run away.

10. Where does the story take place?

    Ⓐ near a lake
    Ⓑ outside in the yard
    Ⓒ in the basement of the house
    Ⓓ at the school

Question 11 is based on the story below.

The Haunted House on Rio Vista Drive

The neighborhood of Rio Vista Drive had two parts to it. On one side of Riverside Avenue were about 14 houses. Each house had approximately three bedrooms, two baths, an extremely grand living area, kitchen, washroom, and most often a small office area. The backyards were all chain linked hurricane fences of around 1.2 acres with a covered garage, back driveway and security locked gate. Most of the front yards were unique to themselves and had a theme which was painted on a plaque on the outside of the house itself. The realtors said that the architect had named each house as he had built it and decorated the fronts to match the names.

However, on the other side of Rio Vista Drive at the end of the block- a dead end, stood a rickety two story house assumed to be about 50-75 years old. This was dubbed the Haunted House. There was an old woman, Widow Crankston, who lived there. The kids say she would come out in the evening and sit on her porch. Several thought they saw her carrying a black cat and presumed she was a witch of sorts. Briars grew up along the fence line and sidewalks. The windows were covered in cobwebs and the like. It had been years and years since the house had been painted or anything in the yard taken care of either. Many a dare had been made among the neighborhood kids to go and ring the doorbell or knock on the door. Most dares were made on Halloween or around that time.

So it was on the night before Halloween that Howard, Ernie and Edward were riding their bikes down Rio Vista Drive. Up one side and down the other, quickly turning around before they reached Widow Crankston's Haunted House! Suddenly, Howard came to a screeching stop right in front of the house.

"Ok, dare ya' to do it!" He hollered at Ernie.
"No, dare you!" Ernie screamed back.
"Scaredy Cats!" Laughed Edward!! "I will do it!"

So off he went, straight up to the front door. He rang the doorbell, but no one answered. Hurriedly he turned around and was running down the steps when he heard a tiny voice behind him.

"Yes, young man, may I help you?" Inquired Widow Crankston, as she peeped out the massive door. "Is today Halloween, I thought it was tomorrow. Let me get you some chocolate brownies and a caramel apple. Do your friends want some, too? Haven't had young- ins come here in ages. Please sit on the porch while I get y'all treats and some cold milk."

Edward stopped in his tracks. She wasn't an old witch, but just a kind hearted little old lady. He motioned for Howard and Ernie. Both came running up the sidewalk just in time to eat the goodies!

Now the other kids in the neighborhood aren't sure yet what to think. There are no more briars, no more cobwebs, and the fresh paint on the house looks wonderful. The boys have a part-time job cleaning and painting while enjoying good company and great snacks!

11. What is the setting of the story? Write your answer in the box below.

Question 12 is based on the story below.

Going Mudding with Dad

Jeff and his dad love to go mudding on their four wheelers. Mudding is great fun, but can be dangerous! Jeff has his own four wheeler, too. It is not as massive as his dad's but can go fast and sling mud everywhere. Mudding has become a sort of sports in the swamp country in Louisiana where they live. So picture this in your mind. A four wheeler with a kid on it going through muddy paths covered in moss and vines. The mud is thick and water is everywhere. Get the picture, if you like mud like they do, it is a blast. The object of mudding is to see who can go the fastest, beat the other "mudders" while getting the most mud and filth on them as well.

There are several things to remember and keep in mind when preparing to drive and while driving four wheelers through mud. First, never go out alone. Buddy up is the best policy. Always wear plenty of clothing. Jeff and his dad wear long sleeve shirts, jeans, and high top hunting boots.

Never go on a four wheeler without wearing a helmet for protection. Most of them have seat belts, so buckle up. Take water or a vitamin sports drink and a healthy snack with you. Keep a first aid kit in your four wheeler, too. If you are going out on a path that has several trails, take strips of cloth and tie on branches along the way to find your way back. Be sure to inspect your vehicle before going out. Check the basic like oil, gas, clean off any mud left before hand and make sure that your vehicle starts and stops when needed. While driving do not turn your four wheeler too sharp at any time as this could cause it to flip over. If the curve ahead of you looks sharp, slow down before you approach, or you might have an accident, as well. Safety is more important than winning or being the muddiest one out there!

Then hit the trails, have fun and enjoy the mud!

12. Review the list of tips on mudding and mark all that apply.

Ⓐ Do not worry about going out alone.

Ⓑ Buddy up, buckle up, and wear plenty of clothing.

Ⓒ Take a first aid kit, take water and snacks, mark your path and inspect your vehicle before going out.

Ⓓ Wear a helmet, slow down on sharp curves, and do not turn sharp.
Do not take snacks or drinks with you.

Question 13 is based on the story below.

Disneyworld- Here We Come

It was a hot summer day in June. My grandmother, Mom, my brother Daniel, my cousin Valerie, and I were headed out for a long vacation. We were first going to Mississippi and then on to Florida to Disneyworld. Talk about excitement!!! I couldn't contain myself and didn't sleep much at all the night before. Valerie was visiting us because her mom had gotten sick. My wonderful mom had volunteered for her to stay with us the entire summer. It was so cool. Valerie and I were best friends already, much less best cousins. We did everything together all the time. So having her come along was just another treat for me. Of course, I had rather my little snoopy brother, Daniel, didn't come, but oh well! After all, who can complain when you are going to Disneyworld!

We had to stop in Mississippi to leave my grandmother off at her house before the vacation. That wasn't such a bad idea either, because I loved my grandmother's house, the creek to fish and swim in and all of her things. The night before we had packed everything we needed. I just couldn't get to sleep. Finally I must have fallen asleep because the alarm was going off and everyone was hurrying about the house. Dad had made us breakfast. He couldn't go due to his work schedule, but insisted we go and have fun. He even told me to ride the Teacups for him and the Train! Dad is such a laugh.

The car was packed, we had double checked everything and were waving goodbye! Another reason for the stop in Mississippi was for rest. It was going to be a long ride to even get that far in one day. Mom turned on the a/c in the car along with the radio and we settled in. She had it on her favorite country music, so we sang along a few songs of Merle Haggard and Johnny Cash.

I must have fallen asleep right after we left the house. The next thing I knew, Mom was waking me up. We had stopped for lunch at a Whataburger restaurant. My favorite, too! She said to eat hearty as we would not stop again until we reached my grandmother's house. I ate a whole Whataburger with fries and an ice tea. Valerie did, too! Daniel had a Jr. Whataburger and so did my grandmother. Mom had a salad with chicken. Back in the car, Valerie and I decided to play, I spy. It is loads of fun! I was spying all kinds of things from license plates from Washington to blue jays in trees. Daniel tried to join in but would get mad if we guessed his too quickly. So he got out his video game and played it. Mom had to stop for gas one time right before we made it to the Mississippi state line. We always honk the horn when we cross over into Mississippi, but she said she was not going to do that since it was now getting dark and it might upset other drivers. I have a very smart mom.

Part 2

Soon enough we were at my grandmother's. Mom had made us pack one light bag with just enough for each of us our night clothes, and a clean outfit for the next day. That way we didn't have to take so much out at my grandmother's house. We were ready for a light soup supper and off to bed.

Before we knew it, it was daylight again. Mom was hustling us out of bed and into the kitchen for breakfast. She said to eat hearty as we had many more miles to go before we reached our final destination. So thankful that my grandmother cooked her best oatmeal for us topped with cinnamon, brown sugar, strawberries, and whipped cream! Who could ask for anything more? Yummy!!

Then it was load back into the car and get on the road. This time Mom found an oldies radio station and she was singing along with Patsy Cline, Tennessee Ernie Ford, and Frank Sinatra. Talk about strange music that none of us knew except her! Valerie and I played a game of travel trivia which was sort of fun and of course, Daniel, was back on his video games!

For lunch we stopped at a roadside park and had the sandwiches our grandmother had packed for us along with an apple and sweet iced tea. When we got back on the road, not a sound could be heard. I figured out later that all of us kids had fallen asleep.

A loud bang woke us as Mom clapped her hands and proclaimed our arrival to the Holiday Inn at Disneyworld! I could not tell you who was the most excited as we were all yelling sounds of glee and running around the car to get our luggage out. Mom registered us for our room and we were giggling uncontrollably.

Part 3

When we were settled in to our room, Mom explained the sleeping arrangements. Valerie and I would get one of the queen size beds to share, Daniel would get the fold out couch in the living area, and Mom would get the other bed. She said that is night number one, then we will switch on the second night. I love it when my mom thinks of everyone and being fair to all. We were so happy we could have slept on the floor and not minded!! Mom called Dad to let him know we made it safe and sound. Then she called our grandmother, too. She also called Valerie's mom in the hospital so Valerie could talk to her and let her know all was well. Valerie's mom's health was improving daily, too.

Mom ordered pizza for us the first night. We went to bed without any complaining, so excited to be going to Disneyworld the next day!

Mom had picked up a map of the park when she had registered us, so she was busy planning our day while we were falling asleep.

The morning came with a clap and thunder outside of our room. What was going on, we had wondered? Mom explained that it was raining and that we would have breakfast in the hotel lobby and then see what happened. She did tell us that the hotel manager had explained to her that quite often the rains would start and stop during the summers at Kissimmee, Florida. We were not too disappointed after she said that. The hotel offers a free breakfast for everyone. That was definitely a plus in Mom's opinion.

Sure enough after we had eaten the sun came out. The hotel offered a trolley bus to the theme parks, so we opted to take that rather than worrying about parking and walking. Disneyworld stays open all day and late into the evening. Mom said she had mapped out our route to take so we could get to see most everything in our two days along with purchasing us the fast passes to avoid long line delays.

What a cool Mom, right?

Part 4

The awesome view, the rides, the larger than life Disney characters, people laughing and having fun everywhere. Yes, Welcome to Disneyworld! First we started following the crowds that were going down the main street with shops galore. Then Mom got out her map and starting us on our route. By lunchtime, we had already seen more than imaginable. We had ridden the Liberty Square Riverboat, gone to the Swiss Family Treehouse, enjoyed the birds at the Enchanted Tiki Room, and countless of stops to listen to theatrical groups perform. Mom had thought of packing a lunch, but had decided against that. We had hot dogs, chips and a soda. Mom said the prices might be a bit high, but it was well worth it!

In the afternoon, the rain began to return, so we went inside a western style dance hall and listened to a group of singers dance and perform. It was really quite entertaining. Then it was time for more rides. Space Mountain was indeed worth it! Scary, and adventurous and well, mostly scary! My little brother couldn't go it and he pouted about that. So we switched directions and went to a kind of petty zoo afterwards, and to ride the Mad Tea Party (Dad's Teacups) to keep him happy. Valerie and I did not mind a bit. Mom steadily had her phone out taking pictures to post and to make copies for us. Needless to say, by the end of the day, we were all exhausted and a little sun burned, too.

Mom said we would stay the second night for the parade and fireworks. She said it was time to call it a day. We all moaned, but happily boarded the trolley back to our hotel. Once at the hotel, we settled for the buffet dinner. They let kids eat free at this hotel if you choose the buffet.

That night we all chatted about the rides and all of the attractions we saw. Mom didn't even have to tell us to go to bed. We bathed and took to the sheets! The morning was just around the corner.

Part 5

Again on the second day, we had the free breakfast and rode the trolley. It wasn't raining this time at all. Mom got out her map and we began our day. Daniel wanted to go back and ride the Mad Tea Party again, but thankfully Mom said no to that.

We were able to go to Splash Mountain, the Jungle Cruise, the 7 Dwarf's Mine Train and much more. Mom did make a request of her own. She wanted to meet Mickey and Minnie Mouse who were scheduled to appear outside of the Cinderella Castle. She also said she wanted to listen to the Enchanted Tales with Belle and ride the Prince Charming Regal Carrousel. What a crazy silly Mom!

What we didn't know was that she had a plan. It was right after we left the carrousel that we heard fantastic sounds coming down the main street. Yes, parade time right before our eyes. Mom told us to come and sit. There we were on the side of the castle sitting on the ledge in perfect view of the parade. We asked her how she knew to stop there. She said one of the hotel clerks had told her how to find the spot and when to be there. The parade was magnificent to say the least. The characters actually stopped in front of us and performed. Wow! We couldn't have planned it any better.

After the parade we went to A Pirate's Adventure and Tomorrowland Speedway, andBig Thunder Mountain. Mom said we needed to head toward the front entrance as it was time for fireworks and we needed to be ready. We got there just in time. The lights lit up the sky behind the Cinderella Castle and throughout Disneyworld. Just picture it!

What a perfect ending to our vacation.

13. In thinking about the entire vacation story, answer the following questions. Arrange the events in order as they happened in the story and write it in the boxes given below.

A. They were able to see the parade and fireworks.
B. It rained as soon as they got up on their first day at Disneyworld.
C. They stopped off in Mississippi before going to Disneyworld.
D. They had the car packed the night before they left on their vacation.
E. They rode the Liberty Square Riverboat.
F. Mom assigned sleeping arrangements.
G. Mom had to wake the kids when they arrived at the hotel.

1.

2.

3.

4.

5.

6.

7.

Question 14 is based on the story below.

THE THREE GOLDEN APPLES, Part - 2

So he journeyed on and on, still making the same inquiry, until, at last, he came to the brink of a river where some beautiful young women sat twining wreaths of flowers.

"Can you tell me, pretty maidens," asked the stranger, "whether this is the right way to the garden of the Hesperides?"

The young women had been having a fine time together, weaving the flowers into wreaths, and crowning one another's heads. And there seemed to be a kind of magic in the touch of their fingers that made the flowers more fresh and dewy, and of brighter lines, and sweeter fragrance while they played with them than even when they had been growing on their native stems. But, on hearing the stranger's question, they dropped all their flowers on the grass, and gazed at him with astonishment.

"The garden of the Hesperides!" cried one. "We thought mortals had been weary of seeking it, after so many disappointments. And pray, adventurous traveler, what do you want there?"

"A certain king, who is my cousin," replied he, "has ordered me to get him three of the golden apples."

"Most of the young men who go in quest of these apples," observed another of the damsels, "desire to obtain them for themselves, or to present them to some fair maiden whom they love. Do you, then, love this king, your cousin, so very much?"

"Perhaps not," replied the stranger, sighing. "He has often been severe and cruel to me. But it is my destiny to obey him."

"And do you know," asked the damsel who had first spoken, "that a terrible dragon, with a hundred heads, keeps watch under the golden apple-tree?"

"I know it well," answered the stranger, calmly. "But, from my cradle upwards, it has been my business, and almost my pastime, to deal with serpents and dragons."

The young women looked at his massive club, and at the shaggy lion's skin which he wore, and likewise at his heroic limbs and figure; and they whispered to each other that the stranger appeared to be one who might reasonably expect to perform deeds far beyond the might of other men. But, then, the dragon with a hundred heads! What mortal, even if he possessed a hundred lives, could hope to escape the fangs of such a monster? So kind-hearted were the maidens, that they could not bear to see this brave and, handsome traveler attempt what was so very dangerous, and devote himself, most probably, to become a meal for the dragon's hundred ravenous mouths.

"Go back," cried they all,—"go back to your own home! Your mother, beholding you safe and sound, will shed tears of joy; and what can she do more, should you win ever so great a victory? No matter for the golden apples! No matter for the king, your cruel cousin! We do not wish the dragon with the hundred heads to eat you up!"

The stranger seemed to grow impatient at these remonstrances. He carelessly lifted his mighty club, and let it fall upon a rock that lay half buried in the earth, near by. With the force of that idle blow, the great rock was shattered all to pieces. It cost the stranger no more effort to achieve this feat of a giant's strength than for one of the young maidens to touch her sister's rosy cheek with a flower.

"Do you not believe," said he, looking at the damsels with a smile, "that such a blow would have crushed one of the dragon's hundred heads?"

14. **What were the young women doing when the stranger came upon them? Write your answer in the box below.**

[blank answer box]

Question 15 is based on the story below.

THE THREE GOLDEN APPLES, Part - 4

Going on with his wonderful narrative, he informed the maidens that as strange an adventure as ever happened was when he fought with Geryon, the six-legged man. This was a very odd and frightful sort of figure, as you may well believe. Any person, looking at his tracks in the sand or snow, would suppose that three sociable companions had been walking along together. On hearing his footsteps at, a little distance, it was no more than reasonable to judge that several people must be coming. But it was only the strange man Geryon clattering onward, with his six legs!

Six legs, and one gigantic body! Certainly, he must have been a very queer monster to look at; and, my stars, what a waste of shoe-leather!

When the stranger had finished the story of his adventures, he looked around at the attentive faces of the maidens.

"Perhaps you may have heard of me before," said he, modestly. "My name is Hercules!"

"We had already guessed it," replied the maidens; "for your wonderful deeds are known all over the world. We do not think it strange, any longer, that you should set out in quest of the golden apples of the Hesperides. Come, sisters, let us crown the hero with flowers!"

Then they flung beautiful wreaths over his stately head and mighty shoulders, so that the lion's skin was almost entirely covered with roses. They took possession of his ponderous club, and so entwined it about with the brightest, softest, and most fragrant blossoms, that not a finger's breadth of its oaken substance could be seen. It looked all like a huge bunch of flowers. Lastly, they joined hands, and danced around him, chanting words which became poetry of their own accord, and grew into a choral song, in honor of the illustrious Hercules.

And Hercules was rejoiced, as any other hero would have been, to know that these fair young girls had heard of the valiant deeds which it had cost him so much toil and danger to achieve. But, still, he was not satisfied. He could not think that what he had already done was worthy of so much honor, while there remained any bold or difficult adventure to be undertaken.

"Dear maidens," said he, when they paused to take breath, "now that you know my name, will you not tell me how I am to reach the garden of the Hesperides?"

"Ah! Must you go so soon?" they exclaimed. "You—that have performed so many wonders, and spent such a toilsome life—cannot you content yourself to repose a little while on the margin of this peaceful river?"

Hercules shook his head.

"I must depart now," said he.

"We will then give you the best directions we can," replied the damsels. "You must go to the sea-shore, and find out the Old One, and compel him to inform you where the golden apples are to be found."

"The Old One!" repeated Hercules, laughing at this odd name. "And, pray, who may the Old One be?"

"Why, the Old Man of the Sea, to be sure!" answered one of the damsels. "He has fifty daughters, whom some people call very beautiful; but we do not think it proper to be acquainted with them, because they have sea-green hair, and taper away like fishes. You must talk with this Old Man of the Sea. He is a sea-faring person, and knows all about the garden of the Hesperides; for it is situated in an island which he is often in the habit of visiting."

Hercules then asked whereabouts the Old One was most likely to be met with. When the damsels had informed him, he thanked them for all their kindness,—for the bread and grapes with which they had fed him, the lovely flowers with which they had crowned him, and the songs and dances wherewith they had done him honor,—and he thanked them, most of all, for telling him the right way,—and immediately set forth upon his Journey.

But, before he was out of hearing, one of the maidens called after him.

"Keep fast hold of the Old-One, when you catch him!" cried she, smiling, and lifting her finger to make the caution more impressive. "Do not be astonished at anything that may happen. Only hold him fast, and he will tell you what you wish to know."

Hercules again thanked her, and pursued his way, while the maidens resumed their pleasant labor of making flower-wreaths. They talked about the hero, long after he was gone.

"We will crown him with the loveliest of our garlands," said they, "when he returns hither with the three golden apples, after slaying the dragon with a hundred heads."

15. What can you infer that the Old Man of the Sea was known to do when approached? Write your answer in the box below.

Chapter 2

Lesson 7: Describing Events

You can scan the QR code given below or use the url to access additional EdSearch resources including videos and mobile apps related to *Describing Events*.

 Search

Describing Events

URL	QR Code
http://www.lumoslearning.com/a/rl44	

Question 1 and 2 based on the story below.

Timothy

Timothy is a student at my school. He is well-liked by all of the teachers and students. We all know that we can count on Timothy to keep our secrets, to help us if we ask, and to always be on time. We know that he is always honest and expects others to be honest as well.

Last summer, Timothy got a job walking dogs each morning. When school started this year, everyone encouraged him to quit his job, but he decided to keep it. He knew it would be hard to get up every morning at 5 a.m. in order to get all of the dogs walked and then go to school all day. Additionally, he planned to sing in the chorus, play basketball, and be a mentor in the tutoring program this year. He knows it will not be easy, but he thinks his hard work will be worth it. He is trying to save enough money to go to a youth camp next summer.

1. According to the above passage, Timothy is saving his money for what upcoming event?

Ⓐ a football game
Ⓑ a chorus trip
Ⓒ youth camp
Ⓓ a basketball game

2. Timothy gets up at 5 a.m. every morning to:

Ⓐ practice basketball
Ⓑ walk dogs
Ⓒ do his homework
Ⓓ tutor a classmate

Question 3-5 are based on the story below.

After reading the story, enter the details in the map below. This will help you to answer the questions that follow.

Fred Goes to the Dentist

Fred had never been to the dentist. All of his life he had heard horror stories about the buzzing drills, the huge needles, and the scary tools that the dentist used to torture his patients. Since none of his teeth were hurting, Fred just couldn't understand why his mom was insisting on taking him to the dentist. She told him that it was important to visit the dentist each year to have his teeth checked and cleaned. This seemed silly to Fred because he cleaned his teeth everyday by brushing and flossing them, but nothing would change his mother's mind. He found it hard to believe that she would think it was a good idea to take him somewhere to be tortured. However, he had no choice but to go.

On the way to the dentist, Fred's imagination went wild. He pictured walking into a room with a huge chair that the dentist would strap him to. He could just see the dentist pulling out a huge drill and drilling his tooth while his mother and several others held him in the chair. By the time he got to the dentist's office, he was shaking all over.

Surprisingly, the office was nothing like he expected. The dentist was friendly, and the chair was comfortable. It didn't have any straps. He looked around the room and didn't see any huge drills or torture devices. He was relieved when all the dentist did was look in his mouth, show him how to properly brush and floss his teeth, and give him a balloon. His mom made another appointment to have his teeth cleaned in six months. Maybe this wouldn't be as bad as he had thought it would be.

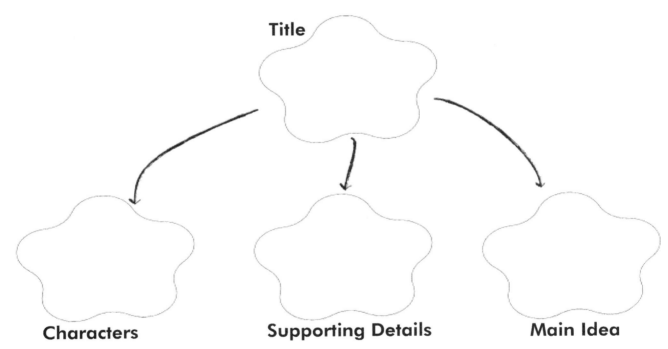

3. Which detail shows that Fred is worried about going to the dentist?

Ⓐ "To his surprise, the office was nothing like he expected."
Ⓑ "Since none of his teeth were hurting, Fred just couldn't understand the reason that his mom was insisting on taking him to a dentist."
Ⓒ "By the time he got to the dentist he was shaking all over."
Ⓓ "Maybe this wouldn't be as bad as he thought it would be."

4. What did Fred imagine was going to happen to him at the dentist office?

Ⓐ The dentist would pull a tooth and then give him a balloon.
Ⓑ The dentist would tie him to the chair and use a huge drill on him.
Ⓒ His mother would hold him down, and the dentist would clean his teeth.
Ⓓ The dentist would tie him down and floss his teeth.

5. What actually happened at the dentist office?

Ⓐ The dentist showed him how to brush and floss his teeth.
Ⓑ The dentist pulled a tooth.
Ⓒ The dentist drilled his tooth.
Ⓓ The dentist pulled a tooth and gave him a balloon.

Question 6 is based on the story below.

Adam lives with his dad and his older brother Stanley. Adam and Stanley share a room. Most of the time Adam enjoys sharing a room with his brother, but there are times that he wishes he had his own room. Being brothers, they have a lot in common; however, they are different in many ways.

Adam likes to spend time with his friends. If he is not with them, he is texting them or playing games with them online. Adam is always busy. He cannot stand to sit around and do nothing. In fact, the only time he is still is when he is sleeping. Adam plays football, basketball, soccer, and baseball. He loves to be involved in school activities or at the town's youth volunteering center. He spends a lot of his time encouraging people to recycle. Although he loves spending time with his friends, he is willing to give up time with them to help others.

Stanley, on the other hand, loves to stay at home. He enjoys activities that can be done alone such as reading, drawing, and spending time with his dogs. Most days after school he can be found at home enjoying one of his favorite activities. He thinks recycling is important and makes sure his family does it. Although he likes being alone, he enjoys volunteering at the youth center with his brother. He thinks it is important to make a difference in the lives of others, which is the reason that he thinks he would like to be a doctor. Adam and Stanley have some differences, but they do join together to make an impact in their community.

6. According to the passage, what do Adam and Stanley enjoy doing together?

Ⓐ Playing football
Ⓑ Drawing cartoons
Ⓒ Playing video games
Ⓓ Volunteering at the youth center

Question 7 is based on the story below.

Mary loves writing stories

"The Elephant Who Saw the World," Mary started speaking. It was Friday, and the students had to share their creative writing stories of the week.

Mary loved writing, and this part of the week, when they were able to make up stories for creative writing, was her favorite part. She enjoyed it so much that she became really good at it. When she was home on the weekends and she didn't have much homework, she would sit in her room for hours and create stories to share with her friends and family. Her parents always supported her and were her biggest fans.

However, there was one part about every Friday at school that Mary did not enjoy, and that was when she had to share her story in front of the class. The teacher made all of the children share on Friday afternoons, and this made Mary very nervous. She was shy, and although she knew her teacher was right, she didn't like it.

After sitting and listening to the other children's share, Mary finally heard her name called. She knew it was her turn to share. She got out of her seat slowly, walked to the front of the room and began.

7. Which event in the above passage made Mary nervous?

Ⓐ writing a story
Ⓑ talking to the teacher
Ⓒ sharing her work in front of the class
Ⓓ showing her family what she had done

Question 8 and 9 are based on the story below.

"Dad and I need to go out of town this weekend," said Mom. "We'll be back on Monday, so the three of you are going to spend the weekend with your two aunts. "

Lindsay, Scarlet, and Austin loved their aunts and were really excited. They ran upstairs and started getting their things together to take with them. They put everything in one bag that they would need for school. They were going to stay with Aunt Margaret for two nights and the last night with their Auntie Josephine.

At the end of the school day, the children came running out of classroom doors from all different directions. Aunt Margaret was waiting for her nieces and nephew at the entrance of the school. She was wearing a bright red suit with a sparkly cat pin on it. She also had on a proper wool hat to match. She noticed a scuff on her shoes when her nieces and nephew ran up to her.

She cried, "Oh, my goodness! I am so happy you are here. The children at your school are just a bunch of toughies. I was nearly trampled while I was standing here! Let's get into the car." Aunt Margaret pointed to a large, green, four-door station wagon that was parked in the lot.

The next day, a funny-sounding honk came from the front of the house. The children ran outside and saw Auntie Jo sitting in her convertible. She was wearing a big cowboy hat. She wore a pair of polka dot shorts with a too large shirt.

8. What most likely happened to Aunt Margaret while she was waiting for her nieces and nephew?

   Ⓐ The children ambushed her while she was waiting in the parking lot.
   Ⓑ She was in a bad mood already and called the children "toughies" for no reason.
   Ⓒ Mean spirited children knocked her down because she was a stranger.
   Ⓓ The school children were excited that school was out and they bumped into her in their hurry to get home and to after school activities.

9. Why did the children need to stay with their two aunts?

   Ⓐ Their parents needed to hang decorations around the house.
   Ⓑ Their parents were celebrating their anniversary.
   Ⓒ Their parents needed to go out of town.
   Ⓓ Their parents needed to help their little brother Austin go shopping for school.

Question 10 is based on the passage below.

This year Jim and I had the most wonderful vacation compared to the one we took last year. This year Jim and I went to Hawaii, which is a much better place to visit than a hunting lodge in Alaska. The hotel we stayed in was a luxury suite. It included a big screen TV with all of the movie channels, a hot tub on the balcony, a small kitchen stocked with local fruits and vegetables, and a huge bed shaped like a pineapple. The weather in Hawaii could not have been any better. We enjoyed many hours on the beach sunbathing and playing volleyball. When we were not on the beach, we were in the ocean swimming or riding the waves on a surf board. Each night we enjoyed eating and dancing with all of our friends at a luau. Our week in Hawaii rushed by, making us wish we had planned a two-week vacation.

On the other hand, the hunting lodge we stayed in Alaska had no TV, a shower with barely warm water, a small cooler for our food, and cots to sleep on each night. The room wasn't even the worst part of the vacation. The weather was terrible. It rained the entire time we were there. Even with the rain, our guide expected us to go on the all-day fishing trip that was part of our vacation package. All we caught on that fishing trip was a cold from the rain. After the third day, we decided to cut our trip short and head for home. Without a doubt, we will be going back to Hawaii next year on our vacation.

10. What event in the above passage caused the writer to catch a cold?

   Ⓐ A day of surfing
   Ⓑ Attending a luau
   Ⓒ Swimming
   Ⓓ Fishing in the rain

Question 11 is based on the story below.

The Mall - What Fun

Santiago and Felix wanted to go to the mall on Saturday. They had both saved up their money from lawn mowing and yard work. Each had been working for 3 weeks on Saturdays and Sunday afternoons to earn money. Their favorite place in the mall was around the food court and video arcade.

Santiago's older sister, Felicia, offered to drive them since she was going to get her hair done at Pro-Cuts there anyway. Felicia told them to be ready by her car at 9:45 Saturday morning. The mall opened at 10:00 and it would take them about 15 minutes or so to get there. Felix had a tendency to be late all the time, so Santiago was a little worried that he wouldn't show up on time. Santiago had a plan to make sure that didn't happen this time.

He asked his mother on Friday after school, if Felix could spend the night. Luckily she agreed if they didn't stay up late and if he cleaned his room before Felix came over. So Santiago quickly called Felix to see if he could come over and spend the night. Felix was elated! "Sure thing, buddy! I will be there in a jiffy!"

"Don't come too soon, I have to clean my room! Mama made me promise to do it!" Santiago said. "No worries, dude, I can help." Felix replied.

So it was set. Santiago did ask his mama if Felix could help him clean his room. His mama just laughed and said, "Sure, you boys are so silly."

As soon as Felix got there, the boys started on their room cleaning project. This gave Felicia an idea, too.

"Guys, if I am giving you a ride to the mall tomorrow, how about cleaning my room, too?"
"No way! Not a girl's room!!" They both exclaimed at the same exact time.
"Oh, well, can't blame a girl for trying!" Laughed Felicia. "Don't worry, I will still take you."

That night the boys played video games and watched a combat movie. About 10:30pm, Santiago remembered what his mama said about not staying up late. He told Felix, "We better get to bed, Mama said not to stay up late if you came over."

"No problem, let's hit the sack," Said Felix.

The next morning, they were up, bathed, dressed, and had eaten breakfast by the time Felicia was ready to go.

"Wow, on time both of you and ready. This must be a special mall day for y'all!" She said.

When they got to the mall, Felicia told them to be sure to keep an eye on their watches. She also told them to meet her back at the door they came in exactly at 12:30. Her hair appointment would take one hour and then she wanted to meet friends to shop, as well. The boys agreed.

Their first stop was the video arcade where they met up with other friends and started playing games. It wasn't long before Felix wanted to go get a snack at the food court. You could say Felix liked food. He wasn't over weight or anything, he just liked to eat. Santiago was in the middle of a game and said he would be there shortly. Well, you guessed it, shortly didn't happen. Felix had his snack and waited for about 30 minutes for Santiago to show up. He didn't know what to do. So he headed back to the video arcade. He did notice that his watch showed it to be 12:10. They only had 20 minutes left and they had not even gone to any shops. Felix felt a sick feeling that he better find Santiago fast or Felicia would not be happy. She might not ever take them again if they did not make it back on time. Felix started almost running around a corner and splat! He ran right into Santiago!

"What took you so long, dude? I had my snack and waited on you forever!" Felix said in a bit of a disgruntled voice.

"My fault, all my fault! I was beating the game and didn't want to stop! Sorry. You are my best friend and I feel bad for letting you down." Replied Santiago.

"No worries, we better get going back to the door we came in at and meet Felicia." Said Felix.

When they got to the meeting place, Felicia was just walking up.

"Hey guys, y'all want to stay longer?" She said.

The guys grinned and nodded yes.

"Great, meet me here at 2:30. I am going to the movies with my friends. I already called Mama to let her know we would be staying longer."

Happily the boys went to shop with their money, bought new sneakers, ate lunch and even got to play video games again.

11. Sequence the events in order as they happened. Write the steps in the correct sequence in the boxes given below.

    A. Santiago and Felix get to go to the shops and eat lunch.
    B. Felicia tells the boys to meet her back at 12:30.
    C. Mama allows Santiago to have Felix over to spend the night.
    D. The boys clean Santiago's bedroom and do not stay up late.
    E. Santiago forgets to meet Felix at the food court and Felix waits for him.

1.

2.

3.

4.

5.

Question 12 is based on the story below.

The Haunted House on Rio Vista Drive

The neighborhood of Rio Vista Drive had two parts to it. On one side of Riverside Avenue were about 14 houses. Each house had approximately three bedrooms, two baths, an extremely grand living area, kitchen, washroom, and most often a small office area. The backyards were all chain linked hurricane fences of around 1.2 acres with a covered garage, back driveway and security locked gate. Most of the front yards were unique to themselves and had a theme which was painted on a plaque on the outside of the house itself. The realtors said that the architect had named each house as he had built it and decorated the fronts to match the names.

However, on the other side of Rio Vista Drive at the end of the block- a dead end, stood a rickety two story house assumed to be about 50-75 years old. This was dubbed the Haunted House. There was an old woman, Widow Crankston, who lived there. The kids say she would come out in the evening and sit on her porch. Several thought they saw her carrying a black cat and presumed she was a witch of sorts. Briars grew up along the fence line and sidewalks. The windows were covered in cobwebs and the like. It had been years and years since the house had been painted or anything in the yard taken care of either. Many a dare had been made among the neighborhood kids to go and ring the doorbell or knock on the door. Most dares were made on Halloween or around that time.

So it was on the night before Halloween that Howard, Ernie and Edward were riding their bikes down Rio Vista Drive. Up one side and down the other, quickly turning around before they reached Widow Crankston's Haunted House! Suddenly, Howard came to a screeching stop right in front of the house.

"Ok, dare ya' to do it!" He hollered at Ernie.

"No, dare you!" Ernie screamed back.

"Scaredy Cats!" Laughed Edward!! "I will do it!"

So off he went, straight up to the front door. He rang the doorbell, but no one answered. Hurriedly he turned around and was running down the steps when he heard a tiny voice behind him.

"Yes, young man, may I help you?" Inquired Widow Crankston, as she peeped out the massive door. "Is today Halloween, I thought it was tomorrow. Let me get you some chocolate brownies and a caramel apple. Do your friends want some, too? Haven't had young- ins come here in ages. Please sit on the porch while I get y'all treats and some cold milk."

Edward stopped in his tracks. She wasn't an old witch, but just a kind hearted little old lady. He motioned for Howard and Ernie. Both came running up the sidewalk just in time to eat the goodies!

Now the other kids in the neighborhood aren't sure yet what to think. There are no more briars, no more cobwebs, and the fresh paint on the house looks wonderful. The boys have a part-time job cleaning and painting while enjoying good company and great snacks!

12. Write the sequence of events in the story in the correct order in the boxes given below.

    A. The boys help paint the house and fix it up.
    B. Edward decides to take the dare.
    C. The house is in bad shape with briars, cobwebs, and needs painting.
    D. It is the night before Halloween.
    E. Widow Crankston offers them treats to eat and cold milk to drink.
    F. There are two parts of Rio Vista Drive.
    G. Some kids believe Widow Crankston is a witch because of her black cat.

    1. (_____)

    2. (_____)

    3. (_____)

4. _____

5. _____

6. _____

7. _____

Question 13 is based on the story below.

The Case of the Missing Lasagna

It was a bright and sunny afternoon at Everton Middle School. Fourth-grade students were returning from lunch. The tardy bell was about to ring. Mr. Hart sat at his teacher's desk with a smudged red stain on the sleeve of his shirt, while Mrs. Waterton told students to find their seats.

"Best lunch I can remember eating in a long time!" Mr. Hart exclaimed. "What was it like for the cafeteria lunch today?" He didn't get a reply from the students. Instead they all just looked at him rather puzzled by that comment.

Out of the blue, Mr. Smith, the Principal, called on the intercom system. He asked Mrs. Waterton to come to the office. When she returned, she asked Mr. Hart to step outside of the classroom. She then told him that Ms. Abernathy's lunch had gone missing, had he seen anything since he had been in her room right before lunch.

Mr. Hart had an astonished look on his face as he quickly returned to the classroom. It was then that he went to his desk and picked up his lunch bag. Splat on the floor went the contents of his bag, 2 lettuce wraps and a banana. "Hmmm," he said to the class while laughing, "Got any ideas about where a missing plate of lasagna for Ms. Abernathy could have gone?"

13. Part A

Consider all of the evidence in the story and determine who you think might have taken Ms. Abernathy's lunch.

List the pieces of evidence from the story that make you think that. Write your answer in the box below.

Part B

Why do these pieces of evidence make you think that this person took Ms. Abernathy's lunch? Explain and Write your answer in the box below.

Question 14 is based on the story below.

A Chosen Child

Mary Ann Woods was a bright and happy 10 year old. She loved playing with her friends outside and working on arts and craft projects with her mother. Mary Ann even helped her dad out in the yard with the garden, weed eating, mowing, and clipping hedges. Mary Ann was an only child and often longed to have a baby brother or sister. She truly envied her neighborhood friends that had many siblings.

Her house was just as large as most of the other houses, but several bedrooms were empty. Not that they didn't have furniture in them, it was that no one lived or slept in the rooms unless guests came for a visit. Mary Ann liked to go in the rooms and pretend that her make-believe sister lived there. She would sit on the bed and pretend to be talking to her, smiling and even laughing out loud at times.

While she was doing just that one day, her mom walked down the hall. She heard talking and laughing, but it wasn't coming from Mary Ann's bedroom. Puzzled, her mom peered around the corner to one of the guest bedrooms and spotted Mary Ann on the bed looking up to the ceiling.

"Child, what on Earth are you doing?" questioned her mother.
"Oh, sorry, Mom, didn't mean to scare you or mess up the bed." She replied.
"I was talking to Josephine."
"And WHO is Josephine, might I ask?"

"My imaginary sister!" And with that reply, Mary Ann hopped off the bed and scurried out of the room.

Her mother was in a quandary, as she wondered why Mary Ann would need an imaginary sister, when she had friends galore. That evening after dinner, Mary Ann's mother told her dad about what had occurred earlier in the day. "Sam, I am quite concerned about her behaving in this manner. What do you think we should do?"

"Do? Why do anything, Sheila? It is normal for kiddos to have pretend friends." Replied Sam, Mary Ann's dad.

"Do you think we need to tell her now? You know we said we would when she got old enough to understand."

Mary Ann's dad breathed a deep sigh and agreed it was time for the dreaded talk. You see Sheila and Sam couldn't have children and they had adopted Mary Ann when she was only a few days old. The adoption had cost them quite a bit of money. In fact, it was all of their savings at the time. They were so thrilled to be able to have Mary Ann as their baby, they did not care about the expense. It was only later as Mary Ann grew up when they wanted to adopt another child that they realized it was not feasible with the costs. They had moved into the large house so that Mary Ann could be in a neighborhood full of other children to be her playmates.

How to break the news was on both of their minds as they tried to prepare for bed. As always, Mary Ann had helped with the dishes and was about to make her way upstairs. Her dad asked her to come sit in the living room with him and her mom. Thinking nothing of it, Mary Ann skipped into the room.

"What's up, Dad?"

Her dad began to tell the story of her adoption. Mary Ann sat quietly, face wrinkled, and listened intently to every word. Her mom held one hand and her dad the other. They were both in tears as they explained that due to health reasons, they could not have children of their own. They grinned as they told of how excited they were to be able to adopt her. Words of love and commitment flowed from their mouths. When they had finished, they looked Mary Ann in the eyes and said, "You are our chosen child!"

Mary Ann hugged them both fiercely and exclaimed with her own sigh of relief, "No wonder I do not have brown eyes like either of you! I love being chosen! My turn to choose! So now I choose you, too, forever to be my chosen parents!"

14. Sequence arrange the events of the story in order in the boxes given below.

    A. Mary Ann is an only child.
    B. Mary Ann's parents tell her she is adopted.
    C. Mary Ann likes to go into the empty bedrooms, and pretend her make believe sister lives there.
    D. Mary Ann's mother is worried about her behavior.
    E. Mary Ann skipped into the living room.

1. _____

2. _____

3. _____

4. _____

5. _____

Question 15 is based on the story below.

Disneyworld- Here We Come! Part - V

Again on the second day, we had the free breakfast and rode the trolley. It wasn't raining this time at all. Mom got out her map and we began our day. Daniel wanted to go back and ride the Mad Tea Party again, but thankfully Mom said no to that.

We were able to go to Splash Mountain, the Jungle Cruise, the 7 Dwarf's Mine Train and much more. Mom did make a request of her own. She wanted to meet Mickey and Minnie Mouse who were scheduled to appear outside of the Cinderella Castle. She also said she wanted to listen to the Enchanted Tales with Belle and ride the Prince Charming Regal Carrousel.   What a crazy silly Mom!

What we didn't know was that she had a plan. It was right after we left the carrousel that we heard fantastic sounds coming down the main street. Yes, parade time right before our eyes. Mom told us to come and sit. There we were on the side of the castle sitting on the ledge in perfect view of the parade. We asked her how she knew to stop there. She said one of the hotel clerks had told her how to find the spot and when to be there. The parade was magnificent to say the least. The characters actually stopped in front of us and performed. Wow! We couldn't have planned it any better.

After the parade we went to A Pirate's Adventure and Tomorrowland Speedway, and Big Thunder Mountain. Mom said we needed to head toward the front entrance as it was time for fireworks and we needed to be ready. We got there just in time. The lights lit up the sky behind the Cinderella Castle and throughout Disneyworld. Just picture it!

What a perfect ending to our vacation

15. **Explain the events that led up to them being able to see the parade from a wonderful view. Be sure to use details from the story to support your evidence. Write your answer in the box below.**

Chapter 2

Lesson 8: Figurative Language

You can scan the QR code given below or use the url to access additional EdSearch resources including videos and mobile apps related to *Figurative Language*.

ed Search

Figurative Language

URL	QR Code
http://www.lumoslearning.com/a/rl44	

1. Identify the simile used in the below sentence.

Her eyes twinkled like diamonds as she looked lovingly at her new kitten.

Ⓐ her eyes twinkled
Ⓑ as she looked lovingly
Ⓒ at her new kitten
Ⓓ twinkled like diamonds

2. Identify the metaphor in the below sentence.

Elaine has no sympathy for others. You know she has a heart of stone.

Ⓐ no sympathy for others
Ⓑ a heart of stone
Ⓒ no sympathy
Ⓓ she has a heart

3. Identify the sentence that contains a metaphor.

Ⓐ She is as sweet as sugar.
Ⓑ She is as blind as a bat.
Ⓒ The sound of the chirping birds is music to my ears.
Ⓓ Billy is as stubborn as a mule.

4. Suzy eats like a bird.

This simile means that Suzy:

Ⓐ eats nuts and seeds
Ⓑ eats many large meals
Ⓒ eats while flying
Ⓓ eats very little

5. The metaphor in the below sentence compares his wife to:

My wife is my compass that guides me to the correct paths in life.

Ⓐ a passage
Ⓑ compass
Ⓒ a guide
Ⓓ life

6. The metaphor in this sentence is used to let you know that the car:

I really got a bad deal on the used car I bought. That <u>car was a real lemon</u>.

- Ⓐ was a good buy
- Ⓑ had a very low price
- Ⓒ was yellow
- Ⓓ didn't run well

7. Choose the answer that contains a simile.

- Ⓐ Your room is a pig pen. How do you even find your bed?
- Ⓑ It has rained cats and dogs all day long. I wish the rain would stop.
- Ⓒ Our math home work was a breeze.
- Ⓓ I could not eat Susan's biscuits because they were as hard as a rock.

8. Janice is such an angel means that Janice:

- Ⓐ is mean
- Ⓑ is annoying
- Ⓒ is kind
- Ⓓ has wings

9. Jimmy is an ox.

   The metaphor 'is an ox' means what?

- Ⓐ He is weak.
- Ⓑ He is blind.
- Ⓒ He is strong.
- Ⓓ He is deaf.

10. What is the metaphor in the sentence below?

   Linda is a road hog. She drives too fast.

- Ⓐ She drives too fast.
- Ⓑ Linda is a road hog.
- Ⓒ Linda is.
- Ⓓ She drives.

Question 11 is based on the story below.

Disneyworld Here We Come! Part -II

Soon enough we were at my grandmother's. Mom had made us pack one light bag with just enough for each of us our night clothes, and a clean outfit for the next day. That way we didn't have to take so much out at my grandmother's house. We were ready for a light soup supper and off to bed. Before we knew it, it was daylight again. Mom was hustling us out of bed and into the kitchen for breakfast. She said to eat hearty as we had many more miles to go before we reached our final destination. So thankful that my grandmother cooked her best oatmeal for us topped with cinnamon, brown sugar, strawberries, and whipped cream! Who could ask for anything more? Yummy!!
Then it was load back into the car and get on the road. This time Mom found an oldies radio station and she was singing along with Patsy Cline, Tennessee Ernie Ford, and Frank Sinatra. Talk about strange music that none of us knew except her! Valerie and I played a game of travel trivia which was sort of fun and of course, Daniel, was back on his video games!

For lunch we stopped at a roadside park and had the sandwiches our grandmother had packed for us along with an apple and sweet iced tea. When we got back on the road, not a sound could be heard. I figured out later that all of us kids had fallen asleep.

A loud bang woke us as Mom clapped her hands and proclaimed our arrival to the Holiday Inn at Disneyworld! I could not tell you who was the most excited as we were all yelling sounds of glee and running around the car to get our luggage out. Mom registered us for our room and we were giggling uncontrollably.

11. Select and write from the following list of words.

out of control/unable to stop
strong/healthy
hurrying
something to wear

Part A

What do you think the following words mean based on the story?

hustling means _____

Part B

outfit means _____

Part C

uncontrollably means _____

Part D

hearty means _____

Question 12 is based on the story below.

GRAINS, GRAINS, GRAINS

Everyone knows that grains are an important healthy part of a good diet. It is important to make sure that you are eating the right amount of grains daily.

To make sure this happens include grains in half of your diet each day. Whole grain and wheat help to keep your digestive system in order and run smoothly as well.

Did you know that whole grains and whole grain foods are made up of all three layers of the grain seed or kernel?

Here are the layers and explanations that will help you to understand.

1. The bran (outer layer): give you all of the fiber as well as B vitamins; minerals such as magnesium, iron and zinc, and some protein.

2. The endosperm (middle layer): makes up for most of the weight of the grain and is made up mainly of carbohydrate and protein.

3. The germ (inner layer): has B vitamins, unsaturated fats, vitamin E, and minerals.

Most whole grains are quite tasty such as brown rice, barley, whole oats or oatmeal, wheat and rye breads.

When you go shopping with your parents, do the healthy choice thing and read labels.

Whole grain foods will have the words 'whole' or 'whole grain' followed by the name of the grain as one of the first ingredients.

12. Match the term with its definition

	germ (inner layer)	endosperm (middle layer)	bran (outer layer)
the weight of the grain			
the fiber			
unsaturated fats			

Question 13 is based on the story below.

THE THREE GOLDEN APPLES
By Nathaniel Hawthorne

Part - 3

Then he sat down on the grass, and told them the story of his life, or as much of it as he could remember, from the day when he was first cradled in a warrior's brazen shield. While he lay there, two immense serpents came gliding over the floor, and opened their hideous jaws to devour him; and he, a baby of a few months old, had griped one of the fierce snakes in each of his little fists, and strangled them to death. When he was but a stripling, he had killed a huge lion, almost as big as the one whose vast and shaggy hide he now wore upon his shoulders. The next thing that he had done was to fight a battle with an ugly sort of monster, called a hydra, which had no less than nine heads, and exceedingly sharp teeth in every one of them.

"But the dragon of the Hesperides, you know," observed one of the damsels, "has a hundred heads!"

"Nevertheless," replied the stranger, "I would rather fight two such dragons than a single hydra. For, as fast as I cut off a head, two others grew in its place; and, besides, there was one of the heads that could not possibly be killed, but kept biting as fiercely as ever, long after it was cut off. So I was forced to bury it under a stone, where it is doubtless alive, to this vary day. But the hydra's body, and its eight other heads, will never do any further mischief."

The damsels, judging that the story was likely to last a good while, had been preparing a repast of bread and grapes, that the stranger might refresh himself in the intervals of his talk. They took pleasure in helping him to this simple food; and, now and then, one of them would put a sweet grape between her rosy lips, lest it should make him bashful to eat alone.

The traveler proceeded to tell how he had chased a very swift stag, for a twelve-month together, without ever stopping to take breath, and had at last caught it by the antlers, and carried it home alive. And he had fought with a very odd race of people, half horses and half men, and had put them all to death, from a sense of duty, in order that their ugly figures might never be seen any more. Besides all this, he took to himself great credit for having cleaned out a stable.

"Do you call that a wonderful exploit?" asked one of the young maidens, with a smile. "Any clown in the country has done as much!"

"Had it been an ordinary stable," replied the stranger, "I should not have mentioned it. But this was so gigantic a task that it would have taken me all my life to perform it, if I had not luckily thought of turning the channel of a river through the stable-door. That did the business in a very short time!"

Seeing how earnestly his fair auditors listened, he next told them how he had shot some monstrous birds, and had caught a wild bull alive, and let him go again, and had tamed a number of very wild horses, and had conquered Hippolyta, the warlike queen of the Amazons. He mentioned, likewise, that he had taken off Hippolyta's enchanted girdle, and had given it to the daughter of his cousin, the king.

"Was it the girdle of Venus," inquired the prettiest of the damsels, "which makes women beautiful?" "No," answered the stranger. "It had formerly been the sword-belt of Mars; and it can only make the wearer valiant and courageous."

"An old sword-belt!" cried the damsel, tossing her head. "Then I should not care about having it!" "You are right," said the stranger.

13. **The stranger told the damsels (young women) many things about his life and his strength. Mark all answers that apply to his story.**

   (A) He killed snakes as a baby.
   (B) He killed a lion as a young child.
   (C) He killed a monster with many heads.
   (D) He had been to the garden but forgot how to get back there.

Question 14 is based on the story below.

THE THREE GOLDEN APPLES, Part - 4

Going on with his wonderful narrative, he informed the maidens that as strange an adventure as ever happened was when he fought with Geryon, the six-legged man. This was a very odd and frightful sort of figure, as you may well believe. Any person, looking at his tracks in the sand or snow, would suppose that three sociable companions had been walking along together. On hearing his footsteps at, a little distance, it was no more than reasonable to judge that several people must be coming. But it was only the strange man Geryon clattering onward, with his six legs!

Six legs, and one gigantic body! Certainly, he must have been a very queer monster to look at; and, my stars, what a waste of shoe-leather!
When the stranger had finished the story of his adventures, he looked around at the attentive faces of the maidens.

"Perhaps you may have heard of me before," said he, modestly. "My name is Hercules!"
"We had already guessed it," replied the maidens; "for your wonderful deeds are known all over the world. We do not think it strange, any longer, that you should set out in quest of the golden apples of the Hesperides. Come, sisters, let us crown the hero with flowers!"
Then they flung beautiful wreaths over his stately head and mighty shoulders, so that the lion's skin was almost entirely covered with roses. They took possession of his ponderous club, and so entwined it about with the brightest, softest, and most fragrant blossoms, that not a finger's breadth of its oaken substance could be seen. It looked all like a huge bunch of flowers. Lastly, they joined hands, and danced around him, chanting words which became poetry of their own accord, and grew into a choral song, in honor of the illustrious Hercules.

And Hercules was rejoiced, as any other hero would have been, to know that these fair young girls had heard of the valiant deeds which it had cost him so much toil and danger to achieve. But, still, he was not satisfied. He could not think that what he had already done was worthy of so much honor, while there remained any bold or difficult adventure to be undertaken.
"Dear maidens," said he, when they paused to take breath, "now that you know my name, will you not tell me how I am to reach the garden of the Hesperides?"

"Ah! Must you go so soon?" they exclaimed. "You—that have performed so many wonders, and spent such a toilsome life—cannot you content yourself to repose a little while on the margin of this peaceful river?"
Hercules shook his head.
"I must depart now," said he.
"We will then give you the best directions we can," replied the damsels. "You must go to the seashore, and find out the Old One, and compel him to inform you where the golden apples are to be found."

"The Old One!" repeated Hercules, laughing at this odd name. "And, pray, who may the Old One be?"

"Why, the Old Man of the Sea, to be sure!" answered one of the damsels. "He has fifty daughters, whom some people call very beautiful; but we do not think it proper to be acquainted with them, because they have sea-green hair, and taper away like fishes. You must talk with this Old Man of the Sea. He is a sea-faring person, and knows all about the garden of the Hesperides; for it is situated in an island which he is often in the habit of visiting."

Hercules then asked whereabouts the Old One was most likely to be met with. When the damsels had informed him, he thanked them for all their kindness,—for the bread and grapes with which they had fed him, the lovely flowers with which they had crowned him, and the songs and dances wherewith they had done him honor,—and he thanked them, most of all, for telling him the right way,—and immediately set forth upon his Journey.

But, before he was out of hearing, one of the maidens called after him.
"Keep fast hold of the Old-One, when you catch him!" cried she, smiling, and lifting her finger to make the caution more impressive. "Do not be astonished at anything that may happen. Only hold him fast, and he will tell you what you wish to know."

Hercules again thanked her, and pursued his way, while the maidens resumed their pleasant labor of making flower-wreaths. They talked about the hero, long after he was gone.
"We will crown him with the loveliest of our garlands," said they, "when he returns hither with the three golden apples, after slaying the dragon with a hundred heads."

14. Who was this stranger?

Question 15 is based on the story below.

THE THREE GOLDEN APPLES, Part - 7

It was in this journey, if I mistake not, that he encountered a prodigious giant, who was so wonderfully contrived by nature, that, every time he touched the earth, he became ten times as strong as ever he had been before. His name was Antreus. You may see, plainly enough, that it was a very difficult business to fight with such a fellow; for, as often as he got a knock-down blow, up he started again, stronger, fiercer, and abler to use his weapons, than if his enemy had let him alone, Thus, the harder Hercules pounded the giant with his club, the further be seemed from winning the victory. I have sometimes argued with such people, but never fought with one. The only way in which Hercules found it possible to finish the battle, was by lifting Antreus off his feet into the air, and squeezing, and squeezing, and squeezing him, until, finally, the strength was quite squeezed out of his enormous body.

When this affair was finished, Hercules continued his travels, and went to the land of Egypt, where he was taken prisoner, and would have been put to death, if he had not slain the king of the country, and made his escape. Passing through the deserts of Africa, and going as fast as he could, he arrived at last on the shore of the great ocean. And here, unless he could walk on the crests of the billows, it seemed as if his journey must needs be at an end.

Nothing was before him, save the foaming, dashing, measureless ocean. But, suddenly, as he looked towards the horizon, he saw something, a great way off, which he had not seen the moment before. It gleamed very brightly, almost as you may have beheld the round, golden disk of the sun, when it rises or sets over the edge of the world. It evidently drew nearer; for, at every instant, this wonderful object became larger and more lustrous. At length, it had come so nigh that Hercules discovered it to be an immense cup or bowl, made either of gold or burnished brass. How it had got afloat upon the sea, is more than I can tell you. There it was, at all events, rolling on the tumultuous billows, which tossed it up and down, and heaved their foamy tops against its sides, but without ever throwing their spray over the brim.

"I have seen many giants, in my time," thought Hercules, "but never one that would need to drink his wine out of a cup like this!"
And, true enough, what a cup it must have been! It was as large—as large—but, in short, I am afraid to say how immeasurably large it was. To speak within bounds, it was ten times larger than a great mill-wheel; and, all of metal as it was, it floated over the heaving surges more lightly than an acorn-cup adown the brook. The waves tumbled it onward, until it grazed against the shore, within a short distance of the spot where Hercules was standing.

As soon as this happened, he knew what was to be done; for he had not gone through so many re-markable adventures without learning pretty well how to conduct himself, whenever anything came to pass a little out of the common rule. It was just as clear as daylight that this marvellous cup had been set adrift by some unseen power, and guided hitherward, in order to carry Hercules across the sea, on his way to the garden of the Hesperides. Accordingly, without a moment's delay, he clambered over the brim, and slid down on the inside, where, spreading out his lion's skin, he proceeded to take a little repose. He had scarcely rested, until now, since he bade farewell to the damsels on the margin of the river. The waves dashed, with a pleasant and ringing sound, against the circumference of the hollow cup; it rocked lightly to and fro, and the motion was so soothing that, it speedily rocked Hercules into an agreeable slumber.

15. Use vocabulary from the story to complete the following sentences.

The cup had been set _____ by some unseen power and guided _____, in order to carry Hercules across the sea, on his way to the garden of the _____.

Chapter 2

Lesson 9: Text Structure

Before answering the questions, it is important to understand the meaning of different text structure.

This standard mentions the word "structure" and lists several examples of literary structures. You need to understand that a literary structure refers to the way the text is organized. To identify the structure used in a text you have been assigned to read, you need to understand the kinds of literary structures and how to recognize them. Here are several commonly used literary structures:

- *Narrative*: text that tells a story (characters, setting, and actions) with a plot (conflict or problem) that ends with a resolution (or solving) of the problem. James and the Giant Peach and Diary of a Wimpy Kid are good examples of stories with a narrative structure.

- *Chronological*: text whose actions move along a time period. Example: A story about a family going on vacation starts with packing for the trip, the trip itself, reaching the destination, describing what happens there, and the trip home.

- *Comparison and Contrast*: text with this structure compares two things and points out similarities and differences between them. Examples: living in a desert compared with living in a forest; playing basketball and playing soccer.

- *Cause and Effect*: text that describes an event (a hurricane; a championship game) and the effects that the event has on people or things (flooding and trees blown over; joy and celebration or sadness and despair).

- *Inductive*: text that describes an idea or event and then expands that idea or event to include a larger audience or a larger result.

  Examples:
  1. The person who discovered the first and only fast food restaurant owned by the McDonald brothers imagined that the idea of fast food could be expanded to many locations in the United States.
  2. Steve Jobs imagined that a telephone could be made small enough to be carried in a person's pocket and could be used to do more than place and receive calls; the Apple iPhone was the result.

- *Deductive*: text that describes things about a person or an idea or event from which the reader or listener reaches a conclusion.

Examples:
1. Human beings cannot exist in extremely cold temperatures without protective clothing. The arctic areas of the world have extremely cold temperatures. Therefore, people planning to visit the arctic must take protective clothing.
2. There are internet users who use software to invade computers to steal information. There are companies who develop software to protect computers from invasion. Therefore, internet users should purchase protective software.

You can scan the QR code given below or use the url to access additional EdSearch resources including videos and mobile apps related to *Text Structure*.

ed Search	**Text Structure**
URL	**QR Code**
http://www.lumoslearning.com/a/rl45	

1. **Which text structure is used in the classic story "The Three Little Pigs?"**

   (A) Cause and effect
   (B) Compare and contrast
   (C) Problem and solution
   (D) Sequence

2. **What is the structure of the below text?**

I saw the most unusual chair in a furniture store today while walking around the mall. The chair was shaped like a high-heeled shoe. The seat was created from the toe of the shoe, and the high heel and back of the shoe created the chair's back. Hot pink velvet covered the top portion of the chair. Black velvet covered the bottom and heel of the chair. Along the sides of the toes and heel, huge rhinestones were glued to the velvet. I wonder who would want this type of chair.

   (A) Cause and effect
   (B) Compare and contrast
   (C) Problem and solution
   (D) Description

Question 3 is based on the story below.

"Dad and I need to go out of town this weekend," said Mom. "We'll be back on Monday, so the three of you are going to spend the weekend with your two aunts. "

Lindsay, Scarlet, and Austin loved their aunts and were really excited. They ran upstairs and started getting their things together to take with them. They put everything in one bag that they would need for school. They were going to stay with Aunt Margaret for two nights and the last night with their Auntie Josephine.

At the end of the school day, the children came running out of classroom doors from all different directions. Aunt Margaret was waiting for her nieces and nephew at the entrance of the school. She was wearing a bright red suit with a sparkly cat pin on it. She also had on a proper wool hat to match. She noticed a scuff on her shoes when her nieces and nephew ran up to her.

She cried, "Oh, my goodness! I am so happy you are here. The children at your school are just a bunch of toughies. I was nearly trampled while I was standing here! Let's get into the car." Aunt Margaret pointed to a large, green, four-door station wagon that was parked in the lot.

The next day, a funny-sounding honk came from the front of the house. The children ran outside and saw Auntie Jo sitting in her convertible. She was wearing a big cowboy hat. She wore a pair of polka dot shorts with a too large shirt.

3. What is the structure of the text?

Ⓐ a play
Ⓑ a comedy
Ⓒ a poem
Ⓓ a narrative

4. What is the structure of the below text?

Before going to bed on Friday night, Susie's parents told her that they had a surprise planned for the weekend and that she would have to wake up really early on Saturday morning. When she woke up, they left the house quickly and started driving. While in the car, Susie looked outside to see if she could figure out where they were going. She noticed that it was getting really hot out and the sun was shining brightly. Then she noticed that the surfboards were in the car. Finally, they stopped, and Susie said, "I know where we are going!"

Ⓐ Cause and effect
Ⓑ Problem and solution
Ⓒ Sequence
Ⓓ Description

5. What is the structure of the below text?

One day James went to town to buy new clothes. First, he tried on a pair of trousers. He didn't like the trousers, so he gave them back to the shopkeeper. Then, he tried on a robe which was the same price as the trousers. James was pleased with the robe, and he left the shop. Before he climbed on his donkey to ride home, the shopkeeper and the shop-assistant ran out.

Ⓐ Descriptive
Ⓑ Problem and solution
Ⓒ Cause and effect
Ⓓ Sequence

6. What is the text structure of this passage?

Beau was a nine-year-old boy who wanted a pet dog very badly. Every day, he asked his parents for a dog. They always told him no, because they didn't think he was responsible enough to take care of a dog. One day, Beau negotiated with his parents. He told them that he would keep his room clean and do other household chores for an entire month to prove he was responsible enough to have a pet. Beau did exactly as he promised, and his parents got him a fluffy, white puppy that he named Snow White.

Ⓐ Description
Ⓒ Compare and contrast

Ⓑ Cause and effect
Ⓓ Problem and solution

Question 7 is based on the passage below.

The blue whale is quite an extraordinary creature. To begin with, it is a mammal that lives its entire life in the ocean. The size of its body is amazing. This whale can grow up to 98 feet long and weigh as much as 200 tons, making it the largest known animal to have ever existed. Its body is long and elegantly tapered, unlike other whales which have a rounder, stockier build. Their build, along with their extreme size, gives them a unique appearance and the ability to move more gracefully and at greater speeds than one might imagine. They can reach speeds up to 31 mph for short periods. Their normal traveling speed is around 12 mph, but they slow to 3.1 mph when feeding. Although they are extremely large animals, they eat small shrimp-like creatures called krill. Since the krill are so small, the blue whale eats about four tons daily as they swim deep in the ocean.

Unlike other whales that live in small, close-knit groups called pods, blue whales live and travel alone or with one other whale. While traveling through the ocean, they surface to breathe air into their lungs through blowholes. They emerge from the ocean, spewing water out of their blowhole, roll, and re-enter the water with a grand splash of their large tail. They make loud, deep, and rumbling low-frequency sounds that travel great distances, which allow them to communicate with other whales as far as 100 miles away. Their cries can be felt as much as heard. Their resonating call makes them the loudest animal on Earth. If you ever have the opportunity to see or hear a blue whale, it will be an experience you will not soon forget.

7. What is the structure of the text in the first paragraph of this passage?

- Ⓐ Descriptive
- Ⓑ Compare and contrast
- Ⓒ Problem and solution
- Ⓓ Sequence or chronological

8. What is the structure of the below text?

When I was little my mom gave me a diary. She told me that it was something really personal and special and I could use it to write down all of my thoughts and ideas. She said that some famous people kept diaries and when they died, their diary was published into a book. Anne Frank is some-one who did this. She was originally from Germany. During the time of World War II, the Nazi soldiers were in power in Germany; they did not like Jews. Anne and her family were Jewish so they had to hide. They went to Amsterdam in the Netherlands. Her diary tells the story of the time when they lived in hiding in concealed rooms in Amsterdam.

- Ⓐ Chronological
- Ⓑ Cause and Effect
- Ⓒ Descriptive
- Ⓓ Problem and Solution

Question 9 is based on the passage below.

This year Jim and I had the most wonderful vacation. Especially, compared to the one we took last year. We went to Hawaii, which was a better place to visit than last year's hunting lodge in Alaska. The hotel we stayed in was a luxury suite; it included a big screen TV with all of the movie channels, a hot tub on the balcony, a small kitchen stocked with local fruits and vegetables, and a huge bed shaped like a pineapple. The weather in Hawaii was superb. We enjoyed many hours on the beach sunbathing and playing volleyball. When we were not on the beach, we were in the ocean swimming or riding the waves on a surf board. Each night we enjoyed eating and dancing with all of our friends at a luau. Our week in Hawaii rushed by, making us wish we had planned a two-week vacation. Without a doubt, we will be going back to Hawaii next year for our vacation.

The hunting lodge in Alaska had a shower with hardly any warm water, a small cooler for our food, and cots to sleep on each night. But, the room wasn't even the worst part of the vacation. The weather was terrible; it rained the entire time we were there. Even with the rain, our guide expected us to go on an all-day fishing trip that was part of our vacation package. All we caught on that fishing trip was a cold from the rain. After the third day in Alaska, we decided to end our nightmare, cut our trip short, and head for home.

9. Choose the text structure used in this passage.

   Ⓐ Cause and effect
   Ⓑ Compare and contrast
   Ⓒ Problem and solution
   Ⓓ Sequence

10. What is the structure of the below text?

A science book might have a lesson about a child who catches an illness from germs that are spread. The child has to see a doctor who cures the illness. Then the Physician tells the child how to prevent the illness in the future. The child learns about hand-washing as one way to prevent disease.

   Ⓐ Cause and effect
   Ⓑ Compare and contrast
   Ⓒ Problem and solution
   Ⓓ Sequence or chronological

Question 11 is based on the story below.

The Mall - What Fun

Santiago and Felix wanted to go to the mall on Saturday. They had both saved up their money from lawn mowing and yard work. Each had been working for 3 weeks on Saturdays and Sunday afternoons to earn money. Their favorite place in the mall was around the food court and video arcade.

Santiago's older sister, Felicia, offered to drive them since she was going to get her hair done at Pro-Cuts there anyway. Felicia told them to be ready by her car at 9:45 Saturday morning. The mall opened at 10:00 and it would take them about 15 minutes or so to get there. Felix had a tendency to be late all the time, so Santiago was a little worried that he wouldn't show up on time. Santiago had a plan to make sure that didn't happen this time.

He asked his mother on Friday after school, if Felix could spend the night. Luckily she agreed if they didn't stay up late and if he cleaned his room before Felix came over. So Santiago quickly called Felix to see if he could come over and spend the night. Felix was elated! "Sure thing, buddy! I will be there in a jiffy!"

"Don't come too soon, I have to clean my room! Mama made me promise to do it!" Santiago said. "No worries, dude, I can help." Felix replied.

So it was set. Santiago did ask his mama if Felix could help him clean his room. His mama just laughed and said, "Sure, you boys are so silly."

As soon as Felix got there, the boys started on their room cleaning project. This gave Felicia an idea, too.
"Guys, if I am giving you a ride to the mall tomorrow, how about cleaning my room, too?"
"No way! Not a girl's room!!" They both exclaimed at the same exact time.
"Oh, well, can't blame a girl for trying!" Laughed Felicia. "Don't worry, I will still take you."

That night the boys played video games and watched a combat movie. About 10:30pm, Santiago remembered what his mama said about not staying up late. He told Felix, "We better get to bed, Mama said not to stay up late if you came over."

"No problem, let's hit the sack," Said Felix.
The next morning, they were up, bathed, dressed, and had eaten breakfast by the time Felicia was ready to go.

"Wow, on time both of you and ready. This must be a special mall day for y'all!" She said.

When they got to the mall, Felicia told them to be sure to keep an eye on their watches. She also told them to meet her back at the door they came in exactly at 12:30. Her hair appointment would take one hour and then she wanted to meet friends to shop, as well. The boys agreed.

Their first stop was the video arcade where they met up with other friends and started playing games. It wasn't long before Felix wanted to go get a snack at the food court. You could say Felix liked food. He wasn't over weight or anything, he just liked to eat. Santiago was in the middle of a game and said he would be there shortly. Well, you guessed it, shortly didn't happen. Felix had his snack and waited for about 30 minutes for Santiago to show up. He didn't know what to do. So he headed back to the video arcade. He did notice that his watch showed it to be 12:10. They only had 20 minutes left and they had not even gone to any shops. Felix felt a sick feeling that he better find Santiago fast or Felicia would not be happy. She might not ever take them again if they did not make it back on time. Felix started almost running around a corner and splat! He ran right into Santiago!

"What took you so long, dude? I had my snack and waited on you forever!" Felix said in a bit of a disgruntled voice.

"My fault, all my fault! I was beating the game and didn't want to stop! Sorry. You are my best friend and I feel bad for letting you down." Replied Santiago.

"No worries, we better get going back to the door we came in at and meet Felicia." Said Felix.

When they got to the meeting place, Felicia was just walking up.

"Hey guys, y'all want to stay longer?" She said.

The guys grinned and nodded yes.

"Great, meet me here at 2:30. I am going to the movies with my friends. I already called Mama to let her know we would be staying longer."

Happily the boys went to shop with their money, bought new sneakers, ate lunch and even got to play video games again.

11. How did Felicia save the day for the boys?

Write a sentence in the box below using evidence from the story to support your answer.

Question 12 is based on the story below.

Disneyworld- Here We Come! Part - I

It was a hot summer day in June. My grandmother, Mom, my brother Daniel, my cousin Valerie, and I were headed out for a long vacation. We were first going to Mississippi and then on to Florida to Disneyworld. Talk about excitement!!! I couldn't contain myself and didn't sleep much at all the night before. Valerie was visiting us because her mom had gotten sick. My wonderful mom had volunteered for her to stay with us the entire summer. It was so cool. Valerie and I were best friends already, much less best cousins. We did everything together all the time. So having her come along was just another treat for me. Of course, I had rather my little snoopy brother, Daniel, didn't come, but oh well! After all, who can complain when you are going to Disneyworld!

We had to stop in Mississippi to leave my grandmother off at her house before the vacation. That wasn't such a bad idea either, because I loved my grandmother's house, the creek to fish and swim in and all of her things. The night before we had packed everything we needed. I just couldn't get to sleep. Finally I must have fallen asleep because the alarm was going off and everyone was hurrying about the house. Dad had made us breakfast. He couldn't go due to his work schedule, but insisted we go and have fun. He even told me to ride the Teacups for him and the Train! Dad is such a laugh.

The car was packed, we had double checked everything and were waving goodbye! Another reason for the stop in Mississippi was for rest. It was going to be a long ride to even get that far in one day. Mom turned on the a/c in the car along with the radio and we settled in. She had it on her favorite country music, so we sang along a few songs of Merle Haggard and Johnny Cash. I must have fallen asleep right after we left the house. The next thing I knew, Mom was waking me up. We had stopped for lunch at a Whataburger restaurant. My favorite, too! She said to eat hearty as we would not stop again until we reached my grandmother's house. I ate a whole Whataburger with fries and an ice tea. Valerie did, too! Daniel had a Jr. Whataburger and so did my grandmother. Mom had a salad with chicken. Back in the car, Valerie and I decided to play, I spy. It is loads of fun! I was spying all kinds of things from license plates from Washington to blue jays in trees. Daniel tried to join in but would get mad if we guessed his too quickly. So he got out his video game and played it. Mom had to stop for gas one time right before we made it to the Mississippi state line. We always honk the horn when we cross over into Mississippi, but she said she was not going to do that since it was now getting dark and it might upset other drivers. I have a very smart mom.

12. Write a sentence that tells why the author is not too upset about her little brother going on vacation. Write your answer in the box below.

Question 13 is based on the story below.

THE THREE GOLDEN APPLES, Part - 2

So he journeyed on and on, still making the same inquiry, until, at last, he came to the brink of a river where some beautiful young women sat twining wreaths of flowers.

"Can you tell me, pretty maidens," asked the stranger, "whether this is the right way to the garden of the Hesperides?"

The young women had been having a fine time together, weaving the flowers into wreaths, and crowning one another's heads. And there seemed to be a kind of magic in the touch of their fingers that made the flowers more fresh and dewy, and of brighter lines, and sweeter fragrance while they played with them than even when they had been growing on their native stems. But, on hearing the stranger's question, they dropped all their flowers on the grass, and gazed at him with astonishment.

"The garden of the Hesperides!" cried one. "We thought mortals had been weary of seeking it, after so many disappointments. And pray, adventurous traveler, what do you want there?"

"A certain king, who is my cousin," replied he, "has ordered me to get him three of the golden apples."

"Most of the young men who go in quest of these apples," observed another of the damsels, "desire to obtain them for themselves, or to present them to some fair maiden whom they love. Do you, then, love this king, your cousin, so very much?"

"Perhaps not," replied the stranger, sighing. "He has often been severe and cruel to me. But it is my destiny to obey him."

"And do you know," asked the damsel who had first spoken, "that a terrible dragon, with a hundred heads, keeps watch under the golden apple-tree?"

"I know it well," answered the stranger, calmly. "But, from my cradle upwards, it has been my business, and almost my pastime, to deal with serpents and dragons."

The young women looked at his massive club, and at the shaggy lion's skin which he wore, and likewise at his heroic limbs and figure; and they whispered to each other that the stranger appeared to be one who might reasonably expect to perform deeds far beyond the might of other men. But, then, the dragon with a hundred heads! What mortal, even if he possessed a hundred lives, could hope to escape the fangs of such a monster? So kind-hearted were the maidens, that they could not bear to see this brave and, handsome traveler attempt what was so very dangerous, and devote himself, most probably, to become a meal for the dragon's hundred ravenous mouths.

"Go back," cried they all,—"go back to your own home! Your mother, beholding you safe and sound, will shed tears of joy; and what can she do more, should you win ever so great a victory? No matter for the golden apples! No matter for the king, your cruel cousin! We do not wish the dragon with the hundred heads to eat you up!"

The stranger seemed to grow impatient at these remonstrances. He carelessly lifted his mighty club, and let it fall upon a rock that lay half buried in the earth, near by. With the force of that idle blow, the great rock was shattered all to pieces. It cost the stranger no more effort to achieve this feat of a giant's strength than for one of the young maidens to touch her sister's rosy cheek with a flower.

"Do you not believe," said he, looking at the damsels with a smile, "that such a blow would have crushed one of the dragon's hundred heads?"

13. What would you have told the stranger if he had asked you directions? Explain why.

Write your answer in the box below.

Question 14 is based on the story below.

THE THREE GOLDEN APPLES, Part - 5
THE THREE GOLDEN APPLES, By Nathaniel Hawthorne

Part 5

Meanwhile, Hercules travelled constantly onward, over hill and dale, and through the solitary woods. Sometimes he swung his club aloft, and splintered a mighty oak with a downright blow. His mind was so full of the giants and monsters with whom it was the business of his life to fight, that perhaps he mistook the great tree for a giant or a monster. And so eager was Hercules to achieve what he had undertaken, that he almost regretted to have spent so much time with the damsels, wasting idle breath upon the story of his adventures. But thus it always is with persons who are destined to perform great things. What they have already done seems less than nothing. What they have taken in hand to do seems worth toil, danger, and life itself.

Persons who happened to be passing through the forest must have been affrighted to see him smite the trees with his great club. With but a single blow, the trunk was riven as by the stroke of lightning, and the broad boughs came rustling and crashing down.

Hastening forward, without ever pausing or looking behind, he by and by heard the sea roaring at a distance. At this sound, he increased his speed, and soon came to a beach, where the great surf-waves tumbled themselves upon the hard sand, in a long line of snowy foam. At one end of the beach, however, there was a pleasant spot, where some green shrubbery clambered up a cliff, making its rocky face look soft and beautiful. A carpet of verdant grass, largely intermixed with sweet-smelling clover, covered the narrow space between the bottom of the cliff and the sea. And what should Hercules espy there, but an old man, fast asleep!

But was it really and truly an old man? Certainly, at first sight, it looked very like one; but, on closer inspection, it rather seemed to be some kind of a creature that lived in the sea. For, on his legs and arms there were scales, such as fishes have; he was web-footed and web-fingered, after the fashion of a duck; and his long beard, being of a greenish tinge, had more the appearance of a tuft of sea-weed than of an ordinary beard. Have you never seen a stick of timber, that has been long tossed about by the waves, and has got all overgrown with barnacles, and, at last drifting ashore, seems to have been thrown up from the very deepest bottom of the sea? Well, the old man would have put you in mind of just such a wave-tost spar! But Hercules, the instant he set eyes on this strange figure, was convinced that it could be no other than the Old One, who was to direct him on his way.

14. Describe in your own words, what the Old Man in the Sea looked like to Hercules. Use details from the selection and write your answer in the box below.

Question 15 is based on the story below.

THE THREE GOLDEN APPLES, Part - 8

His nap had probably lasted a good while, when the cup chanced to graze against a rock, and, in consequence, immediately resounded and reverberated through its golden or brazen substance, a hundred times as loudly as ever you heard a church-bell. The noise awoke Hercules, who instantly started up and gazed around him, wondering whereabouts he was. He was not long in discovering that the cup had floated across a great part of the sea, and was approaching the shore of what seemed to be an island. And, on that island, what do you think he saw?

No; you will never guess it, not if you were to try fifty thousand times! It positively appears to me that this was the most marvelous spectacle that had ever been seen by Hercules, in the whole course of his wonderful travels and adventures. It was a greater marvel than the hydra with nine heads, which kept growing twice as fast as they were cut off; greater than the six-legged man-monster; greater than Antreus; greater than anything that was ever beheld by anybody, before or since the days of Hercules, or than anything that remains to be beheld, by travelers in all time to come. It was a giant!

But such an intolerably big giant! A giant as tall as a mountain; so vast a giant, that the clouds rested about his midst, like a girdle, and hung like a hoary beard from his chin, and flitted before his huge eyes, so that he could neither see Hercules nor the golden cup in which he was voyaging. And, most wonderful of all, the giant held up his great hands and appeared to support the sky, which, so far as Hercules could discern through the clouds, was resting upon his head! This does really seem almost too much to believe.

Meanwhile, the bright cup continued to float onward, and finally touched the strand. Just then a breeze wafted away the clouds from before the giant's visage, and Hercules beheld it, with all its enormous features; eyes each of them as big as yonder lake, a nose a mile Long, and a mouth of the same width. It was a countenance terrible from its enormity of size, but disconsolate and weary, even as you may see the faces of many people, nowadays, who are compelled to sustain burdens above their strength. What the sky was to the giant, such are the cares of earth to those who let themselves be weighed down by them. And whenever men undertake what is beyond the just measure of their abilities, they encounter precisely such a doom as had befallen this poor giant.

Poor fellow! He had evidently stood there a long while. An ancient forest had been growing and decaying around his feet; and oak-trees, of six or seven centuries old, had sprung from the acorn, and forced themselves between his toes.

15. **The narrator uses two sentences to intrigue and motivate the reader to go on. Choose the two sentences below from the passage that are evidence of this.**

Ⓐ And, on that island, what do you think he saw?
Ⓑ Poor fellow!
Ⓒ No; you will never guess it, not if you were to try fifty thousand times!
Ⓓ None of the above

Chapter 2

Lesson 10: Point of view

Before answering the questions, it is important to understand the meaning of different points of view.

Author's Point of View

As an author, you need to decide from which point of view you are writing to the reader: first person, second person or third person. Also, if you are reading a work written by some other author, you should be able to compare your opinion with from what the author is saying or writing about.

First person: The author is the one telling the story to the reader. The story may be about a topic the author has actually experienced or seen (nonfiction), or a topic that the author made-up (fiction). When writing in the first person, the author does not give directions or instructions to the reader. Also, the author uses the personal pronouns I, we, me, us, my, mine, our or ours in the essay.

Second person: The author is addressing the reader, giving instructions or suggestions for the reader to follow. The author will use the personal pronouns you or yours in the essay.

Third person: The author is not a character in the story, but is a narrator telling the story as an outside observer. The narrator may or may not know all the thoughts and feelings of one or more characters in the story. The author will use the personal pronouns he, she, it, him, his, her, hers, it or its in the essay.

You can scan the QR code given below or use the url to access additional EdSearch resources including videos and mobile apps related to *Point of View*.

ed)Search

Point of View

URL	QR Code
http://www.lumoslearning.com/a/rl46	

LumosLearning.com

1. The below passage uses which style of narration?

You are not the kind of guy who would be at a place like this at this time of the morning. But here you are, and you cannot say that the terrain is entirely unfamiliar, although the details are fuzzy. —Opening lines of Jay McInerney's Bright Lights, Big City (1984)

Ⓐ First person
Ⓑ Second person
Ⓒ Third person
Ⓓ Fourth person

2. The below passage uses which style of narration?

I was so scared when I first learned that I would be having my tooth pulled. I didn't sleep at all the night before the procedure. I was terrified that it would hurt more than I could tolerate. I was shaking when I sat in the dentist's chair. He promised me that it would not hurt, but I certainly had my doubts. The dentist gave me some medicine. When I awoke, my tooth was gone, and I didn't remember a thing.

Ⓐ First person
Ⓑ Second person
Ⓒ Third person
Ⓓ Fourth person

3. The below passage uses which style of narration?

Huckleberry Hound ran through the yard and into the field next to his house. Suddenly, he put his nose to the ground and started sniffing as he walked. Yep, he definitely smelled a rabbit. He raised his head and howled loudly to let the other dogs know what he had found. Then, he shot after the rabbit like a bolt of lightning. He chased the rabbit for what seemed like hours, but he never caught it. He returned to his yard with his head hanging and his tail tucked between his legs.

Ⓐ First person
Ⓑ Second person
Ⓒ Third person
Ⓓ Fourth person

4. The below passage uses which style of narration?

You didn't want to ask for a loan, but you had no choice. You spent all of your allowance at the ballgame, and now you don't have the money to buy your mom a birthday present.

Ⓐ First person
Ⓑ Second person
Ⓒ Third person
Ⓓ Fourth person

5. The below passage uses which style of narration?

Max went for a bike ride in the park. While on the ride, he saw his best friend, Sammy. They decided to go to the movies instead of bike riding in the park. Max called his mom and asked if it would be alright to go to the movie with his friend. She said yes, so Max and Sammy jumped on their bikes and went to see The Emoji Movie.

Ⓐ First person
Ⓑ Second person
Ⓒ Third person
Ⓓ Fourth person

6. The below passage uses which style of narration?

I had been craving chocolate ice cream all day. Finally, school was over and I could get a huge chocolate ice cream cone. The line was long, but it was worth the wait. The first taste of my ice cream cone was delicious. Then, the worst thing imaginable happened. I bumped into the person behind me and dropped my ice cream cone and it fell on the floor.

Ⓐ First person
Ⓑ Second person
Ⓒ Third person
Ⓓ Fourth person

7. The below passage uses which style of narration?

I wanted to learn how to knit, so I asked my grandmother to teach me. She agreed, so I went to the store and bought yarn and knitting needles. I had my first lesson last week. I quickly learned that knitting is much harder than I thought it would be. I don't think I want to learn to knit anymore.

Ⓐ First person
Ⓑ Second person
Ⓒ Third person
Ⓓ Fourth person

8. The below passage uses which style of narration?

I wonder why Mindy didn't come to the meeting. Did I forget to tell her about it? Did she forget about it? I think I will call her and see why she isn't here.

Ⓐ First person
Ⓑ Second person
Ⓒ Third person
Ⓓ Fourth person

9. The below passage uses which style of narration?

Opal walked into the store not wanting to do what she had planned. She knew when she took the makeup without paying for it that it was wrong. She felt so guilty. She knew she couldn't keep the makeup. So, gathering up all her courage, she walked over to the security officer and confessed what she had done.

Ⓐ First person
Ⓑ Second person
Ⓒ Third person
Ⓓ Fourth person

10. What style of narration is the below text?

One day James went to town to buy new clothes. First, he tried on a pair of trousers. He didn't like the trousers, so he gave them back to the shopkeeper. Then, he tried on a robe which was the same price as the trousers. James was pleased with the robe, and he left the shop. Before he climbed on his donkey to ride home, the shopkeeper and the shop-assistant ran out.

- (A) First person
- (B) Second person
- (C) Third person
- (D) Fourth person

Question 11 is based on the story below.

The Mall - What Fun

Santiago and Felix wanted to go to the mall on Saturday. They had both saved up their money from lawn mowing and yard work. Each had been working for 3 weeks on Saturdays and Sunday afternoons to earn money. Their favorite place in the mall was around the food court and video arcade.

Santiago's older sister, Felicia, offered to drive them since she was going to get her hair done at Pro-Cuts there anyway. Felicia told them to be ready by her car at 9:45 Saturday morning. The mall opened at 10:00 and it would take them about 15 minutes or so to get there. Felix had a tendency to be late all the time, so Santiago was a little worried that he wouldn't show up on time. Santiago had a plan to make sure that didn't happen this time.

He asked his mother on Friday after school, if Felix could spend the night. Luckily she agreed if they didn't stay up late and if he cleaned his room before Felix came over. So Santiago quickly called Felix to see if he could come over and spend the night. Felix was elated! "Sure thing, buddy! I will be there in a jiffy!"

"Don't come too soon, I have to clean my room! Mama made me promise to do it!" Santiago said. "No worries, dude, I can help." Felix replied.

So it was set. Santiago did ask his mama if Felix could help him clean his room. His mama just laughed and said, "Sure, you boys are so silly."

As soon as Felix got there, the boys started on their room cleaning project. This gave Felicia an idea, too.
"Guys, if I am giving you a ride to the mall tomorrow, how about cleaning my room, too?"
"No way! Not a girl's room!!" They both exclaimed at the same exact time.

"Oh, well, can't blame a girl for trying!" Laughed Felicia. "Don't worry, I will still take you."

That night the boys played video games and watched a combat movie. About 10:30pm, Santiago remembered what his mama said about not staying up late. He told Felix, "We better get to bed, Mama said not to stay up late if you came over."

"No problem, let's hit the sack," Said Felix.

The next morning, they were up, bathed, dressed, and had eaten breakfast by the time Felicia was ready to go.

"Wow, on time both of you and ready. This must be a special mall day for y'all!" She said.

When they got to the mall, Felicia told them to be sure to keep an eye on their watches. She also told them to meet her back at the door they came in exactly at 12:30. Her hair appointment would take one hour and then she wanted to meet friends to shop, as well. The boys agreed.

Their first stop was the video arcade where they met up with other friends and started playing games. It wasn't long before Felix wanted to go get a snack at the food court. You could say Felix liked food. He wasn't over weight or anything, he just liked to eat. Santiago was in the middle of a game and said he would be there shortly. Well, you guessed it, shortly didn't happen. Felix had his snack and waited for about 30 minutes for Santiago to show up. He didn't know what to do. So he headed back to the video arcade. He did notice that his watch showed it to be 12:10. They only had 20 minutes left and they had not even gone to any shops. Felix felt a sick feeling that he better find Santiago fast or Felicia would not be happy. She might not ever take them again if they did not make it back on time. Felix started almost running around a corner and splat! He ran right into Santiago!

"What took you so long, dude? I had my snack and waited on you forever!" Felix said in a bit of a disgruntled voice.

"My fault, all my fault! I was beating the game and didn't want to stop! Sorry. You are my best friend and I feel bad for letting you down." Replied Santiago.

"No worries, we better get going back to the door we came in at and meet Felicia." Said Felix.

When they got to the meeting place, Felicia was just walking up.

"Hey guys, y'all want to stay longer?" She said.

The guys grinned and nodded yes.

"Great, meet me here at 2:30. I am going to the movies with my friends. I already called Mama to let her know we would be staying longer."

Happily the boys went to shop with their money, bought new sneakers, ate lunch and even got to play video games again.

11. If you could change the ending of the story, what would have happen? Write your answer in the box below.

```




```

Question 12 is based on the story below.

The Haunted House on Rio Vista Drive

The neighborhood of Rio Vista Drive had two parts to it. On one side of Riverside Avenue were about 14 houses. Each house had approximately three bedrooms, two baths, an extremely grand living area, kitchen, washroom, and most often a small office area. The backyards were all chain linked hurricane fences of around 1.2 acres with a covered garage, back driveway and security locked gate. Most of the front yards were unique to themselves and had a theme which was painted on a plaque on the outside of the house itself. The realtors said that the architect had named each house as he had built it and decorated the fronts to match the names.

However, on the other side of Rio Vista Drive at the end of the block- a dead end, stood a rickety two story house assumed to be about 50-75 years old. This was dubbed the Haunted House. There was an old woman, Widow Crankston, who lived there. The kids all say she would come out in the evening and sit on her porch. Several thought they saw her carrying a black cat and presumed she was a witch of sorts. Briars grew up along the fence line and sidewalks. The windows were covered in cobwebs and the like. It had been years and years since the house had been painted or anything in the yard taken care of either. Many a dare had been made among the neighborhood kids to go and ring the doorbell or knock on the door. Most dares were made on Halloween or around that time.

So it was on the night before Halloween that Howard, Ernie and Edward were riding their bikes down Rio Vista Drive. Up one side and down the other, quickly turning around before they reached Widow Crankston's Haunted House! Suddenly, Howard came to a screeching stop right in front of the house.

"Ok, dare ya' to do it!" He hollered at Ernie.
"No, dare you!" Ernie screamed back.
"Scaredy Cats!" Laughed Edward!! "I will do it!"

So off he went, straight up to the front door. He rang the doorbell, but no one answered. Hurriedly he turned around and was running down the steps when he heard a tiny voice behind him.

"Yes, young man, may I help you?" Inquired Widow Crankston, as she peeped out the massive door. "Is today Halloween, I thought it was tomorrow. Let me get you some chocolate brownies and a cara-mel apple. Do your friends want some, too? Haven't had young- ins come here in ages. Please sit on the porch while I get y'all treats and some cold milk."

Edward stopped in his tracks. She wasn't an old witch, but just a kind hearted little old lady. He motioned for Howard and Ernie. Both came running up the sidewalk just in time to eat the goodies!

Now the other kids in the neighborhood aren't sure yet what to think. There are no more briars, no more cobwebs, and the fresh paint on the house looks wonderful. The boys have a part-time job cleaning and painting while enjoying good company and great snacks!

12. What do you think the author's purpose is in this story?

Write a sentence or two to explain your answer using evidence supported in the passage. Write your answer in the box below.

Question 13 is based on the story below.

Disneyworld- Here We Come

It was a hot summer day in June. My grandmother, Mom, my brother Daniel, my cousin Valerie, and I were headed out for a long vacation. We were first going to Mississippi and then on to Florida to Disneyworld. Talk about excitement!!! I couldn't contain myself and didn't sleep much at all the night before. Valerie was visiting us because her mom had gotten sick. My wonderful mom had volunteered for her to stay with us the entire summer. It was so cool. Valerie and I were best friends already, much less best cousins. We did everything together all the time. So having her come along was just another treat for me. Of course, I had rather my little snoopy brother, Daniel, didn't come, but oh well! After all, who can complain when you are going to Disneyworld!

We had to stop in Mississippi to leave my grandmother off at her house before the vacation. That wasn't such a bad idea either, because I loved my grandmother's house, the creek to fish and swim in and all of her things. The night before we had packed everything we needed. I just couldn't get to sleep. Finally I must have fallen asleep because the alarm was going off and everyone was hurrying about the house.   Dad had made us breakfast. He couldn't go due to his work schedule, but insisted we go and have fun. He even told me to ride the Teacups for him and the Train! Dad is such a laugh.

The car was packed, we had double checked everything and were waving goodbye! Another reason for the stop in Mississippi was for rest. It was going to be a long ride to even get that far in one day. Mom turned on the a/c in the car along with the radio and we settled in. She had it on her favorite country music, so we sang along a few songs of Merle Haggard and Johnny Cash. I must have fallen asleep right after we left the house. The next thing I knew, Mom was waking me up. We had stopped for lunch at a Whataburger restaurant. My favorite, too! She said to eat hearty as we would not stop again until we reached my grandmother's house. I ate a whole Whataburger with fries and an ice tea. Valerie did, too! Daniel had a Jr. Whataburger and so did my grandmother. Mom had a salad with chicken. Back in the car, Valerie and I decided to play, I spy. It is loads of fun! I was spying all kinds of things from license plates from Washington to blue jays in trees. Daniel tried to join in but would get mad if we guessed his too quickly. So he got out his video game and played it. Mom had to stop for gas one time right before we made it to the Mississippi state line. We always honk the horn when we cross over into Mississippi, but she said she was not going to do that since it was now getting dark and it might upset other drivers. I have a very smart mom.

Part 2

Soon enough we were at my grandmother's. Mom had made us pack one light bag with just enough for each of us our night clothes, and a clean outfit for the next day. That way we didn't have to take so much out at my grandmother's house. We were ready for a light soup supper and off to bed.

Before we knew it, it was daylight again. Mom was hustling us out of bed and into the kitchen for breakfast. She said to eat hearty as we had many more miles to go before we reached our final destination. So thankful that my grandmother cooked her best oatmeal for us topped with cinnamon, brown sugar, strawberries, and whipped cream! Who could ask for anything more? Yummy!!

Then it was load back into the car and get on the road. This time Mom found an oldies radio station and she was singing along with Patsy Cline, Tennessee Ernie Ford, and Frank Sinatra. Talk about strange music that none of us knew except her! Valerie and I played a game of travel trivia which was sort of fun and of course, Daniel, was back on his video games!

For lunch we stopped at a roadside park and had the sandwiches our grandmother had packed for us along with an apple and sweet iced tea. When we got back on the road, not a sound could be heard. I figured out later that all of us kids had fallen asleep.

A loud bang woke us as Mom clapped her hands and proclaimed our arrival to the Holiday Inn at Disneyworld! I could not tell you who was the most excited as we were all yelling sounds of glee and running around the car to get our luggage out. Mom registered us for our room and we were giggling uncontrollably.

Part 3

When we were settled in to our room, Mom explained the sleeping arrangements. Valerie and I would get one of the queen size beds to share, Daniel would get the fold out couch in the living area, and Mom would get the other bed. She said that is night number one, then we will switch on the second night. I love it when my mom thinks of everyone and being fair to all. We were so happy we could have slept on the floor and not minded!! Mom called Dad to let him know we made it safe and sound. Then she called our grandmother, too. She also called Valerie's mom in the hospital so Valerie could talk to her and let her know all was well. Valerie's mom's health was improving daily, too.

Mom ordered pizza for us the first night. We went to bed without any complaining, so excited to be going to Disneyworld the next day!

Mom had picked up a map of the park when she had registered us, so she was busy planning our day while we were falling asleep.

The morning came with a clap and thunder outside of our room. What was going on, we had wondered? Mom explained that it was raining and that we would have breakfast in the hotel lobby and then see what happened. She did tell us that the hotel manager had explained to her that quite often the rains would start and stop during the summers at Kissimmee, Florida. We were not too disappointed after she said that. The hotel offers a free breakfast for everyone. That was definitely a plus in Mom's opinion.

Sure enough after we had eaten the sun came out. The hotel offered a trolley bus to the theme parks, so we opted to take that rather than worrying about parking and walking. Disneyworld stays open all day and late into the evening. Mom said she had mapped out our route to take so we could get to see most everything in our two days along with purchasing us the fast passes to avoid long line delays.

What a cool Mom, right?

Part 4

The awesome view, the rides, the larger than life Disney characters, people laughing and having fun everywhere. Yes, Welcome to Disneyworld! First we started following the crowds that were going down the main street with shops galore. Then Mom got out her map and starting us on our route. By lunchtime, we had already seen more than imaginable. We had ridden the Liberty Square Riverboat, gone to the Swiss Family Treehouse, enjoyed the birds at the Enchanted Tiki Room, and countless of stops to listen to theatrical groups perform. Mom had thought of packing a lunch, but had decided against that. We had hot dogs, chips and a soda. Mom said the prices might be a bit high, but it was well worth it!

In the afternoon, the rain began to return, so we went inside a western style dance hall and listened to a group of singers dance and perform. It was really quite entertaining. Then it was time for more rides. Space Mountain was indeed worth it! Scary, and adventurous and well, mostly scary! My little brother couldn't go it and he pouted about that. So we switched directions and went to a kind of petty zoo afterwards, and to ride the Mad Tea Party (Dad's Teacups) to keep him happy. Valerie and I did not mind a bit. Mom steadily had her phone out taking pictures to post and to make copies for us.

Needless to say, by the end of the day, we were all exhausted and a little sun burned, too. Mom said we would stay the second night for the parade and fireworks. She said it was time to call it a day. We all moaned, but happily boarded the trolley back to our hotel. Once at the hotel, we settled for the buffet dinner. They let kids eat free at this hotel if you choose the buffet.

That night we all chatted about the rides and all of the attractions we saw. Mom didn't even have to tell us to go to bed. We bathed and took to the sheets! The morning was just around the corner.

Part 5

Again on the second day, we had the free breakfast and rode the trolley. It wasn't raining this time at all. Mom got out her map and we began our day. Daniel wanted to go back and ride the Mad Tea Party again, but thankfully Mom said no to that.

We were able to go to Splash Mountain, the Jungle Cruise, the 7 Dwarf's Mine Train and much more. Mom did make a request of her own. She wanted to meet Mickey and Minnie Mouse who were scheduled to appear outside of the Cinderella Castle. She also said she wanted to listen to the Enchanted Tales with Belle and ride the Prince Charming Regal Carrousel. What a crazy silly Mom!

What we didn't know was that she had a plan. It was right after we left the carrousel that we heard fantastic sounds coming down the main street. Yes, parade time right before our eyes. Mom told us to come and sit. There we were on the side of the castle sitting on the ledge in perfect view of the parade. We asked her how she knew to stop there. She said one of the hotel clerks had told her how to find the spot and when to be there. The parade was magnificent to say the least. The characters actually stopped in front of us and performed. Wow! We couldn't have planned it any better.

After the parade we went to A Pirate's Adventure and Tomorrowland Speedway, andBig Thunder Mountain. Mom said we needed to head toward the front entrance as it was time for fireworks and we needed to be ready. We got there just in time. The lights lit up the sky behind the Cinderella Castle and throughout Disneyworld. Just picture it!

What a perfect ending to our vacation.

13. If you were the author, how would you change your story?

   Write at least two sentences to show what you would do differently. Write your answer in the box below.

Question 14 is based on the story below.

Celia Cruz

She was born in Havana, Cuba in 1925. She was told by her grandmother that she could sing before she could talk. Her grandmother used to laugh and tell the family that she practiced her singing at night. (She was thought to have cried most of the night.) Cruz' work in radio during the 1940's in Cuba led to her fame and she traveled throughout Latin America with a female band. She won her first award singing on an amateur hour TV show. Cruz sang a version of a tango song that was very popular in Cuba.

In the 1950's Celia Cruz joined the Sonora Mantancera as a lead female singer. Then she was able to go to the Tropicana, the best establishment for Cuban music. If you performed at the Tropicana, you had made it in the singing world of Cubans.

She then went to Mexico for a one year contract right before Fidel Castro took over Cuba. She and her band never returned. Cruz moved to New York in 1961. By this time she was a well- known Cuban singer and independent from her band. She became known as the "Salsa Queen" due to her style of music. During the 1990's she gained great popularity among the younger generations, as her music reappeared. Cruz has been honored by five Presidents of the United States. She died of brain cancer in 2003, but her music and legend continue to thrive throughout the world.

14. If you were to be a musician such as Celia Cruz, what type of music would you perform, where and why? Write your answer in the box below.

Question 15 is based on the story below.

The Endangered Species Act.

The Act was originated in 1973, and is one of many US environmental laws passed in the 1970's. The law protects species from extinction. The United States Fish and Wildlife Service and the National Oceanic and Atmospheric Administration help to administer the act.

It was amended in 1978 to add economic considerations and again in 1982 which prevented economic considerations.

To be considered for listing, the species must meet one of five criteria (section 4(a)(1)):
1. There is the present or threatened destruction, modification, or curtailment of its habitat or range.
2. An over utilization for commercial, recreational, scientific, or educational purposes.
3. The species is declining due to disease or predation.
4. There is an inadequacy of existing regulatory mechanisms.
5. There are other natural or manmade factors affecting its continued existence.

15. In thinking about and considering types of endangered species, animals in particular, which one would you most be concerned with?

Which of the 5 listed criteria supports your concern? Write your answer in the box below.

Chapter 2

Lesson 11: Visual Connections

You can scan the QR code given below or use the url to access additional EdSearch resources including videos and mobile apps related to *Visual Connections*.

ed Search	Visual Connections	
URL		**QR Code**
http://www.lumoslearning.com/a/rl47		

Question 1 is based on the story below.

Mary loves writing stories

"The Elephant Who Saw the World," Mary started speaking. It was Friday, and the students had to share their creative writing stories of the week.

Mary loved writing, and this part of the week, when they were able to make up stories for creative writing, was her favorite part. She enjoyed it so much that she became really good at it. When she was home on the weekends and she didn't have much homework, she would sit in her room for hours and create stories to share with her friends and family. Her parents always supported her and were her biggest fans.

However, there was one part about every Friday at school that Mary did not enjoy, and that was when she had to share her story in front of the class. The teacher made all of the children share on Friday afternoons, and this made Mary very nervous. She was shy, and although she knew her teacher was right, she didn't like it.

After sitting and listening to the other children's share, Mary finally heard her name called. She knew it was her turn to share. She got out of her seat slowly, walked to the front of the room and began.

1. Which picture below best represents what's happening in the story?

Ⓓ None of the above

2. **Which text below best represents what is happening in the picture?**

Ⓐ Thelma watched her two baby lions, Louis and Lisa as they played. They were playing well until they started fighting over something the zoo keeper had thrown into the enclosure.

Ⓑ Thelma watched her two baby meerkats, Louis and Lisa, as they played. They were playing well until they started fighting over something the zoo keeper had thrown into the enclosure.

Ⓒ Thelma watched her two baby monkeys, Louis and Lisa, as they played. They were playing well until they started fighting over something the zoo keeper had thrown into the enclosure.

Ⓓ Thelma watched her two baby koala bears, Louis and Lisa, as they played. They were playing well until they started fighting over something the zoo keeper had thrown into the enclosure.

3. Which paragraph would be an appropriate description for the picture above?

Ⓐ One day last spring I was out walking as it was a beautiful spring day. I came across an empty forest and heard a noise. It sounded like a baby but it couldn't have been a baby since there was no one else there. I walked over to where I thought the noise was coming from and stopped in front of a large hollow tree. It looked as if it had been there for a very long time. I stopped and listened. I heard the noise again and it was definitely coming from inside the tree. I looked inside and I saw a little kitten.

Ⓑ One day last spring I was out walking as it was a beautiful spring day. I came across an empty parking lot and heard a noise. It sounded like a baby but it couldn't have been a baby since there was no one else there. I walked over to where I thought the noise was coming from and stopped in front of a large box. It looked like some thing someone may have used for moving. I stopped and listened. I heard the noise again and it was definitely coming from inside the box. I looked inside and I saw a little kitten.

Ⓒ One day last spring I was out walking as it was a beautiful spring day. I came across a construction site and heard a noise. It sounded like a baby but it couldn't have been a baby since there was no one else there. I walked over to where I thought the noise was coming from and stopped in front of a large cement pipe. It looked like some thing they might use to transport water underground. I stopped and listened. I heard the noise again and it was definitely coming from inside the pipe. I looked inside and I saw a little kitten.

Ⓓ At first the kitten was scared but eventually, with lots of coaxing, the kitten came to one of the open ends of the tree. I was able to see that it was a little black and white kitten who was probably very hungry and scared. I took the kitten home and it became my companion from that day on.

4. Which of the statements below most accurately reflects the picture?

Ⓐ Many people like to act, even if they don't act very well. Acting helps them express how they are feeling. Sometimes acting makes them feel happy. Not everyone wants to be a professional, though. Professional actors like to entertain other people. Their skill is usually a combination of talent and training.

Ⓑ Many people like to dance, even if they don't dance very well. Dancing helps them express how they are feeling. Sometimes dancing makes them feel happy. Not every one wants to be a professional, though. Professional dancers like to entertain other people. Their skill is usually a combination of talent and training.

Ⓒ Many people like to sing, even if they don't sing very well. Singing helps them express how they are feeling. Sometimes singing makes them feel happy. Not everyone wants to be a professional, though. Professional singers use their voices to entertain other people. Their skill is usually a combination of talent and training.

Ⓓ Their skill is usually a combination of talent and training. Most professional dancers work with a coach. They usually start training at a young age. Many of them get their first experience by being in school musicals. Talent and training are not enough to make a successful career, though. Young people who want to be dancers should also have poise, good stage presence, creativity, and the ability to deal with change. They must be healthy and strong, too.

5. Which paragraph would be an appropriate description for the picture above?

Ⓐ Summer is probably my favorite season. One of my most favorite things to do is to go watch a sandcastle building contest they have every year in San Diego, California. We can see amazing sandcastles that people spend hours and days building. This year one of the winners of the contest made this really large superhero to honor their love of comic books.

Ⓑ Summer is probably my favorite season. One of my most favorite things to do is to go watch a sandcastle building contest they have every year in San Diego, California. We can see amazing sandcastles that people spend hours and days building. This year one of the winners of the contest made this really long snake to honor their Mexican heritage.

Ⓒ Summer is probably my favorite season. One of my most favorite things to do is to go watch a sandcastle building contest they have every year in San Diego, California. We can see amazing sandcastles that people spend hours and days building. This year one of the winners of the contest made this really big pyramid to honor their Egyptian heritage.

Ⓓ Summer is probably my favorite season. One of my most favorite things to do is to go watch a sandcastle building contest they have every year in San Diego, California. We can see amazing sandcastles that people spend hours and days building. This year one of the winners of the contest made this really long dragon to honor their Chinese heritage.

Question 6 is based on the passage below.

Sandy's Soccer

Sandy Thomas enrolled in soccer when she was in first grade. She had loved to watch the soccer games on TV with her dad. Sandy's dad was a high school soccer coach. It was his passion, as well as hers. Sandy was elated when she convinced her parents to let her play soccer rather than take ballet. Her friends were astonished as they had all signed up for ballet and expected her to, as well.

The team she was on this year was called, The Blue Jets. She was playing her favorite position, goalie. She practices at home with a goal her dad made for her. He tries to make the goal and she blocks it almost every time.

6. If the pattern stays exactly the same, what will game 3 score results be? Fill in the chart.

Game #	Team Blue Jets	Opposing Team	Difference + or -
1	10	8	+2
2	8	6	+2
3			

7. Choose a team sport and write a sentence telling what position you would play and how you would practice with a family member or a friend.

Write your answer in the box below.

Question 8 and 9 are based on the passage below.

Going Mudding with Dad

Jeff and his dad love to go mudding on their four wheelers. Mudding is great fun, but can be dangerous! Jeff has his own four wheeler, too. It is not as massive as his dad's but can go fast and sling mud everywhere. Mudding has become a sort of sports in the swamp country in Louisiana where they live. So picture this in your mind. A four wheeler with a kid on it going through muddy paths covered in moss and vines. The mud is thick and water is everywhere. Get the picture, if you like mud like they do, it is a blast. The object of mudding is to see who can go the fastest, beat the other "mudders" while getting the most mud and filth on them as well.

There are several things to remember and keep in mind when preparing to drive and while driving four wheelers through mud. First, never go out alone. Buddy up is the best policy. Always wear plenty of clothing. Jeff and his dad wear long sleeve shirts, jeans, and high top hunting boots. Never go on a four wheeler without wearing a helmet for protection. Most of them have seat belts, so buckle up. Take water or a vitamin sports drink and a healthy snack with you. Keep a first aid kit in your four wheeler, too. If you are going out on a path that has several trails, take strips of cloth and tie on branches along the way to find your way back. Be sure to inspect your vehicle before going out. Check the basic like oil, gas, clean off any mud left before hand and make sure that your vehicle starts and stops when needed. While driving do not turn your four wheeler too sharp at any time as this could cause it to flip over. If the curve ahead of you looks sharp, slow down before you approach, or you might have an accident, as well. Safety is more important than winning or being the muddiest one out there!

Then hit the trails, have fun and enjoy the mud!

8. If you were to go bike riding, which of the tips for mudding that were listed in the passage could apply? List three. Write your answer in the box below.

9. Find and write the two sentences in the first paragraph that help you to visualize mudding.

Question 10 is based on the poem below.

YOUNG NIGHT THOUGHT

All night long and every night,
When my mama puts out the light
I see the people marching by,
As plain as day, before my eye.
Armies and emperors and kings,
All carrying different kinds of things,
And marching in so grand a way,
You never saw the like by day.
So fine a show was never seen
At the great circus on the green;
For every kind of beast and man
Is marching in that caravan.
At first they move a little slow,
But still the faster on they go,
And still beside them close I keep
Until we reach the Town of Sleep.

By Robert Louis Stevenson

10. The poet uses many descriptions in his poem to help the reader picture what he is referring to.

Draw a picture or write what you are seeing in your mind as you read this poem.

Question 11 is based on the passage below.

Roses are Red

Everyone knows the poem that goes- Roses are Red, Violets are blue, Sugar is sweet and so are you!

But I am not talking poetry right now. I am talking about the roses that Aunt Molly has in her yard.

Yeah, you see the pictures of them. Aren't they so beautiful? How does she get them that way?

Notice the two pictures on the page. The white roses come from a huge rose bush. I call it a tree it is so big! My aunt started that one with a branch cut off of our Great Grandma Witt's rose bush down in Centerville. She brought it home when Great Grandma was still alive. Grandma Witt told her to cut it off, wrap it in wet paper towels, put it in a bucket of red clay dirt from her front yard and take it home. So my aunt did.

When she got home with it, she dug a deep hole in her backyard. She put the clay dirt in first, then made another hole in the middle of that. Next, she put in rose fertilizer to help it grow. Then she put in the branch from the rose bush. After that, she pushed the dirt in real tight. When she got ready to water it, she didn't water it straight at the branch. Instead, she watered it slightly to the side of the hole at an angle. She also took a banana peel the next day and wrapped it around where the bottom of the branch was at. An old man had told her to do that whenever she planted rose bushes. I had no idea that you could grow a rose bush just from a branch. You can. The rose bush will start to make new roots under the soil. Bingo, a rose bush!

Now, look at the second red rose picture. This is a rose bush from Tyler, Texas. That town is world famous for growing the best roses. Aunt Molly bought that one about a year ago. It was on sale, she said, or she would never have paid full price for it. She put it on the side of her house near the carport. She had wanted to grow roses there for a long time. At first, she told me that it was not looking very healthy, and she knew why it had been on sale. However, she kept pampering it, adding fresh clay soil around it. Of course, she had to do the banana peel thing to it, too! During the winter, Aunt Molly was afraid it was dead. But to her surprise, it came back bigger than ever. She said it produces cluster roses almost every week.

Well, apparently she knows how to grow roses. It all seems to work just fine for Aunt Molly.

11. Part A
   What did you notice about the two pictures that are the same? Write your answer in the box below.

Part B.
What might be different? Write your answer in the box below.

Chapter 2

Lesson 12: Comparing and Contrasting

Compare means to find the similarities in two texts while Contrast means to find the differences in two texts.

Let us understand the concept with an example.

The following essays present two different opinions about global warming. The literacy standard shown above asks students to compare the two essays to show where they agree and where they disagree.

Definition: What is global warming? Global warming is an increase in the earth's atmospheric and oceanic temperatures believed to be caused by the increase of certain gases (such as carbon dioxide) in the atmosphere. These gases form a blanket that traps the warmth from the sun in the Earth's atmosphere. This is called the greenhouse effect.

Opinion #1: Global warming and the greenhouse effect are occurring, and human activities are the principal causes of these changes.

Global warming is occurring. Here are some scientific facts as proof:

- Average temperatures have climbed 1.4 degrees Fahrenheit around the world since 1880, much of this in recent decades, according to NASA's Goddard Institute for Space Studies.
- Arctic ice is rapidly disappearing, and the region may have its first completely ice-free summer by 2040 or earlier. Polar bears and indigenous cultures are already suffering from the sea-ice loss.
- Glaciers and mountain snows are rapidly melting.
- In the Northern Hemisphere, thaws come a week earlier in spring and freezes begin a week later.

Conclusions:

1. An IPCC (United Nations' Intergovernmental Panel on Climate Change) report, based on the work of some 2,500 scientists in more than 130 countries, concluded that humans have caused all or most of the current planetary warming, because of industrialization (large increases in the number of manufactured products), deforestation (cutting down forests and replacing them with buildings) and pollution have greatly increased greenhouse gases that help trap heat near Earth's surface.
2. Humans are pouring carbon dioxide into the atmosphere much faster than plants and oceans can absorb it.
3. Reports by the IPCC warned that global warming could lead to large-scale food and water shortages and have catastrophic effects on wildlife, and sea level could rise between 7 and 23 inches by century's end, resulting in flooding in many low-lying areas on Earth.

Opinion #2: Global warming is not just a recent event, but is a natural phenomenon that has been occurring for thousands of years as part of a cycle of warming and cooling of the earth's atmosphere, and that human activity is only a minor contributor.

We agree that global warming is taking place, there is enough evidence to prove that.

One survey concluded that there are thousands of scientists who say there is "no convincing evidence" that humans have been or will be the primary cause of global warming. Instead, we believe that the increase in global average temperatures are caused mostly by natural, not human, factors. Natural cycles in Earth's orbit can alter the planet's exposure to sunlight, which may explain the current trend. Earth has experienced warming and cooling cycles roughly every hundred thousand years due to these orbital shifts, but such changes have occurred over the span of several centuries.

Adding to the argument that humans are not the major causes of climate change are a discovery in late November 2009 by hackers of hundreds of emails at a university in the United Kingdom that exposed private conversations among top-level British and U.S. climate scientists discussing whether certain data should be released to the public. The email exchanges also refer to statistical tricks used to illustrate climate change trends. Climate change skeptics have pointed out that these emails reveal an attempt to fool the public about the causes of climate change.

The standard asks you to **Compare and contrast the treatment of similar themes**.

The themes in Opinion #1 and Opinion #2 are the same: climate change. And both opinions agree that climate change has occurred. And both use scientist's opinions to support their points of view. But that is all they agree on.

Opinion #1 believes human actions (industrialization, deforestation and pollution) are the major causes of global warming. Opinion #2 believes that natural forces, such as the earth's orbit in relation to its exposure to the sun, are the major causes of global warming and that human activities are only a minor cause.

The standard also asks you to **Compare and contrast... patterns of events in stories, myths, and traditional literature from different cultures.** Here is an example of what you might write. Note that two different cultures are included.

Bastille Day Compared With Independence Day

Bastille Day is celebrated in July in France. It celebrates the day when thousands of French people stormed the Bastille, a prison for those who opposed the policies of King Louis XVI. Ordinary French citizens had had enough suffering from food shortages and high taxes during King Louis's reign, and it was the attack on the Bastille prison that started the French Revolution. The French Revolution overthrew the monarchy of King Louis and replaced it with a republic, under which a council of leaders were formed to fairly represent the citizens of the country. France has never been ruled by a king again, from then to today (although France was ruled by dictator Napoleon for about 10 years in which he created a French Empire, which delayed for about 10 years France from becoming a true republic).

Independence Day in the United States is also celebrated in July, and it also led to freedom from oppressive rule. In this case, the oppressive rule was not directly by a king, but by the country of Great Britain, ruled by a king and Parliament, which regarded the 13 original colonies (which were the beginnings of the United States) as part of the British Empire. Citizens of the 13 colonies became very angry at the taxes imposed by Great Britain on the colonies, over which they had no control (they were not allowed to have any representatives in the British Parliament).

Independence Day celebrates not an attack on a prison but the adoption of the Declaration of Independence by the Continental Congress, which declared the independence of the 13 colonies from the British Empire. As with the attack on the Bastille which started the French Revolution, the Declaration of Independence led to the Revolutionary War fought by the 13 colonies against Great Britain.

The most important fact that Bastille Day and Independence Day have in common is that they resulted in greater freedom, or independence, for the citizens of both countries.

You can scan the QR code given below or use the url to access additional EdSearch resources including videos and mobile apps related to *Comparing and Contrasting.*

ed)Search	*Comparing and Contrasting*
URL	**QR Code**
http://www.lumoslearning.com/a/rl49	

Question 1 is based on the passage below.

Fred Goes to the Dentist

Fred had never been to the dentist. All of his life he had heard horror stories about the buzzing drills, the huge needles, and the scary tools that the dentist used to torture his patients. Since none of his teeth were hurting, Fred just couldn't understand why his mom was insisting on taking him to the dentist. She told him that it was important to visit the dentist each year to have his teeth checked and cleaned. This seemed silly to Fred because he cleaned his teeth everyday by brushing and flossing them, but nothing would change his mother's mind. He found it hard to believe that she would think it was a good idea to take him somewhere to be tortured. However, he had no choice but to go.

On the way to the dentist, Fred's imagination went wild. He pictured walking into a room with a huge chair that the dentist would strap him to. He could just see the dentist pulling out a huge drill and drilling his tooth while his mother and several others held him in the chair. By the time he got to the dentist's office, he was shaking all over.

Surprisingly, the office was nothing like he expected. The dentist was friendly, and the chair was comfortable. It didn't have any straps. He looked around the room and didn't see any huge drills or torture devices. He was relieved when all the dentist did was look in his mouth, show him how to properly brush and floss his teeth, and give him a balloon. His mom made another appointment to have his teeth cleaned in six months. Maybe this wouldn't be as bad as he had thought it would be.

1. **Compare the way Fred felt about going to the dentist before his visit to the way he felt after his first visit.**

   Ⓐ Fred was excited about going but became afraid once he arrived.
   Ⓑ Fred was afraid of going and was even more afraid after he met the dentist.
   Ⓒ Fred was afraid of going but felt relieved after he met the dentist.
   Ⓓ Fred was excited about going and loved it once he arrived.

Question 2-4 are based on the passages below.

Passage 1:

Timothy

Timothy got a job walking dogs each morning. When school started this year, everyone encouraged him to quit his job, but he decided to keep it. He knew it would be hard to get up every morning at 5 a.m. in order to get all of the dogs walked and then go to school all day. Additionally, he planned to sing in the chorus, play basketball, and be a mentor in the tutoring program this year. He knows it will not be easy, but he thinks his hard work will be worth it. He is trying to save enough money to go to a youth camp next summer.

Passage 2:

Adam likes to spend time with his friends. If he is not with them, he is texting them or playing games with them online. Adam is always busy. He cannot stand to sit around and do nothing. In fact, the only time he is still is when he is sleeping. Adam plays football, basketball, soccer, and baseball. He loves to be involved in whatever is going on at school or at the town's youth center. He spends a lot of his time encouraging people to recycle and even volunteers at the youth center. Although he loves spending time with his friends, he is willing to give up time with them to help others.

Passage 3:

Stanley loves to stay at home. He enjoys activities that can be done alone such as reading, drawing, and spending time with his dogs. Most days after school you can find him at home enjoying one of his favorite activities. He also thinks recycling is important and makes sure his family does it. Although he likes being alone, he enjoys volunteering at the youth center with his brother. He thinks it is important to make a difference in the lives of others, which is why he thinks he would like to be a doctor. Adam and Stanley may be different in many ways, but they join together and make a difference in their community.

2. If you compare Timothy and Adam, which statement is correct?

   Ⓐ   Timothy participates in extracurricular activities, but Adam does not.
   Ⓑ   Timothy does not participate in extracurricular activities, but Adam does.
   Ⓒ   Timothy and Adam both participate in extracurricular activities.
   Ⓓ   Neither Timothy nor Adam participates in extracurricular activities.

3. If you contrast Timothy and Stanley, which statement is correct?

   Ⓐ   Stanley participates in many extracurricular activities such as sports and chorus, but Timothy does not.
   Ⓑ   Stanley and Timothy both participate in extracurricular activities such as sports and chorus.
   Ⓒ   Neither Stanley nor Timothy participates in extracurricular activities.
   Ⓓ   Stanley enjoys solitary activities such as drawing, but Timothy enjoys group activities such as chorus and sports.

4. Compare and contrast Adam and Stanley. Which statement is true?

   Ⓐ   Both Adam and Stanley believe in recycling.
   Ⓑ   Neither Adam nor Stanley believes in recycling.
   Ⓒ   Adam believes in recycling, but Stanley does not.
   Ⓓ   Adam does not believe in recycling, but Stanley does.

Question 5 is based on the passage below.

This year Jim and I had the most wonderful vacation. Especially, compared to the one we took last year. We went to Hawaii, which was a better place to visit than last year's hunting lodge in Alaska. The hotel we stayed in was a luxury suite; it included a big screen TV with all of the movie channels, a hot tub on the balcony, a small kitchen stocked with local fruits and vegetables, and a huge bed shaped like a pineapple. The weather in Hawaii was superb. We enjoyed many hours on the beach sunbathing and playing volleyball. When we were not on the beach, we were in the ocean swimming or riding the waves on a surf board. Each night we enjoyed eating and dancing with all of our friends at a luau. Our week in Hawaii rushed by, making us wish we had planned a two-week vacation. Without a doubt, we will be going back to Hawaii next year for our vacation.

The hunting lodge in Alaska had a shower with hardly any warm water, a small cooler for our food, and cots to sleep on each night. But, the room wasn't even the worst part of the vacation. The weather was terrible; it rained the entire time we were there. Even with the rain, our guide expected us to go on an all-day fishing trip that was part of our vacation package. All we caught on that fishing trip was a cold from the rain. After the third day in Alaska, we decided to end our nightmare, cut our trip short, and head for home.

5. Compare and contrast the Alaskan and Hawaiian vacations. Which statement is correct?

- Ⓐ Both had beautiful hotel rooms with nice accommodations.
- Ⓑ The weather in Alaska was beautiful, but it rained the entire time they were in Hawaii.
- Ⓒ The Hawaiian vacation was much more enjoyable than the Alaskan vacation.
- Ⓓ The Alaskan vacation was much more enjoyable than the Hawaiian vacation.

Question 6 and 7 are based on the passage below.

"Dad and I need to go out of town this weekend," said Mom. "We'll be back on Monday, so the three of you are going to spend the weekend with your two aunts. "

Lindsay, Scarlet, and Austin loved their aunts and were really excited. They ran upstairs and started getting their things together to take with them. They put everything in one bag that they would need for school. They were going to stay with Aunt Margaret for two nights and the last night with their Auntie Josephine.

At the end of the school day, the children came running out of classroom doors from all different directions. Aunt Margaret was waiting for her nieces and nephew at the entrance of the school. She was wearing a bright red suit with a sparkly cat pin on it. She also had on a proper wool hat to match. She noticed a scuff on her shoes when her nieces and nephew ran up to her.

She cried, "Oh, my goodness! I am so happy you are here. The children at your school are just a bunch of toughies. I was nearly trampled while I was standing here! Let's get into the car." Aunt Margaret pointed to a large, green, four-door station wagon that was parked in the lot.

The next day, a funny-sounding honk came from the front of the house. The children ran outside and saw Auntie Jo sitting in her convertible. She was wearing a big cowboy hat. She wore a pair of polka dot shorts with a too large shirt.

6. Compare and contrast the way the two different aunts dressed.

Ⓐ Auntie Jo and Aunt Margaret dressed the same.
Ⓑ Auntie Jo dressed very casually while Aunt Margaret dressed very formally.
Ⓒ Auntie Jo was wearing a skirt and Aunt Margaret was wearing a dress.
Ⓓ None of the above

7. Compare and contrast the cars that the aunts drove.

Ⓐ Auntie Jo had a convertible, and Aunt Margaret had a station wagon.
Ⓑ The two aunts had the same car.
Ⓒ Auntie Jo had a sedan, and Aunt Margaret had a convertible.
Ⓓ Neither Aunt liked to wear skirts or dresses.

Question 8 and 9 are based on the passage below.

The red tail hawk noticed something was happening to all of the other animals living in Running Brook during the spring. The birds seemed to be losing their feathers. The bears were losing their fur. Mountain goats were complaining that their feet hurt. The beavers had cavities, and the deer all seemed to be catching cold. The red squirrels had gotten so fat that they almost could not make it across the road.

Hawk made an observation. He was pretty sure that everything started happening when the town's first fast food restaurant opened. Forest Fawn thought he brought a great idea to the town and that he could make some extra money. He opened an eatery where food was easy to prepare, order, and eat quickly. Forest Fawn knew how difficult it was to find food during the winter months. He thought that he was doing his friends a favor.

The restaurant sold birdseed in five different flavors. Forest Fawn sold artificially flavored honey, salmon cakes, and deep-fried berries for the bears. Salted tree moss with lichen-flavored chips was on the shelf for the mountain goats and deer.

8. What was Hawk's theory of what was causing the animals' complaints?

Ⓐ Birds were losing their feathers, and bears were losing patches of fur.
Ⓑ Beavers got cavities, and deer had colds.
Ⓒ Bad things were happening to the animals because of the food that they were eating.
Ⓓ The squirrels were getting fat and the mountain goats complained about their feet.

9. Compare what happened to the beavers and the birds.

Ⓐ The birds lost their feathers, and the beavers had cavities.
Ⓑ The birds had cold, and the beavers lost their fur.
Ⓒ The birds liked the candy, and the beavers liked the syrup
Ⓓ The birds had sore feet and the beavers gained weight.

Question 10 is based on the passage below.

Beatrice was so excited. This was truly a special day for her. She looked down and saw that her cup was sparkling with clean and cold water. She couldn't believe that it was real! She had never seen water like this before. Slowly, she took a sip and it tasted so fresh. Her mother had always told her about the importance of water.

Beatrice used to get water from a ditch near her home. Also, they could walk for miles to reach other areas with water. The water wasn't very clean in the stream. In fact, most of the time, the water had a putrid smell and was brown in color. Beatrice and her family knew it wasn't acceptable but they didn't have any choice. The water that they drank was unclean, making Beatrice feel sick often.

The water they mostly use is from streams, rivers, and lakes and is used for cooking, taking baths, and washing clothes. This water is contaminated with chemicals in the products they use and can cause diseases, such as typhus, cholera, dysentery, and malaria.

10. How did Beatrice get her water in the past compared to how she gets her water now?

Ⓐ They have always gotten their water from a faucet in their kitchen.
Ⓑ They used to get it from the well and now they'll get it from the faucet.
Ⓒ They used to get it from the dirty stream, and now they will have a well in the village.
Ⓓ None of the above

Question 11 is based on the passage below.

GRAINS, GRAINS, GRAINS

Everyone knows that grains are an important healthy part of a good diet. It is important to make sure that you are eating the right amount of grains daily.

To make sure this happens include grains in half of your diet each day. Whole grain and wheat help to keep your digestive system in order and run smoothly as well.

Did you know that whole grains and whole grain foods are made up of all three layers of the grain seed or kernel?

Here are the layers and explanations that will help you to understand.

1. The bran (outer layer): give you all of the fiber as well as B vitamins; minerals such as magnesium, iron and zinc, and some protein.

2. The endosperm (middle layer): makes up for most of the weight of the grain and is made up mainly of carbohydrate and protein.

3. The germ (inner layer): has B vitamins, unsaturated fats, vitamin E, and minerals.

Most whole grains are quite tasty such as brown rice, barley, whole oats or oatmeal, wheat and rye breads.

When you go shopping with your parents, do the healthy choice thing and read labels.

Whole grain foods will have the words 'whole' or 'whole grain' followed by the name of the grain as one of the first ingredients.

11. How can you help when you are out shopping with your parents to be sure healthy choices are made? Write your answer in the box below.

Question 12 and 13 are based on the passage below.

John F. Kennedy and Martin Luther King, Jr.

John F. Kennedy

John Fitzgerald "Jack" Kennedy (May 29, 1917 – November 22, 1963)

President John F. Kennedy, our 35th President of the United States, has often been referred to as simply JFK. He was President from January 1961 until he was assassinated in November 1963. He is known for his famous quote, "Ask not what your country can do for you. Ask what you can do for your country." He was the youngest US President elected and the only Roman Catholic to serve office. He is also the only US President to win the famed Pulitzer's Prize.

He is well known for his advancements in aiding the Civil Rights Movement. During his term, the Peace Corps was established, the "New Frontier" domestic program, and the Cuban Missile Crisis also occurred.

He was killed by Lee Harvey Oswald in Dallas, Texas. It is thought that there was a conspiracy to commit the murder. Jack Ruby then killed Oswald in a jail corridor. The majority of Americans alive during the time believed that it was not done simply by just one man.

Martin Luther King, Jr. 1929-1968

Martin Luther King, Jr. was born in 1929 in Atlanta, Georgia. He was the son of a Baptist preacher and became a Baptist minister himself, too. He followed the beliefs of Gandhi to be non-violent in his actions. He was the greatest supporter of the Civil Rights Movement during his time. He believed in boycotting, refusing to buy merchandise from those people who were considered racists. He was known for the March on Washington for Jobs and Freedom in 1963. King became a sort of national hero for the movement of African-Americans.

He is best known today for this and for his historic speech, "I Have a Dream". Martin Luther King, Jr. won the Nobel Peace Prize in 1964. The Civil Rights Act was passed that year, and he was the greatest influence in its passing. He was against discrimination of all kinds, but especially that against the African-American population. He was killed in 1968.

12. In what ways do you find both President Kennedy and Martin Luther King, Jr. alike? List three and Write your answer in the box below.

13. Had you been alive during this time, what do you think your thoughts might be in ways to promote civil rights to all? Could these thoughts still help today?

   Write two sentences in the box below to show how you would feel then and how you could help then and now.

Question 14 is based on the passage below.

Lionel Sosa and Sam Walton

Lionel Sosa grew up in San Antonio, Texas. He was expected to follow his family tradition and learn a trade and become a Democrat. However, he chose to follow the ideal of the American Dream and also to become a Republican.

In doing so, he ran a small ad- agency. It was then that US Senator John Tower employed Sosa's company to run his election ad campaign. This gained Tower his re-election by focusing on the Hispanic vote. Sosa was then approached by clients such as Dr Pepper to help gain the Latino market sales. Sosa and Associates became the largest and most profitable US Hispanic ad agency in the country.

Since then, he was able to work on many presidential campaigns including that of Ronald Reagan.

He now spends his retirement time painting and writing.

Sam Walton (1918-1992) founded Walmart and Sam's Club. He opened the first Wal-Mart Discount City in 1962 after having several franchise Ben Franklin stores. His main effort was to market American made products. Although after his death, this practice was not continued. He placed his stores close to distribution centers, thereby having stores in multiple areas, not just in major cities.

He was listed as the richest man in the US from 1982 to 1988. Walmart and Sam's Club stores operate in the US and in 15 other countries including, Canada, Japan, Mexico, and the UK.

14. Part A
   How do you think the two men were alike in the business deals? Write your answer in the box below.

Part B

How did they differ? Write your answer in the box below.

Question 15 is based on the poem below.

The Fish

wade
through black jade.
    Of the crow-blue mussel-shells, one keeps
    adjusting the ash-heaps;
        opening and shutting itself like

an
injured fan.
    The barnacles which encrust the side
    of the wave, cannot hide
        there for the submerged shafts of the

sun,
split like spun
    glass, move themselves with spotlight swiftness
    into the crevices—
        in and out, illuminating

the
turquoise sea
     of bodies. The water drives a wedge
     of iron through the iron edge
        of the cliff; whereupon the stars,

pink
rice-grains, ink-
     bespattered jelly fish, crabs like green
     lilies, and submarine
        toadstools, slide each on the other.

All
external
     marks of abuse are present on this
     defiant edifice—
        all the physical features of

ac-
cident—lack
     of cornice, dynamite grooves, burns, and
     hatchet strokes, these things stand
        out on it; the chasm-side is

dead.
Repeated
     evidence has proved that it can live
     on what can not revive
        its youth. The sea grows old in it.

15. Part A

If you were to write such a poem, not using rhyming patterns, what might you write about? Write your answer in the box below.

Part B

Give at least two lines of your poem. Write your answer in the box below.

End of Reading: Literature

Answer Key and Detailed Explanations

Chapter 2: Reading: Literature

Lesson 1: Finding Detail in the Story

Question No.	Answer	Detailed Explanations
1	B	The second choice is correct. When Mary began reading her story to her class, those were the first words that she read. The title of a story goes at the top of the page, and those are the first words read when sharing a story aloud.
2	C	The third choice is correct. The passage states that "However, there was one part about every Friday at school that Mary did not enjoy, and that was when she had to share her story in front of the class."
3	C	The third choice is correct because the passage stated, "The teacher made all of the children share on Friday afternoons."
4	D	The fourth choice is correct. It referred to the vacation as a "nightmare," and it told that they "cut their trip short." If they were enjoying their trip, they would have stayed the whole time as planned instead of leaving early.
5		They packed everything they needed in a bag, her dad cooked the breakfast for them and the author's mom turned on the AC and music for everyone to enjoy the trip.
6		Mom clapped loudly when she arrived at the hotel.
7		The answer is the floor. The fact stated in the story. 'We were so happy we could have slept on the floor and not minded!!'
8	Rain	The correct answer is "rain"
9		The correct order sequence is: 1. She dug a deep hole. 2. She added the clay dirt to the hole. 3. She watered the rose branch at an angle after it was planted. 4. She put a banana peel around the bottom of the branch.
10		Aunt Molly felt that the second rose bush was not looking very healthy when she had bought it an year ago. She took very good care of it by adding fresh clay soil around it. But Aunt Molly was afraid that it was going to die during the winter.
11		When she awoke her Ayah was not there. Instead, there was a strange lady looking down at her.

Question No.	Answer	Detailed Explanations
12	A,B,C	Answer choices A, B and C are correct. All three of these should be selected, as they are all found as details in the story.
13	A,C	Answer choices A and C are correct. Both facts found in the passage.
14		Part A - Hesperides Part B - open-mouthed Part C - Adventurous Part D - wrapt

Lesson 2: Inferring

Question No.	Answer	Detailed Explanations
1	C	The third choice is correct. We know that the poet was surprised to hear a song from the shell, because the poet "listened hard, And it was really true." It makes sense to gather information before confirming a situation is true.
2	C	The third choice is correct. We know that the horse was scared, because the passage said "Realizing that the horse was terrified of its own shadow." Terrified means the same thing as scared.
3	D	The fourth choice is correct. We can infer that Cindy did not like what her mother had cooked, because she asked if she could cook something else (the frozen pizza).
4	B	The second choice is correct. We can infer that Mary began reading her story in front of the class, because the last sentence said that she got out of her seat and walked to the front of the room after her name was called. We know that was the signal to start reading the story.
5	C	The third choice is correct. The passage tells us that Mary really enjoys writing stories. We know that many parents support their children at things they do well.
6	C	The third choice is correct. We can infer that Ben and his dad were going to a mountain, because the passage reads that there was a new blanket of snow outside. Also, his dad told him to grab his skis. Our background knowledge tells us that people ski on snow-covered mountains.
7	C	The third choice is correct. We can infer that this takes place in the early morning at sunrise, because the sky was turning from dark to pinkish-yellow. We know that at nighttime, the sky is dark. We also know that it becomes light in the early morning.
8	D	The fourth choice is correct. The author says she, "lay on the windowsill." These are characteristics specific to a cat. The mention of birds in the 5th sentence is also a clue, because cats prey on birds.
9	A	The first choice is correct. We can infer that it is summer, because the passage tells us that it is hot. We know that people go surfing in the summertime because the hot weather makes the ocean just right for swimming and surfing.

Question No.	Answer	Detailed Explanations
10	B	The second choice is correct. We can infer that Susie's family lives near the beach, because the passage says that they drove there in a car. If they did not live near the beach, they would have to travel for several hours or fly on an airplane to get to the beach. The passage did not imply that they would be traveling a long distance.
11		The answer is: The fireworks.
12	Salsa Queen	She became known as the "Salsa Queen" due to her style of music.
13	No	She then went to Mexico for a one year contract right before Fidel Castro took over Cuba. She and her band never returned. Answer details are in the story.
14	A	The correct answer choice is A.
15		The fox's intent was to gobble up the rooster. This is evident from this line in the passage – 'A Fox, hearing the sound, and wishing to make a breakfast on him, came and stood under the branches, saying how earnestly he desired to make the acquain¬tance of the owner of so sweet a voice'.

Lesson 3: Finding the Theme

Question No.	Answer	Detailed Explanations
1	C	The third choice is correct. Fred spent a lot of time worrying about visiting the dentist and got himself really worked up. When he actually visited the dentist, nothing bad happened to him. He realized that he did not need to worry.
2	B	The second choice is correct. Opal felt really bad when she acted dishonestly. After she told the truth, she instantly felt better.
3	A	The first choice is correct. The quilt did not cost much money, but it had a lot of sentimental value to Libby.
4	B	The second choice is correct. A homemade gift (the quilt) was better than an expensive one, is a detail not the theme.
5	C	The third choice is correct. Rhonda's new school is different than her old one. Rhonda liked the different things at her new school.
6	D	The fourth choice is correct. Telling her little brother that she was sorry didn't make Polly's little brother feel better. Polly's little brother started to feel better when Polly read him a story.
7	C	The third choice is correct. Since Karen worked hard and completed her assignments on time, she received an A in the class.
8	A	The first choice is correct. If Mr. Toad had shared his food, he wouldn't have been so full and would have been able to escape the hunter.
9	C	The third choice is correct. Frank's classmates stopped asking him to hang out, because all he wanted to do was quote information from books.
10	C	The third choice is correct. If the monkey wasn't greedy and just let go of the cookies, his hand wouldn't be stuck in the cookie jar.
11		He is dreaming up a marching band to help him get to sleep.
12	D	Sea Shell Song is the best title, because the main idea of the passage is "a girl discovered that a shell has a song."

Lesson 4: Summarizing the Text

Question No.	Answer	Detailed Explanations
1	B	The second choice is correct, because it tells only the important information from the passage. Option D also gives a summary, but it has additional information that is not needed.
2	A	The first choice is correct, because it tells only the most important information from the passage. Options B. and C do not give enough information. Option D basically retells the entire story instead of just summarizing it.
3	A	The first choice is correct, because it gives only the most important information from the passage. Some of the information in the other answer choices is out of order. Options B and D do not summarize because there is too much information.
4	A	The first choice is correct, because it tells the most important information in the passage. Option B is correct but does not include all of the key information. Options C and D do not summarize the paragraph.
5	B	The second choice is correct, because it tells the most important information in the passage. The other options either give too little or too much information.
6	C	The third choice is correct, because it tells the most important details from the passage. The other options either give too little or too much information.
7	C	The third choice is correct, because writing as a strong point is not discussed in the main idea of the passage. The passage is about Mary being good at creative writing, but being afraid to share her stories in front of her class.
8	A	The first choice is correct, because it tells the main idea and the most important information from the story. The other options either give too little or too much information.
9	C	The third choice is correct, because it gives the main idea of the passage and the most important details. The other options either give too little or too much information.
10	A	The first choice is correct. The first choice is not an important piece of information from the story. The other options are necessary for the summary.

Question No.	Answer	Detailed Explanations
11		He wanted to preserve the land because he was worried about the beauty of the land that was going to be destroyed. He felt that only the government could protect the land and Native Americans by creating a national park.
12	A	Answer choice A is correct. This answer gives the most detail and is found in the passage.
13		The poet is comparing a tree to a poem. This is because he said that fools like him can make a poem, but only God can make a tree. The poem says, " Poems are made by fools like me, but only God can make a tree. The poet says this because humans can not create a tree, but God can.
14		They were afraid for his safety when he would meet the dragon.
15	A,B & C	Answer options A, B and C are correct.

Lesson 5: Describing Characters

Question No.	Answer	Detailed Explanations
1	C	The third choice is correct. We know that Timothy is responsible, because the passage reads that he gets up early every day to perform his dog walking job. We know that Timothy is ambitious, because Timothy believes he can continue his dog walking job and participate in extracurricular activities.
2	B	The second answer is correct. We know that Timothy wouldn't help someone cheat on a test. The passage indicates that "he is always honest and expects others to be honest."
3	B	The second choice is correct. We know that Fred was afraid and didn't understand the reason that he had to go to the dentist. The passage states that he had heard horror stories about the dentist and he thought the dentist would torture him. The passage reads that he didn't understand the reason that his mom thought he needed to go since his teeth weren't hurting.
4	C	The third choice is correct. We know that Fred felt relieved after his visit to the dentist, because he said the chair was comfortable and the dentist was friendly. The last sentence of the passage reads that it wasn't as bad as he thought it would be.
5	A	The first choice is correct. Stanley is solitary, because he likes to spend his time doing things by himself. Stanley is caring, because he volunteers at the recycling center.
6	A	The first choice is correct. We know that Adam and Stanley like and respect each other, because they enjoy volunteering together at the recycling center.
7	B	The second choice is correct. We know that Adam is thoughtful, because he volunteers his time at a recycling center. We know that Adam is outgoing, because he likes to spend all of his time with his friends.
8	A	The first choice is correct. We know that Beau was anxious, because he was in a situation where most kids would be anxious. The passage states that he was fidgeting and playing with his button.
9	A	The first choice is correct. Libby's grandmother was nervous, because she was afraid that Libby would not like the quilt.
10	D	The fourth choice is correct. Libby's grandmother was happy after Libby opened up the quilt, because Libby loved the present.

Question No.	Answer	Detailed Explanations
11 Part A	A,C & E	Answer A, C and E are correct. She is loving, bright and helpful child.
11 Part B		Answer should include adjectives and explanations of how Mary Ann helps out, and laughs, is happy to do chores, etc.
12	B, C	Answer B and C are correct. These are characteristics found in the passage. She was spoiled, selfish, ill-tempered and tyrannical.
13		Stag - proud, conceited Lion - confident, hungry Wolf - conniving, deceitful, analytical, hungry Lamb - young, innocent, Rooster - thoughtful, intelligent, smart, witty Dog - protectorate, fierce, friend, Fox - conniving, deceitful, sly
14		Howard, Ernie, Edward & Widow Crankston The main characters in the story are Howard, Ernie, Edward and Widow Crankston.
15	A,B	Answer choices A and B are correct. These are characteristics of being strong. Although it states he shouldn't have wasted his time, that has nothing to do with being strong.

Lesson 6: Describing the Setting

Question No.	Answer	Detailed Explanations
1	A	The first choice is correct. The first sentence of the passage tells us that the story takes place two thousand five hundred years ago.
2	B	The second choice is correct. The setting for the second paragraph is an automobile, because it tells us that Fred and his mother were on their way to the dentist.
3	A	The first choice is correct. Huckleberry Hound was in the yard at the beginning of the story. The first sentence of the passage provides this information.
4	B	The second choice is correct. Huckleberry Hound chased the rabbit in the field. The second sentence of the passage provides this detail.
5	A	The first choice is correct. Huckleberry Hound was in the yard at the end of the story. The last sentence of the passage tells us so.
6	B	The second choice is correct. The writer was at school. The second sentence of the passage provides the setting.
7	A	The first choice is correct. The writer dropped her ice cream at the ice cream shop. The last sentence of the passage tells us so.
8	C	The third choice is correct. The third paragraph says "at the end of the school day."
9	C	The third choice is correct. The story takes place in a classroom at Mary's school. The whole passage is about one of Mary's classes.
10	B	The second choice is correct. The story takes place outside in a yard. The first sentence of the passage provides the setting.
11		The haunted house neighborhood of Rio Vista Drive, in front of the house.
12	B,C & D	Answer B, C and D are correct options. These are all noted in the passage.

Question No.	Answer	Detailed Explanations
13		The correct order of the event is:
		They had the car packed the night before they left on their vacation.
		They stopped off in Mississippi before going to Disneyworld.
		Mom had to wake the kids when they arrived at the hotel.
		Mom assigned sleeping arrangements.
		It rained as soon as they got up on their first day at Disneyworld.
		They rode the Liberty Square Riverboat.
		They were able to see the parade and fireworks.
14		The young women were weaving flowers into wreaths and crowning each other's heads with them.
15		Although it does not say at this point, one can infer that he tried to get away if held down.

Lesson 7: Describing Events

Question No.	Answer	Detailed Explanations
1	C	The third choice is correct. We know that Timothy is saving up for youth camp, because the last sentence of the passage tells us so.
2	B	The second choice is correct. We know that Timothy gets up at 5 a.m. to walk dogs, because the third sentence of the second paragraph provides the time.
3	C	The third choice is correct. We know that Fred is worried about going to the dentist because people who are scared often tremble.
4	B	The second choice is correct. We know that Fred thinks the dentist will put him in a chair and use a huge drill on him. This information is present in the second paragraph of the passage.
5	A	The first choice is correct. The last paragraph of the passage tells us that the dentist showed Fred how to brush and floss his teeth.
6	D	The fourth choice is correct. The last paragraph of the passage tells us that Adam and Stanley enjoy volunteering at the youth center together.
7	C	The third choice is correct. Sharing her story in front of the class made Mary nervous. The third paragraph in the passage provides this information.
8	D	The fourth choice is correct. The kids were excited about being dismissed from school, and Aunt Margaret happened to be in the way. A scuff is only a very small mark.
9	C	The third choice is correct. The parents are going out of town. The first sentence of the passage tells us this.
10	D	The fourth choice is correct. In the last paragraph of the passage, it tells us that the narrator caught a cold.
11		The correct order: Box 1: Mama allows Santiago to have Felix over to spend the night. Box 2: The boys clean Santiago's bedroom and do not stay up late. Box 3: Felicia tells the boys to meet her back at 12:30. Box 4: Santiago forgets to meet Felix at the food court and Felix waits for him. Box 5: Santiago and Felix get to go to the shops and eat lunch.

Question No.	Answer	Detailed Explanations
12		The correct sequence of events in the story: Box 1: There are two parts of Rio Vista Drive. Box 2: Some kids believe Widow Crankston is a witch because of her black cat. Box 3: The house is in bad shape with briars, cobwebs, and needs painting. Box 4: It is the night before Halloween. Box 5: Edward decides to take the dare. Box 6: Widow Crankston offers them treats to eat and cold milk to drink. Box 7: The boys help paint the house and fix it up.
13 Part A		Mr. Hart took the Ms. Abernathy's lunch. The evidence are: He had been in her room. He had a stain on his shirt. He did not eat his own lunch. He laughed and asked the kids if they knew who took the lunch once he dropped his on the floor.
13 Part B		Answer should include that the evidence leads you to believe it was him based on facts given.
14		The order of events in the story is: Mary Ann is an only child. Mary Ann likes to go into the empty bedrooms, and pretend her make believe sister lives there. Mary Ann's mother is worried about her behavior. Mary Ann skipped into the living room. Mary Ann's parents tell her she is adopted.

Question No.	Answer	Detailed Explanations
15		The events that led to the parade was firstly they rode the trolly and got free breakfast. secondly, they were able to go to the splash mountain, jungle cruise, the seven dwarfs mine train and much more. Finally, they saw the parade on the side of the castle because the hotel clerk told the mother how to find a good seat to view the parade.

Lesson 8: Figurative Language

Question No.	Answer	Detailed Explanations
1	D	"Twinkled like diamonds" is a simile. A simile compares two things using like or as. The way the girl's eyes twinkle is compared to how diamonds twinkle.
2	B	This is a metaphor. A metaphor is a direct comparison of two unlike objects. Her heart is being compared to stone. Stone is hard, and her heart was hard (meaning she was not very sensitive).
3	C	This is a metaphor. The sound the bird made was compared to music, meaning it made a pleasant, entertaining sound.
4	D	Birds eat very little, and Suzy eats very little.
5	B	A compass guides people to the right location. The man's wife guides him to the right paths in life.
6	D	A lemon is sour and unpleasant. A car that doesn't run well is unpleasant.
7	D	A simile compares two objects using like or as. This simile compares the hardness of the biscuits to the hardness of rocks.
8	C	Angels are kind. Janice is kind.
9	C	Oxen are strong. Jimmy is strong.
10	B	A metaphor directly compares two unlike objects. Linda is being compared to a road hog.
11 Part A	hurrying	Hustling means hurrying
11 Part B	something to wear	Outfit means something to wear
11 Part C	out of control/ unable to stop	Uncontrollably means out of control or unable to stop
11 Part D	strong/ healthy	Hearty means strong or healthy

Question No.	Answer	Detailed Explanations		
12			germ (inner layer)	endosperm (middle layer)	bran (outer layer)
		the weight of the grain		●	
		the fiber			●
		unsaturated fats	●		
13	A,B & C	A, B and C answer choices are correct. These details are found in the story.		
14	Hercules	Hercules is the correct answers. He tells them his name, finally.		
15		The cup had been set **adrift** by some unseen power, and guided **hitherward**, in order to carry Hercules across the sea, on his way to the garden of the **Hesperides**.		

Lesson 9: Text Structure

Question No.	Answer	Detailed Explanations
1	D	The Three Little Pigs is told in sequence or chronologically. The events are told in the order that they happened.
2	D	Descriptive texts tell the characteristics of a particular subject.
3	D	This is a narrative text, because the writer is describing an event in his or her life.
4	C	Sequencing texts tell about events in the order that they happened.
5	D	Sequencing and texts tell the events in the order that they happened.
6	D	Problem/Solution texts start out explaining a problem. Then, they offer a solution. The problem in this passage is that Beau wanted a dog. The solution was for him to keep his room clean.
7	A	Descriptive passages tell the characteristics of one particular subject.
8	C	Descriptive text is about providing detail regarding a particular topic. This is the type of unsequenced text used in this passage.
9	B	This is a compare and contrast passage, because it tells the similarities and differences of two different subjects.
10	C	Problem and solution texts describe a problem, then explain a solution to the problem. Germs are a problem, and the passage explains how to eliminate them.
11		She saved the day by deciding to stay longer at the mall and letting her mom know they would be there longer.
12		She was not upset set because her best friend Valerie was coming along with her to the trip to Disneyworld. So who could complain about a little brother coming along? The author is not too upset, on her brother going on vacation, because she was going to Disney world.
13		I would have told the stranger where to go, but would have also told him about the danger ahead about the dragon with 100 heads and would have advised him not to go.
14		Students need to include some of the following adjectives found in the text, sea creature, scales such as fishes have, web-footed, web-fingered, likes a duck, long beard, greenish tinge like seaweed, barnacles, and wave-test spar.
15	A & C	These sentences intrigue the reader to want to read more.

Lesson 10: Point of View

Question No.	Answer	Detailed Explanations
1	B	Second person point of view is when the writer is talking directly to the reader.
2	A	First person point of view is when one of the characters is telling the story. Pronouns such as I and me are used.
3	C	Third person point of view is when the story is told by someone who is not a character in the story.
4	B	Second person point of view is when the writer is speaking directly to the reader.
5	C	Third person point of view is when the story is being told by some-one who is not a character in the story.
6	A	First person point of view is when one of the characters in the story is telling it. Pronouns such as I and me are used.
7	A	First person point of view is when one of the characters in the story is telling the story. Pronouns such as I and me are used.
8	A	First person point of view is when the story is being told by one of the characters in the story. Pronouns such as I and me are used.
9	C	Third person point of view is when the story is told by someone who is not a character in the story.
10	C	Third person point of view is when the story is being told by a per-son who is not a character in the story.
11		The student will choose a different ending for the story . Watch to see that they use the evidence from the story as the basis for the new ending.
12		Author's purpose is to show that not all we assume is correct and that kindness needs to be returned. We think about something we see, may not be correct and we need to help others.
13		I would change the story by going to the beach, have lots of fun, go on every ride and see all the Disney characters.
14		If I were a musician like Celia Cruz, I would play country music, be-cause I love country music and I would like to make people happy by playing country music.

Question No.	Answer	Detailed Explanations
15		The Bengal Tiger is an endangered species, due to habit loss and deforestation. This animal concerns me most because there are only 2,00 Bengal Tigers left in the wild.

Their population is declining due to illegal poaching and there is a demand in the market for their skins, nails, and tooth. Also, their hunting grounds is reducing year after year, due to deforestation. In China, Tigers are bred in captivity and killed for their organs for their cuisine. Due to man's intervention in the forest, their reproduction is also on the decline and they get frequent diseases. |

Lesson 11: Visual Connections

Question No.	Answer	Detailed Explanations
1	B	The picture of the female in front of a chalkboard is appropriate, because this story takes place in a school classroom and Mary is speaking to her class.
2	C	The third choice is correct, because it is about baby monkeys. There are baby monkeys in the picture.
3	C	The third choice is correct, because it is about a kitten at a construction site. The kitten in the picture is in a concrete pipe.
4	C	The third choice is correct, because it is about singing. The girl in the picture is holding a microphone and singing.
5	D	The fourth choice is correct, because it is about a sandcastle shaped like a dragon.
6	6; 4; +2	The pattern on the table shows each game the score decreases by 2 points for both teams, but the Blue Jets still win with +2 over the other teams.

Game #	Team Blue Jets	Opposing Team	Difference + or -
1	10	8	+2
2	8	6	+2
3	**6**	**4**	**+2**

Question No.	Answer	Detailed Explanations
7		Each student may choose their own team sport, and tell what position they would like to play and who would help them to practice.
8		Bike riding tips should include the following: take snacks, buddy up, wear a helmet, slow down, inspect your vehicle.
9		A four wheeler with a kid on it going through muddy paths covered in moss and vines. The mud is thick and water is everywhere. These two sentences in the first paragraph that help you to visualize mudding.
10		Students are required to draw a picture and describe the same in a poem.
11.1		Both are roses, small roses, similar in form and size.
11.2		Color, kind of rose, one is on a large bush, the other a young bush.

Lesson 12: Comparing and Contrasting

Question No.	Answer	Detailed Explanations
1	C	The third choice is correct, because it most accurately describes how Fred was afraid at first and then relieved after he saw the dentist.
2	C	The third choice is correct, because it tells a way that the two boys are alike. Compare means to tell how one or more subjects are alike.
3	D	To contrast means to tell how two subjects are different. The fourth choice tells what both Stanley and Timothy like to do.
4	A	The first choice is correct. Both boys volunteer at the recycling center.
5	C	The third choice is correct, because it tells how the people favored the Hawaiian vacation over the Alaskan vacation.
6	B	The second choice is correct, because it tells how each aunt dresses. The story specifically describes how the two Aunt's dress.
7	A	The first choice is correct, because it tells what kind of car each aunt drives. The story specifically describes the types of vehicles that the two Aunts drive.
8	C	The third choice is correct, because it tells what happened to the animals after the restaurant opened. Each animals had various complaints.
9	A	The first choice is correct, because it describes what happened the birds and to the beavers during spring.
10	C	The third choice is correct, because it correctly tells where the family used to get their water.
11		When we are out shopping with our parents, we should follow the below given measures to be sure that healthy choices are made. The answer may include the following points : 1. Read food nutrition labels. 2. Look for the date of expiry. 3. Choose whole grain foods. 4. Choose fresh/canned/frozen produce. The answers may vary.
12		Answer may vary
13		Answer may vary
14.1		Answer may vary
14.2		Answer may vary
15.1		Answer may vary
15.2		Answer may vary

Chapter 3 - Reading Informational Text

The objective of the Reading Informational Text standards is to ensure that each student is able to read and comprehend informational text (history/social studies, science, and technical texts) related to Grade 4.

This section is to support students to master the necessary skills, an example which will help the student understand the concepts related to the standard is given. Along with this, we encourage the student to go through the resources available online on EdSearch to gain an in depth understanding of these concepts. EdSearch page for each lesson can be accessed with the help of the url or the QR code provided.

A small map is provided after each passage or text in which the student can enter the details as understood from the literary text. Doing this will help the student to refer to key points that help in answering the questions with ease.

Lesson 1: It's All in the Details

Explicit text: When you have been assigned to explain some text explicitly, it means that you have to explain the meaning of the text so clearly and in enough detail that any reader will understand completely what you have written. To do this, you will have to understand the main idea(s) that the author of the text is telling his readers so that you can explain them explicitly. And the best way to do this is to use actual details and examples from the text.

Inference: This is a conclusion reached by a reader after reading the information in a passage. The reader uses the information in the passage to reach this conclusion on his/her own; it has not been stated by the author. For example, the author may write about large population growth in the world and the negative effects of climate change on the production of food. The reader could draw the inference that there will not be enough food to feed the population.

Here are two examples that represent use of the standard.

Example 1: Author Jennifer writes: We think allowing students to bring their smartphones and tablets to school to do school work in class is not a good idea. It provides too great an opportunity for students to play games or go on social media instead of focusing on performing assigned work. We favor the greater control that using school computers provides even though we sacrifice some efficiency. You are assigned to write about Jennifer's article. You disagree with her position on this issue, and will use details and examples from her text in your report, as required by the standard. Here is an example of what you might write.

Jennifer states that "… allowing students to bring their smartphones and tablets to school … provides too great an opportunity for students to play games or go on social media instead of focusing on performing assigned work." I do not agree that this will occur. The teacher can continue to walk around the room and monitor what is on a student's screen, and how much the student has accomplished, during class or even during a study hall.

Jennifer also states that "… even though we sacrifice some efficiency." She minimizes the inefficiency of students only having access to the school's computer center for one period a day. This is because of the large number of classes that need to use the computer center. If students could use their own smartphones or tablets, they could remain in their classrooms to do their work and continue to work during study periods.

Example 2: Author Jimmy writes: I am in favor of research that can create robots who think like humans. They could take the place of humans in call centers by using technology that recognizes words and can match these words with pre-programmed solutions. They would be available 24/7, not taking vacation or sick days.

You are assigned to write about Jimmy's article. You disagree with his position on this issue, and choose to draw an inference (conclusion) to defend your position. Here is an example of what you might write.

While I agree that robots do not take sick days or vacations, I do not agree with Jimmy's conclusion that "They could take the place of humans in call centers." I conclude that robots will not be able to handle requests for information as well as humans can, for several reasons. First, callers may have various accents when speaking English that a robot cannot understand. Second, a caller may not be able to clearly explain the problem, and may not use the keywords that a robot relies on to match to a solution. Third, a human can more accurately understand the need to transfer the caller to someone else, or to lookup additional information relating to the caller's request. Fourth, most callers would rather speak with a human than a robot for two reasons: more friendly feedback, and the capability of a human call center person to have a dialogue that goes beyond the initial question and response.

You can scan the QR code given below or use the url to access additional EdSearch resources including videos and mobile apps related to *It's All in the Details*.

ed Search

It's All in the Details

URL	QR Code
http://www.lumoslearning.com/a/ri41	

Question 1 and 2 are based on the passage below.

The ostrich is the largest bird in the world, but it cannot fly. Its legs are so strong and long that it can travel faster by running. Ostriches use their wings to help them gather speed when they start to run. They also use them as brakes when turning and stopping.

Ostriches have been known to run at speeds of 60 miles per hour. This is faster than horses and matches the average speed of vehicles on a highway.

These huge birds stand as tall as horses and sometimes weigh as much as 298 pounds. In North Africa, they are often seen with other larger animals.

The zebra, which is also a fast runner, seems to be one of their favorite companions.

An ostrich egg weighs one pound, which is as much as two dozen chicken eggs. Ostrich eggs are delicious and are often used for food by people in Africa. The shells are also made into cups and beautiful ornaments.

1. **Why is it a good thing that the Ostrich can run, rather than fly?**

   Ⓐ The Ostrich does not enjoy flying.
   Ⓑ The Ostrich is able to fly.
   Ⓒ The Ostrich does not want to fly.
   Ⓓ The Ostrich can travel faster by running.

2. **Devon says that Ostriches are shy and solitary birds. Which detail in the text proves him wrong?**

   Ⓐ "Ostrich eggs are delicious and are often used for food by people in Africa."
   Ⓑ "An ostrich egg weighs one pound."
   Ⓒ "These huge birds stand as tall as a horse."
   Ⓓ "The zebra, which is also a fast runner, seems to be one of their favorite companions."

Question 3 is based on the passage below.

The blue whale is quite an amazing creature. It is a mammal that lives its entire life in the ocean. The size of its body is also amazing. This whale can grow up to 98 feet long and weigh as much as 200 tons. It is the largest known animal to have ever existed. Its body is long and elegantly tapered, un-like other whales which have a rounder, stockier build. The way that they are built, along with their extreme size, gives them a unique look. It also gives them the ability to move gracefully at greater speeds. Normally they travel around 12 mph, but they slow to 3.1 mph when feeding. They can even reach speeds up to 31 mph for short periods of time! Although they are extremely large animals, they eat small shrimp-like creatures called krill. Since the krill are so small, the blue whale eats about four tons daily as they swim deep in the ocean.

Blue whales do not live in tight-knit groups called pods like other whales. They live and travel alone or with one other whale. While traveling through the ocean, they come to the top to breathe air into their lungs through blowholes. They come from under the ocean, spitting water out of their blowholes. Then they roll and re-enter the water with a grand splash of their large tails. They make loud, deep, and rumbling low-frequency sounds that travel great distances. This allows them to communicate with other whales as far as 100 miles away. Their cries can be felt as much as heard. This resonating call makes them the loudest animal on Earth. If you ever have the opportunity to see or hear a blue whale, it will be an experience you will not soon forget.

3. **Angel argues that the blue whale is a solitary creature. What evidence from the text best supports his point?**

Ⓐ   "Blue whales do not live in tight-knit groups called pods like other whales. They live and travel alone or with one other whale."

Ⓑ   "This whale can grow up to 98 feet long and weigh as much as 200 tons. It is the largest known animal to have ever existed."

Ⓒ   "They make loud, deep, and rumbling low-frequency sounds that travel great distances. This allows them to communicate with other whales as far as 100 miles away."

Ⓓ   "Although they are extremely large animals, they eat small shrimp-like creatures called krill."

Question 4 is based on the passage below.

If you join our music club, you will receive 4 free CDs. These CDs are yours to keep even if you decide to cancel your membership. If you choose to stay a member and buy just 2 CDs at the regular price, you will get to choose 3 more CDs to keep for free. After your first purchase you will receive 10 points for every CD you buy after that. When you collect 30 points, you get to choose another free CD! If you want to earn even more free CDs, then have your friends join, too. When a friend joins and gives your name, you will get 3 more free CDs. The best part is that you get 3 free CDs each time you have another friend join our club, so join today and start collecting your favorite CDs.

4. What detail from the text encourages music club members to get their friends to join the club?

Ⓐ "If you join our music club, you will receive 4 free CDs."
Ⓑ "After your first purchase you will receive 10 points for every CD you buy after that."
Ⓒ "If you want to earn even more free CDs, then have your friends join, too."
Ⓓ "The best part is that you get 3 free CDs each time you have another friend join our club, so join today and start collecting your favorite CDs."

Question 5 is based on the passage below.

Have you ever wondered what happened to the dinosaurs that once roamed the Earth? Well, scientists have developed several theories throughout the years. One such theory is that a gigantic meteorite crashed into our planet, causing a massive dust cloud to cover the Earth. The dust cloud was so enormous that it blocked the rays of the Sun from reaching Earth. This caused all of the plants to die. With nothing to eat, the herbivores died. The large carnivores also died, leaving the planet without dinosaurs.

5. Amelia asserts that dinosaurs definitely died because a giant meteorite crashed into Earth. What key words from the text would help Terrance to make a counterpoint?

Ⓐ "One idea…"
Ⓑ "…a giant meteorite crashed into our planet"
Ⓒ "…leaving the planet with no dinosaurs."
Ⓓ This caused all of the plants to die.

Question 6 is based on the passage below.

Do you like frogs? Do you know what a spring peeper is?

Spring peepers are tiny little tree frogs that live in wooded areas near ponds. Although these frogs are tiny, only about an inch big, they make a very loud sound. They are found mostly in the central and eastern parts of the United States. So, when the weather begins to get warmer after winter, these little frogs start to sing. Their "peep," which is why they are called spring peepers, can be heard for miles around. They live near ponds so they can lay their eggs in the water.

When the weather starts getting colder again, the spring peepers start to go into hiding. They hibernate under logs or any other place they can find in the forest to protect them from the cold. For example, sometimes they hide under fallen leaves or even in a small hole in the ground.

6. **Which paragraph contains details that support Monique's idea that people are most likely to see spring peepers during warm weather months?**

   Ⓐ Paragraphs 1 and 2
   Ⓑ Paragraphs 1 and 3
   Ⓒ Paragraph 3
   Ⓓ Paragraphs 2 and 3

Question 7 is based on the passage below.

Most people think of koalas as koala bears, but they are not bears. They are marsupials and are in the same family as the wombat. Koalas live in a special place called a eucalyptus forest. They can be found in eastern and southeastern Australia. Adult koalas are one of only three animals that can live on a diet of eucalyptus leaves. These leaves contain 50% water. The eucalyptus leaves are mostly the main source of water for koalas.

The koala is a marsupial which means the baby crawls into a pocket, called a pouch, on the mother's tummy as soon as it is born. Baby koalas are called "joeys." When they are born, they cannot see, have no hair, and are less than one inch long. They stay in their mother's pouch for the next six months. First the mother feeds them milk. Then she feeds them a food called "pap" in addition to milk. Joeys continue to drink the mother's milk until they are a year old. The young koala will remain with its mother until another joey is born and comes into the pouch.

7. **What detail in the text explains why someone is not likely to see a koala in northwestern Australia?**

   Ⓐ Koalas live in a special place called a eucalyptus forest.
   Ⓑ They are marsupials and are in the same family as the wombat.
   Ⓒ Koalas live...in eastern and south-eastern Australia.
   Ⓓ When they are born, they are blind, hairless, and less than one inch long.

Question 8 and 9 are based on the passage below.

There are four types of tissues that are created as cells join together and work as a group. Each type of tissue has a unique structure and does a specific job. Muscle tissue is made up of long, narrow muscle cells. Muscle tissue makes the body parts move by tightening and relaxing. Connective tissue is what holds up the body and connects its parts together. The bone is made up of connective tissue. Nerve tissue is made up of long nerve cells that go through the body and carry messages. Epithelial tissue is made of wide, flat epithelial cells. This tissue lines the surfaces inside the body and forms the outer layer of the skin. Groups of tissue join together to form the organs in the body such as the heart, liver, lungs, brain, and kidneys just to name a few. Then these organs work together to form the body systems. Each system works together, and with the other systems of the body.

8. What job does muscle tissue perform in the body? Circle the correct answer choice.

Ⓐ It holds up the body.
Ⓑ It allows the body to move
Ⓒ It allows messages to travel through the body.
Ⓓ It forms the outer layer of skin.

9. What job does the epithelial tissue perform? Circle the correct answer choice.

Ⓐ It holds up the body.
Ⓑ It allows the body to move.
Ⓒ It allows messages to travel through the body.
Ⓓ It forms the outer layer of skin.

Question 10 is based on the passage below.

2362 West Main Street
Jojo, TX 98456

June 16, 2017

Dear Mr. Seymour:

I ordered a Magic Racing Top from your company. The toy was delivered to me today in a package that was badly damaged. I took a picture of the box before I opened it, which I am sending to you as proof of the damage. The toy inside was broken due to the damage of the package during shipping.

This toy was to be a gift for my friend's birthday. There is not enough time before his party to wait for a replacement toy; therefore, I no longer need the toy. I would like you to refund my money. Please send me a prepaid shipping label if you would like me to return the broken toy. Thank you for handling this matter for me. I look forward to hearing from you and hope we can satisfactorily resolve this problem.

Sincerely,
Tim West

10. Dominique argues that the writer of this letter was pleased with the toy company because he says, "please," and "if you would like." Does this evidence do a good job of supporting her argument? Circle the correct answer choice.

Ⓐ Yes. These are very polite words, so he is clearly pleased with the toy company.

Ⓑ Yes. He also says, "Thank you for handling this matter for me."

Ⓒ No. He is being polite, but he also says the package he ordered was, "badly damaged," and, "I would like you to refund my money."

Ⓓ No. He wants to satisfactorily resolve the problem.

Chapter 3

Lesson 2: The Main Idea

Main Idea: It is the main thought or message being conveyed about the topic. To figure out the main idea, ask yourself: What is being said about the person, thing, or idea (the topic). The main idea is usually the first sentence of the passage. The rest of the passage usually has the supporting ideas and details.

An Inference: a logical conclusion that can be reached based on evidence in the passage by reasoning.

You can scan the QR code given below or use the url to access additional EdSearch resources including videos and mobile apps related to *The Main Idea*.

 The Main Idea

URL	QR Code
http://www.lumoslearning.com/a/ri42	

Question 1 and 2 are based on the passage below.

The ostrich is the largest bird in the world, but it cannot fly. Its legs are so strong and long that it can travel faster by running. Ostriches use their wings to help them gather speed when they start to run. They also use them as brakes when turning and stopping.

Ostriches have been known to run at speeds of 60 miles per hour. This is faster than horses and matches the average speed of vehicles on a highway.

These huge birds stand as tall as horses and sometimes weigh as much as 298 pounds. In North Africa, they are often seen with other larger animals.

The zebra, which is also a fast runner, seems to be one of their favorite companions.

An ostrich egg weighs one pound, which is as much as two dozen chicken eggs. Ostrich eggs are delicious and are often used for food by people in Africa. The shells are also made into cups and beautiful ornaments.

1. What is the most appropriate title for this passage?

Ⓐ The Ostrich
Ⓑ The Bird that Cannot Fly
Ⓒ The Ostrich Egg
Ⓓ The Largest Bird in the World

2. What is the main idea of the passage?

Ⓐ Ostriches are great because their eggs are delicious.
Ⓑ The ostrich is the largest bird and can run very fast.
Ⓒ The ostrich is the largest bird but it cannot fly.
Ⓓ The ostrich lives in Africa.

Question 3 is based on the passage below.

Did you know that the coconut tree is very useful to people? Each part of the tree can be used for many different purposes. The coconut fruit, which we get from the tree, is very nutritious and is used to cook varieties of food. Coconut milk, which is taken from the coconut, tastes very delicious. It is used to prepare a variety of sweet dishes.

Oil can be extracted from a dried coconut. Coconut oil is a very good moisturizer. It is used in many beauty products like body wash, face wash, shampoos, and conditioners. The oil is also used for cooking of tropical foods. Some coconut trees grow straight and tall, and some trees are very short. Coconut trees do not have branches. They have long leaves which grow right at the top of the tree. The leaves have many different uses. Leaf ribs are made into brooms. The fiber obtained from the outer cover of the nut is used for mattresses and rugs. The trunk is used to make logs for small boats. It is also used for firewood. The sweet water of the tender coconut quenches thirst during the hot summer months and it is also very healthy.

3. What is the most appropriate title for this passage?

- Ⓐ   The Coconut Tree and Its Uses
- Ⓑ   Trees of the Rainforest
- Ⓒ   Foods that We Get from the Coconut
- Ⓓ   Tall Coconut Trees

4. What would be the main idea of the below story?

Beatrice was so excited. This was truly a special day for her. She looked down and saw that her cup was sparkling with clean and cold water. She couldn't believe it was real as she had never seen water like that before. She slowly took a sip and it tasted so fresh. Her mother always told her how important water is.

The only way that Beatrice was able to get her water in the past was from the dirty water in a ditch not far from her home. Otherwise, they would have to walk for miles to reach other areas that had water. The water there wasn't very clean, either. In fact, most of the time, this water had a horrible smell and was brownish in color. Beatrice and her family knew it wasn't great but they didn't have any choice. The water that they drank from was contaminated making Beatrice feel sick often.

The water they mostly use is from streams, rivers, and lakes and is used for cooking, taking baths, and washing clothes. This water is contaminated from chemicals in the products they use and can cause diseases, such as typhus, cholera, dysentery, and malaria.

Ⓐ Beatrice never had water that tasted so good before.
Ⓑ Beatrice is happy that she and her family will finally have clean drinking water.
Ⓒ Beatrice and her family get their water from the murky stream near the home.
Ⓓ Contaminated water often carries diseases and people can become very ill.

5. Which detail in the below passage tells us that the soil is being polluted?

Pollution hurts the world around us. It upsets the balance of nature, which is very important for our survival. The problems in the environment affect in four areas. The areas affected are the soil, water, air and sound. Large amounts of trash from factories and houses can cause land pollution. Chemicals used in farming pollute the soil. Plastics are wasteful products. Too many animals needing to eat and the cutting down of trees creates deserts and wastelands. Deserts already cover 40 percent of the Earth's surface. Waste in water makes it unhealthy and harmful. Plants and animals in the water are harmed because of the tons of oil that is spilled into the seas and oceans. The air that we breathe is polluted by smoke and dust in the atmosphere. Lung illnesses can occur when the air is polluted. Noise pollution in cities has grown intensely. Pollution has become a serious and invasive problem around the globe.

Ⓐ the oil spills in the seas and oceans.
Ⓑ smoke and dust in the air
Ⓒ large amounts of trash from factories and houses
Ⓓ global warming

Question 6 is based on the passage below.

Beautiful seashells that are washed ashore on beaches by ocean waves have always amazed people. Shells come in a collection of shapes, sizes, and colors. Shells are actually made by marine creatures to serve as their homes. Seashells are quite simply skeletons of mollusks. Mollusks are a class of water animals that have soft bodies and hard outer coverings, called shells. People have bony skeletons on the inside and soft bodies on the outside. But mollusks do just the opposite. Shells protect these soft-bodied animals from rough surfaces that can harm their bodies. Shells also protect mollusks from predators.

Shells are durable and last longer than the soft-bodied animals that make and wear them. Shells may be univalve or bivalve. Univalve shells are made up of just one unit. Bivalve shells have two units or two halves. Snails have univalve shells and oysters have bivalve shells.

6. The main role of a seashell is:

Ⓐ to look beautiful
Ⓑ to serve as a home for mollusks
Ⓒ to float to the shores
Ⓓ to be collected by divers

Question 7 and 8 are based on the passage below.

Sacagawea is a famous Native American from the Shoshone tribe. She became famous when she helped two male explorers named Lewis and Clark, find their way through the unknown west. When she was 12 years old, she was kidnapped by an enemy Native American tribe called the Hidatsa. Then, legend has it, the chief of the Hidatsa tribe sold Sacagawea into slavery.

In 1804, she became a translator and guide for a group of explorers led by Lewis and Clark. She helped them find their way from near the Dakotas to the Pacific Ocean. She became a famous Native American in our history for being brave and helping these men discover unknown territory.

7. What would be a good title for the below story?

Ⓐ Sacagawea: A Shoshone Woman
Ⓑ Sacagawea: An Amazing Woman
Ⓒ Sacagawea: Kidnapped by the Hidatsa
Ⓓ Sacagawea: Sold to a Fur Trader

8. What is the main idea of the story above?

Ⓐ Sacagawea's life was amazing.
Ⓑ Sacagawea was a woman who did so many things that women didn't do at the time.
Ⓒ Sacagawea helped two men explore the west.
Ⓓ What Sacagawea did will be remembered forever.

9. What is the main idea of the below passage?

A Bichon frise is an unusual breed of dog. It has white fluffy hair and tiny, black eyes. Years ago, this funny little breed was used as a circus dog. Many people keep this breed as pets, because it is hypoallergenic. This means that people with allergies aren't allergic to this breed. They don't shed, so they won't leave hair all over your house.

 Ⓐ A Bichon frise is a unique breed of dogs.
 Ⓑ A Bichon frise was used as a circus dog.
 Ⓒ A Bichon frise is hypoallergenic.
 Ⓓ A Bichon frise has white hair and black eyes.

10. Which detail supports the idea that scientists believe a meteorite crashed into the planet and killed off the dinosaurs?

Have you ever thought about what happened to the dinosaurs that once roamed the Earth? Well, scientists have developed several ideas throughout the years. One idea is that a giant meteorite crashed into our planet and caused a huge dust cloud to cover the Earth. The dust cloud was so enormous that it kept the Sun's rays from reaching Earth. This caused all of the plants to die. With nothing to eat, the herbivores died. The large carnivores also died, leaving the planet without dinosaurs.

 Ⓐ Scientists have developed several ideas through the years.
 Ⓑ Have you ever thought about what happened to the dinosaurs that once roamed the Earth?
 Ⓒ The dust cloud was so enormous that it kept the Sun's rays from reaching Earth.
 Ⓓ The planet was left without dinosaurs.

Chapter 3

Lesson 3: Using Details to Explain the Text

Publisher's Note: A **procedure** *tells you how to do something. Examples: the steps that you follow in a recipe are a procedure for making a food item. The steps that a dentist takes to fill a cavity is a procedure.*

A **concept** is an idea about how something might work or get done. Examples: a company has a concept (idea) about how to design a car that drives itself. A teacher has a concept of a program that will solve the bullying problem in her school.

An **epidemic** describes something that affects a lot of humans or plants or animals and occurs suddenly. Example: the Zika virus, carried by mosquitos, has spread quickly through countries with warm climates, infecting thousands of people.

When you are assigned to write about an historical, scientific or technical subject, either as the author or as a reviewer of another author's text, you are expected to explain any events, procedures, ideas or concepts that are related to the subject. You should include in your writing what happened that resulted in the historic, scientific or technical event, and why the event happened.

Here are two examples of how an author could write about a scientific event and a technology event:

- Describe what happened (an **event** such as a disease epidemic, in which thousands of people were infected) and then describe the **ideas** about what caused the disease and how it was transmitted. Also describe any **concepts** of what drug combinations could treat this disease and lastly the **procedures** for educating people to avoid being infected.

- Describe what happened (an **event** such as an epidemic of computers being hacked and the damage that was caused). Then describe the **ideas** about how to protect computer files and any **concepts** about what is needed in software that will identify attempts at unauthorized access to computer files and prevent access to these files. Lastly, describe **procedures** for purchasing and downloading the software when it is available.

You can scan the QR code given below or use the url to access additional EdSearch resources including videos and mobile apps related to *Using Details to Explain the Text*

 ## *Using Details to Explain the Text*

URL	QR Code
http://www.lumoslearning.com/a/ri43	

Question 1 and 2 are based on the passage below.

Digestive System

The digestive system is made up of the esophagus, stomach, liver, gall bladder, pancreas, large and small intestines, appendix, and rectum. Digestion actually begins in the mouth when food is chewed and mixed with saliva. Muscles in the esophagus push food into the stomach. Once there, it mixes with digestive juices. While in the stomach, food is broken down into nutrients, good for you, and turned into a thick liquid. The food then moves into the small intestine where more digestive juices complete breaking it down. It is in the small intestine that nutrients are taken into the blood and carried throughout the body. Anything left over that your body cannot use goes to the large intestine. The body takes water from the leftovers. The rest is passed out of your body.

1. What event begins the digestive process?

Ⓐ The small intestine absorbing nutrients.
Ⓑ Muscles in the esophagus pushing food into the stomach.
Ⓒ Chewing food and allowing it to mix with saliva.
Ⓓ Nutrients are taken into the blood.

2. How do nutrients that are absorbed from food move through the body?

Ⓐ They develop the ability to swim through the body's fluids in a tiny school bus.
Ⓑ The digestive juices in the small intestine break them down.
Ⓒ They move through the esophagus and into the stomach.
Ⓓ They are absorbed into the blood, which carries them to other parts of the body.

Question 3 and 4 are based on the passage below.

The blue whale is quite an amazing creature. It is a mammal that lives its entire life in the ocean. The size of its body is also amazing. This whale can grow up to 98 feet long and weigh as much as 200 tons. It is the largest known animal to have ever existed. Its body is long and elegantly tapered, unlike other whales which have a rounder, stockier build. The way that they are built, along with their extreme size, gives them a unique look. It also gives them the ability to move gracefully at greater speeds. Normally they travel around 12 mph, but they slow to 3.1 mph when feeding. They can even reach speeds up to 31 mph for short periods of time! Although they are extremely large animals, they eat small shrimp-like creatures called krill. Since the krill are so small, the blue whale eats about four tons daily as they swim deep in the ocean.

Blue whales do not live in tight-knit groups called pods like other whales. They live and travel alone or with one other whale. While traveling through the ocean, they come to the top to breathe air into their lungs through blowholes. They come from under the ocean, spitting water out of their blowholes. Then they roll and re-enter the water with a grand splash of their large tails. They make loud, deep, and rumbling low-frequency sounds that travel great distances. This allows them to communicate with other whales as far as 100 miles away. Their cries can be felt as much as heard. This resonating call makes them the loudest animal on Earth. If you ever have the opportunity to see or hear a blue whale, it will be an experience you will not soon forget.

3. How do blue whales breathe?

Ⓐ They use their blowholes to process oxygen found at deep ocean depths.
Ⓑ They spit water out of their blowholes and then rise to the surface to breathe air.
Ⓒ They rise to the surface, spit water out of their blowholes, and then breathe air in through their blowholes.
Ⓓ They roll and re-enter the water with a grand splash of their large tail.

4. How are blue whales able to communicate with other whales from great distances?

Ⓐ They make a loud, deep, low frequency sound that is able to travel as much as 100 miles under water.
Ⓑ They use tiny whale telephones.
Ⓒ They send a high frequency sound that only other whales are able to hear.
Ⓓ Their cries can be heard but never felt.

Question 5-7 are based on the passage below.

All matter, which makes up all things, can be changed in two ways: chemically and physically. Both chemical and physical changes affect the state of matter. Physical changes are those that do not change the actual substance. For example, clay will flatten if squeezed, but it will still be clay. Changing the shape of clay is a physical change and does not change the matter's identity. Chemical changes turn the matter into something new. For example, when paper is burned, it becomes ash and will never be paper again. The difference between them is that physical changes are temporary or only last for a little while. Chemical changes are permanent, which means they last forever. Physical and chemical changes both affect the state of matter.

5. Which sentence below explains the concept of physical change?

Ⓐ Physical change occurs when matter goes through a change that makes something new.
Ⓑ Physical change occurs when a person gains or loses weight.
Ⓒ Physical change is change that occurs naturally and affects the state of matter.
Ⓓ Physical change is change that does not make something new.

6. Which sentence below explains the concept of chemical change?

Ⓐ Chemical change is change that does not make something new.
Ⓑ Chemical changes occur when something new is made
Ⓒ Chemical change occurs when someone mixes unknown chemicals in a beaker.
Ⓓ Chemical change occurs when clay is flattened or squeezed.

7. **What is the primary difference between physical and chemical change?**

Ⓐ Physical changes affect the state of matter, while chemical changes do not.
Ⓑ Chemical changes are temporary, while physical changes are permanent.
Ⓒ Physical changes are temporary, while chemical changes are permanent.
Ⓓ Chemical and physical changes make something entirely new.

Question 8 is based on the passage below.

Lewis and Clark

Sacagawea, also spelled *Sacajawea*, is best known for her role in helping Meriwether Lewis and William Clark during their journey to explore the American West. They set out on their journey on May 14, 1804. They left from near Wood River, Illinois; it was during winter in South Dakota when they met Sacagawea. They reached the Pacific Ocean on the coast of Oregon in November 1805.

The journey was unique. The new frontier was full of unknown native people and the land was dangerous. Without the help of someone who knew the land, Lewis and Clark may not have made it to the Pacific.

Sacagawea was the young Shoshone wife of a French-Canadian fur trapper named Toussaint Charbonneau. Together, she and her husband served as interpreters, guides, and negotiators for Lewis and Clark. Their friendship with Clark was so strong that when they returned, they moved to his hometown of St. Louis. Clark became the guardian of her children after her death.

8. **Which of the following sentences best explains how important Sacagawea was to Lewis and Clark's expedition?**

Ⓐ Sacagawea was a member of the Shoshone tribe of Native Americans.
Ⓑ Because they were travelling unknown territory, they needed the help of a person who knew about the people that they would encounter and the land that they would navigate.
Ⓒ Sacagawea could not have aided the Lewis and Clark expedition without the help of her husband, who was an experienced fur trapper.
Ⓓ Sacagawea was Shoshone by birth and married to a French-Canadian man, and she spoke two languages.

Question 9 and 10 are based on the passage below.

There are many theories about how dinosaurs came to be extinct. Scientists do not all agree about what may have happened. The most recent idea says that a giant meteorite crashed into the earth. It kicked up enough dust and dirt that the Sun's rays did not reach Earth for a very long time. This prevented plants from making their own food via photosynthesis. Plant-eaters and then, meat-eaters died due to a lack of food.

The other leading idea says that dinosaurs died out when the Earth went through a time of volcanoes erupting. Like the meteorite idea, it is thought that the volcanoes spewed enough ash into the air that the Sun's rays were blocked. This also caused plant and animal life to die.

9. According to the passage, how can lack of sunlight cause animals to become extinct? Circle the correct answer choice.

Ⓐ   It disrupts the food chain starting with producers. If plants die out, then plant-eaters have nothing to eat. If plant-eaters starve and die out, then meat-eaters have nothing to eat and also die.

Ⓑ   Dinosaurs became extinct because of widespread volcanic eruptions that blocked sunlight from reaching Earth. When this happened, plants died, beginning a disruption of the food chain that dinosaurs didn't survive.

Ⓒ   One theory suggests a meteorite caused dinosaur extinction, while another claims widespread volcanic eruptions caused the animals to die. Both theories, however, center around the idea that plants did not get needed sunlight and plant-eating and meat-eating animals died as a result.

Ⓓ   It creates a shadow over the entire planet which makes everything very cold. This extreme cold keeps the animals from being able to hunt or eat.

10. Do all scientists agree about how dinosaurs became extinct? Circle the correct answer choice.

Ⓐ   No. The text explains that there are many theories on dinosaur extinction and describes two of them.

Ⓑ   No. Some scientists believe dinosaurs died when a giant meteorite crashed into earth, while others blame extraterrestrials.

Ⓒ   Yes. The scientific community has debated several possibilities, and they agree that dinosaurs died out as the result of widespread volcanic eruptions.

Ⓓ   Yes. The scientists have argued but finally agree that the dinosaurs became extinct when a meteor crashed into Earth.

Chapter 3

Lesson 4: What Does it Mean?

This standard asks the reader to "Determine the meaning" of words or phrases in written text. If you don't know the meaning of a word or phrase, you have to either look it up in a dictionary or thesaurus (contains other words that mean the same thing) or figure it out by reading the other words in the text. But sometimes a word or phrase can have different meanings, so you have to decide what the author of the text wanted the meaning to be.

Here are some examples of words and phrases which are underlined and ways to figure out their meanings.

1. The poor woman was <u>despondent</u> after losing everything she owned in the fire. Losing everything in a fire is a very sad event, so you can figure out that despondent means very sad or feeling hopeless or feeling despair.

2. The sleepy kittens crawled into bed and <u>nestled cozily</u> beside their mother and went to sleep. The kittens were sleepy, they were going to their bed, and it is easy to picture them snuggled together next to their mother (nestled), warm and comfortable (cozy).

3. In certain countries, tigers are an <u>endangered</u> species, so hunting them is against the law. The government is trying to protect them from the danger of being killed, because there are so few still alive that if killing continues there will be none left.

4. <u>Global warming</u> is an increase in the earth's <u>atmospheric and oceanic temperatures</u>. One cause is the <u>greenhouse effect</u>. You can figure out that oceanic has to do with ocean (water) temperatures, and because the earth consists of water and air, then atmospheric temperatures mean air temperatures. If you have ever been in a greenhouse, you know that sunlight shines through the glass covering and warms the air, which cannot escape. The greenhouse effect means that the warm air produced on the earth by the sun cannot escape because of a layer of various gases.

You can scan the QR code given below or use the url to access additional EdSearch resources including videos and mobile apps related to *What Does it Mean?*

 What Does it Mean?

URL	QR Code
http://www.lumoslearning.com/a/ri44	

Question 1 is based on the passage below.

The blue whale is quite an amazing creature. It is a mammal that lives its entire life in the ocean. The size of its body is also amazing. This whale can grow up to 98 feet long and weigh as much as 200 tons. It is the largest known animal to have ever existed. Its body is long and elegantly tapered, un-like other whales which have a rounder, stockier build. The way that they are built, along with their extreme size, gives them a unique look. It also gives them the ability to move gracefully at greater speeds. Normally they travel around 12 mph, but they slow to 3.1 mph when feeding. They can even reach speeds up to 31 mph for short periods of time! Although they are extremely large animals, they eat small shrimp-like creatures called krill. Since the krill are so small, the blue whale eats about four tons daily as they swim deep in the ocean.

Blue whales do not live in tight-knit groups called pods like other whales. They live and travel alone or with one other whale. While traveling through the ocean, they come to the top to breathe air into their lungs through blowholes. They come from under the ocean, spitting water out of their blowholes. Then they roll and re-enter the water with a grand splash of their large tails. They make loud, deep, and rumbling low-frequency sounds that travel great distances. This allows them to communicate with other whales as far as 100 miles away. Their cries can be felt as much as heard. This <u>resonating</u> call makes them the loudest animal on Earth. If you ever have the opportunity to see or hear a blue whale, it will be an experience you will not soon forget.

1. What is the meaning of the word resonating?

Ⓐ low
Ⓑ loud
Ⓒ silent
Ⓓ quiet

Question 2 and 3 are based on the passage below.

Have you ever thought about what happened to the dinosaurs that once roamed the Earth? Well, scientists have developed several ideas throughout the years. One idea is that a giant meteorite crashed into our planet and caused a huge dust cloud to cover the Earth. The dust cloud was so enormous that it kept the Sun's rays from reaching Earth. This caused all of the plants to die. With nothing to eat, the <u>herbivores</u> died. The large <u>carnivores</u> also died, leaving the planet without dinosaurs.

2. What is the meaning of the word herbivore?

Ⓐ a type of plant
Ⓑ an animal that eats only plants
Ⓒ a type of storm
Ⓓ an animal that eats only meat

3. What is the meaning of the word carnivores?

Ⓐ a type of plant
Ⓑ an animal that eats only plants
Ⓒ a type of storm
Ⓓ an animal that eats only meat

4. The rain danced on the roof, tapping a happy tune.
The sentence above gives human qualities to the rain. This is called:

Ⓐ Onomatopoeia
Ⓑ Personification
Ⓒ Assonance
Ⓓ Alliteration

Question 5 is based on the passage below.

In the United States today, we are starting to see more and more of a problem with children who are overweight. Doctors and other health care professionals are trying to do something about it. They are recommending healthier foods and encouraging children get daily <u>vigorous</u> exercise. They also recommend that children go outside and play instead of sitting in front of the tv. They have suggested that children get at least an hour of exercise a day by participating in activities like jumping rope, cycling, or basketball, movement that makes the heart beat faster. This kind of exercise is known as aerobic exercise. Something else they recommend is for children to do exercises that strengthen the bones and muscles. There are a lot of ways that children can do this. One way is running.

5. What is the meaning of "vigorous" in the above text?

Ⓐ slow
Ⓑ growing well
Ⓒ energetic, forceful
Ⓓ weak

6. What word in the sentence below helps you understand what reimburse means?

People who travel on business are usually <u>reimbursed</u> for their travel expenses; that is, they are repaid for money that they have spent for the company.

Ⓐ expenses
Ⓑ representatives
Ⓒ repaid
Ⓓ business

Question 7 is based on the passage below.

Many years ago there weren't any self-serve grocery stores. Shoppers were served by clerks who chose products for them. When the first self-serve market was opened, no one thought that it would be successful. Owners of the full-service grocery stores laughed at the idea and said that the public would probably <u>boycott</u> the stores.

Clarence Saunders, the man who came up with this innovative system, thought that he could save money by having shoppers help themselves from the open shelves. He was warned by many of his competitors that customers would <u>boycott</u> this type of grocery store and put him out of business.

7. What is the meaning of the word boycott in the above text?

Ⓐ to only go to this store and shop there
Ⓑ to get a lot of money
Ⓒ to lose a lot of money
Ⓓ to refuse to buy something

8. Which words in the below text help to understand the meaning of copra?

We get a lot of <u>copra</u> from the Malay Peninsula. <u>Copra</u> is dried coconut meat which is used for making coconut oil. We use coconut oil for cooking and as an ingredient in many beauty products.

Ⓐ coconut oil
Ⓑ coconut meat
Ⓒ Malay Peninsula
Ⓓ beauty products

9. What is the meaning of the underlined word?

The first review of *Despicable Me* was <u>favorable</u>. Many people attended and enjoyed the movie.

Ⓐ clear
Ⓑ negative
Ⓒ positive
Ⓓ unsure

10. **The bomb exploded with a loud BOOM! Did you hear the snake hiss as it crawled along the ground?**
    Boom and hiss are words that imitate the noise made. This is called:

    Ⓐ Onomatopoeia
    Ⓑ Personification
    Ⓒ Assonance
    Ⓓ Alliteration

Chapter 3

Lesson 5: How is it Written?

This standard mentions the word "structure." Structure in written text means the way the text is organized. Literary structure means the way the text is organized in written text.

To describe a literary structure, you need to understand the kinds of literary structures. Here are several commonly used literary structures:

- *Narrative*: text that tells a story in which the characters, setting and actions are all connected. It may be real (non-fiction) or not real (fiction). James and the Giant Peach and Diary of a Wimpy Kid are good examples of stories with a narrative structure.
- *Chronological*: text whose actions move along a time period. Example: A story about a family going on vacation starts with packing for the trip, the trip itself, reaching the destination, describing what happens there, and the trip home.
- *Comparison and Contrast*: text with this structure compares two things and points out similarities and differences between them. Examples: living in a desert compared with living in a forest; playing basketball and playing soccer.
- *Cause and Effect*: text that describes an event (a hurricane; a championship game) and the effects that the event has on people or things (flooding and trees blown over; joy and celebration or sadness and despair).

- *Inductive*: text that describes an idea or event and then expands that idea or event to include a larger audience or a larger result.

   Examples:
   1. The person who discovered the first and only fast food restaurant owned by the McDonald brothers imagined that the idea of fast food could be expanded to many locations in the United States.

   2. Steve Jobs imagined that a telephone could be made small enough to be carried in a person's pocket and could be used to do more than place and receive calls; the Apple iPhone was the result.

- *Deductive*: text that describes things about a person or an idea or event from which the reader or listener reaches a conclusion.

Examples:

1. Human beings cannot exist in extremely cold temperatures without protective clothing. The arctic areas of the world have extremely cold temperatures. Therefore, people planning to visit the arctic must take protective clothing.

2. There are internet users who use software to invade computers to steal information. There are companies who develop software to protect computers from invasion. Therefore, internet users should purchase protective software.

You can scan the QR code given below or use the url to access additional EdSearch resources including videos and mobile apps related to *How is it Written?*

ed Search	*How is it Written?*	
URL		**QR Code**
http://www.lumoslearning.com/a/ri45		

Question 1 and 2 are based on the passage below.

The blue whale is quite an amazing creature. It is a mammal that lives its entire life in the ocean. The size of its body is also amazing. This whale can grow up to 98 feet long and weigh as much as 200 tons. It is the largest known animal to have ever existed. Its body is long and elegantly tapered, unlike other whales which have a rounder, stockier build. The way that they are built, along with their extreme size, gives them a unique look. It also gives them the ability to move gracefully at greater speeds. Normally they travel around 12 mph, but they slow to 3.1 mph when feeding. They can even reach speeds up to 31 mph for short periods of time! Although they are extremely large animals, they eat small shrimp-like creatures called krill. Since the krill are so small, the blue whale eats about four tons daily as they swim deep in the ocean.

Blue whales do not live in tight-knit groups called pods like other whales. They live and travel alone or with one other whale. While traveling through the ocean, they come to the top to breathe air into their lungs through blowholes. They come from under the ocean, spitting water out of their blowholes. Then they roll and re-enter the water with a grand splash of their large tails. They make loud, deep, and rumbling low-frequency sounds that travel great distances. This allows them to communicate with other whales as far as 100 miles away. Their cries can be felt as much as heard. This resonating call makes them the loudest animal on Earth. If you ever have the opportunity to see or hear a blue whale, it will be an experience you will not soon forget.

1. The author used which text structure when writing this passage?

Ⓐ Problem and solution
Ⓑ Cause and effect
Ⓒ Sequence
Ⓓ Descriptive

2. A report that explains how animal cells and plant cells are alike and how they are different would be written using which of the text structures?

Ⓐ Cause and effect
Ⓑ Compare and contrast
Ⓒ Problem and solution
Ⓓ Sequence or chronological

Question 3 is based on the passage below.

Grandma's Chocolate Cake
1 ¾ cups all-purpose flour
2 cups white sugar
2 sticks of room temperature butter
2 eggs
¾ cup cocoa powder
1 cup milk
1 tsp. vanilla extract
1 tsp. salt

Preheat oven to 350 degrees F.
Butter and flour two 8 inch cake pans.
Combine eggs, sugar, milk, vanilla extract, and butter. Beat until smooth.
Sift together the flour, salt, and cocoa powder.
Slowly add the sifted dry ingredients to the wet ingredients.
Mix until batter is smooth.
Pour the batter into the floured and greased cake pans.
Bake for 35 to 40 minutes.
Cool in pans on cooling rack for 30 minutes.
Ice cake with your favorite frosting.

3. Which text structure is used in the second half of the above recipe?

Ⓐ Cause and effect
Ⓑ Compare and contrast
Ⓒ Problem and solution
Ⓓ Sequence

Question 4 is based on the paragraph below.

All matter, which makes up all things, can be changed in two ways: chemically and physically. Both chemical and physical changes affect the state of matter. Physical changes are those that do not change the actual substance. For example, clay will flatten if squeezed, but it will still be clay. Changing the shape of clay is a physical change and does not change the matter's identity. Chemical changes turn the matter into something new. For example, when the paper is burned, it becomes ash and will never be paper again. The difference between them is that physical changes are temporary or only last for a little while. Chemical changes are permanent, which means they last forever. Physical and chemical changes both affect the state of matter.

4. What type of structure did they use to write this paragraph?

   Ⓐ Compare and contrast
   Ⓑ Cause and effect
   Ⓒ Sequence
   Ⓓ Problem and solution

Question 5 and 6 are based on the passage below.

Sacagawea

Sacagawea is a famous Native American woman from the Shoshone tribe. She became famous when she helped two male explorers named Lewis and Clark, find their way through the unknown west. When she was 12 years old, she was kidnapped by an enemy of the Shoshone tribe called the Hidatsa. Legend has it, that the chief of the Hidatsa tribe sold Sacagawea into slavery.

In 1804, she became a translator and guide for a group of explorers led by Lewis and Clark. She helped them find their way from near the Dakotas to the Pacific Ocean. She became a famous Native American woman in US history for being brave and helping these explorers discover unknown territory.

5. How is the text written?

   Ⓐ Compare and contrast
   Ⓑ Cause and effect
   Ⓒ Sequence
   Ⓓ Problem and solution

6. What type of writing is the text above?

   Ⓐ Descriptive
   Ⓑ Informative
   Ⓒ Persuasive
   Ⓓ Narrative

Question 7 is based on the passage below.

Every day after school when I get home, I get certain ingredients to make myself a snack. I get the peanut butter, jelly, and bread and put everything on the counter. Peanut butter and jelly sandwiches are my favorite! Then, I take the lid off all the jars. Next, I take a big spoonful of peanut butter and spread it on one side of the bread and another big spoonful of jelly on the other. After that, I put the two pieces of bread together to make my super yummy peanut butter and jelly sandwich. I can enjoy my snack while starting my homework. It always tastes so good! Each time it seems as if it is the best peanut butter and jelly sandwich I have ever eaten.

7. What is the text structure of the above passage?

(A) Cause and effect
(B) Compare and contrast
(C) Problem and solution
(D) Chronological

8. If the title of an essay was, "Should Students be Allowed to Have Cell Phones in Elementary School?" What type of writing would it be?

(A) Comparative
(B) Informative
(C) Narrative
(D) Persuasive

9. If the title of an essay was "Two Places I've Visited Recently," what type of writing will it be?

(A) Persuasive
(B) Informative
(C) Comparative
(D) Narrative

10. If a title of an essay was "How I Spent My Summer Vacation," what type of writing would it be?

(A) Persuasive
(B) Informative
(C) Narrative
(D) Poetry

Chapter 3

Lesson 6: Comparing Different Versions of the Same Event

A firsthand account (or description) of an event or topic means that the author is the one telling the reader about an event or topic. The author will use I, we, me, us, mine, our or ours when telling the story. The author is not giving the reader directions or telling the reader how to do something.

A secondhand account (or description) of an event or topic means that the author is telling the reader how to do something or making suggestions about how the reader should do something. The author will use you or yours when giving instructions or suggestions.

The standard asks you to compare a firsthand account and a secondhand account of the same event or topic and to describe the differences between them.

Here are two examples that show you how this standard can be used.

The event tells about what happened when the author tried to follow a recipe for making a cake.

Firsthand account:

Tomorrow is my mom's birthday. I am going to surprise her by baking a cake while she is at work. I opened her cookbook to the "Cakes" chapter and read the recipe for a yellow cake.

I found her measuring cup, mixing bowl, baking pan and all the other ingredients and put them on the counter. To grease the baking pan I melted the butter and accidentally burned it, but I spooned it onto the pan anyway and sprinkled it with flour. Then I had to mix a bunch of ingredients together. I did not know how to use the mixing machine so I found a wire whisk and mixed them; it took a lot of work and my fingers really hurt when it was done. I cracked the eggs but some pieces of the shells fell into the mix but I figured no one would notice so I left them in there. I poured the mix into the baking pan, smoothed it out, and set the oven temperature.

In 35 minutes, I was supposed to take it out of the oven but my best friend called and brought over her new kitten and I forgot about the cake. Then she left and I went to the kitchen and smelled something burning. It was the cake. I took it out, but since only the bottom was burned, I figured no one would notice. I added whipped cream on top and put the finished cake into the refrigerator with a birthday card on top. When she came home, she was so surprised and happy and we ate it for dessert. It was pretty good and a little crunchy from the eggshells but my first cake was really a success.

Secondhand account:

Did you ever think of how nice a present baking a cake for someone's birthday would be, instead of just buying it from a bakery? I can tell you exactly how to do it – just follow these steps.

1. You have to find a measuring cup, whisk, baking pan, mixing bowl and these ingredients: flour, baking powder, salt, butter, sugar, vanilla flavoring, eggs and milk.

Publisher's Note: the author would then describe each step you should follow to create the cake. I think you get the idea without me listing all of these steps. So let's move on to see how you would compare and contrast these two descriptions of the same event: baking a cake.

Compare and Contrast these two descriptions of the same event:

These two accounts (or descriptions) have the same focus (or main idea): baking a cake, describing the ingredients, and describing the steps that have to be followed. But that is where the similarities end.

The secondhand account gives the exact details about the quantity (or amount) of each ingredient and the exact steps required by the recipe, but does not give any other information. The firsthand account does not list the quantities (amounts) of each ingredient nor does it give complete details of each step that the recipe requires. But it does describe the thoughts going through the baker's mind, for example "…it took a lot of work and my fingers really hurt when it was done." and "I cracked the eggs but some pieces of the shells fell into the mix but I figured no one would notice so I left them in there."

 The firsthand account also describes details not directly related to the recipe. For example: "Tomorrow is my mom's birthday. I am going to surprise her by baking a cake while she is at work." and "In 35 minutes, I was supposed to take it out of the oven but my best friend called and brought over her new kitten and I forgot about the cake."

Publisher's Note: In the above Compare and Contrast paragraph, can you see where we mentioned what the focus (or main idea) was? Can you also see how we pointed out the similarities and differences (compare and contrast) between the first- and secondhand accounts? These are the things required by this standard.

You can scan the QR code given below or use the url to access additional EdSearch resources including videos and mobile apps related to *Comparing Different Versions of the Same Event.*

ed Search	**Comparing Different Versions of the Same Event**
URL	QR Code
http://www.lumoslearning.com/a/ri46	

Question 1-3 are based on the passage below.

The Parade: A Firsthand Account

When I got there I was dressed from head to toe in sparkly sequins and itchy tights, and I held my baton like a pro. I lined up with others in my squad and we began marching through the streets while the marching band played in front of us. I saw the crowds of people waving and smiling. At first, their happy faces made it seem less cold, but by the second mile the happy faces did not soothe the blisters on my feet. I threw my twirling baton into the air, and this time I did not catch it. In fact, when I turned to retrieve it, I tripped on the girl behind me and caused quite a situation. I was so embarrassed that I contemplated never showing my face again.

The Parade: A Secondhand Account

I read about the Thanksgiving parade in our school newspaper today. It was held downtown last Saturday morning to honor the American holiday that occurs every year on the third Thursday in November. There was a marching band, floats from all of the local businesses, a step team, a ballet studio, and baton twirlers. The temperature outside was forty five degrees, but the sun was shining brightly and helped warm over 600 people who came out to see the parade. All in all, the parade was a huge success, and the city plans to hold it again next year.

1. How is the focus of the firsthand account different from the secondhand account?

Ⓐ   The firsthand account focuses on the parade itself, while the secondhand account focuses on the weather on the day of the parade.

Ⓑ   The firsthand account has a wide focus that represents the parade as a whole, while the secondhand account is narrow and only talks about the crowd who attended the parade.

Ⓒ   The firsthand account is more accurate, while the secondhand account is based on rumor.

Ⓓ   The firsthand account focuses only on the personal experience of the speaker, while the secondhand account gives general information from the newspaper report about the parade.

2. How are the firsthand account and the secondhand account alike?

Ⓐ   They both consider the parade a huge success.

Ⓑ   They both give specific information about the number of people in attendance.

Ⓒ   They both discuss the baton twirlers' sequin costumes.

Ⓓ   They both discuss the weather, the marching band, the baton twirlers, and the crowd.

3. How are the firsthand account and the secondhand account different?

Ⓐ The firsthand account is more personal and includes the speaker's feelings about the parade, while the secondhand account is more objective and includes mostly facts about the parade.
Ⓑ The firsthand account includes more details about the parade, while the secondhand account is more of a broad summary.
Ⓒ The firsthand account is true, while the secondhand account gives false information.
Ⓓ The firsthand account discusses the origins of the parade, while the secondhand account is from a newspaper.

Question 4-6 are based on the passage below.

The Inauguration of Barack Obama: A Firsthand Account

When Barack Obama was inaugurated as America's first African-American president, I was watching from my TV only a couple of miles away. It was a cold, cold, cloudy day, but thousands and thousands of people climbed on jam-packed metro train cars, and busses. Some even walked across the Key Bridge from Arlington, Virginia to get into Washington, D.C. I saw groups of people moving down the street outside of my apartment. They had homemade signs in puffy jackets and happy faces. I wondered what they would eat. I also wondered where they would sleep. I watched from of my warm living room with what I imagined to be, a much better view of a new President taking the oath of office.

The Inauguration of Barak Obama: A Secondhand Account

Barak Obama was inaugurated as our nation's 44th president on Tuesday, January 20, 2009. It was the most attended event in Washington, D.C.'s history. The inauguration was held during the celebration of the 200th year of Abraham Lincoln's birthday. There were many mentions of Lincoln throughout the event. Obama was even sworn into office using the same Bible Lincoln used when he became President.

The event offered welcoming remarks, the oath of office, and an inaugural address. There was music by Aretha Franklin, Yo Yo Ma, and other talented artists. The night was celebrated with a series of inaugural balls, which the new First Family attended.

4. How are the two accounts similar?

Ⓐ They both detail the events of election night.
Ⓑ They both give important details about the inauguration itself.
Ⓒ They both tell true events on the day of Barack Obama's first inauguration.
Ⓓ They both talk about the importance of Abraham Lincoln.

5. How are the two accounts different?

(A) The details in the secondhand account may not be accurate, while the details in the firsthand account have been verified to be true.

(B) The secondhand account is more personal than the firsthand account.

(C) The firsthand account is longer than the secondhand account.

(D) The details in the firsthand account are limited only to what the speaker witnessed, while the secondhand account gives more specific details concerning the inauguration.

6. What is the difference in focus between the two accounts?

(A) The firsthand account focuses on the practical details concerning the people in attendance, while the secondhand account focuses on the details of the inauguration event.

(B) The firsthand account focuses on important details, while the secondhand account is focused on less significant details.

(C) The secondhand account focuses on biographical details about Obama's life, while the first-hand account focuses on details like the music that played at the inauguration.

(D) Both accounts have the same focus.

Question 7-9 are based on the passage below.

John Glenn's Return to Space: a Firsthand Account

President Bill Clinton, The White House, Washington, D.C.

Dear Mr. President,
   This is certainly a first for me, writing to a President from, space, and it may be a first for you in receiving an E mail direct from an orbiting spacecraft.

   In any event, I want to personally thank you and Mrs. Clinton for coming to the Cape to see the launch. I hope you enjoyed it just half as much as we did on board.. It is truly an awesome experience from a personal standpoint, and of even greater importance for all of the great research projects we have on Discovery. The whole crew was impressed that you would be the first President to personally see a shuttle launch and asked me to include their best regards to you and Hillary. She has discussed her interest in the space program with Annie on several occasions, and I know she would like to be on a flight just like this.

   We have gone almost a third of the way around the world in the time it has taken me to write this letter, and the rest of the crew is waiting. Again, our thanks and best regards. Will try to give you a personal briefing after we return next Saturday.

Sincerely,

John Glenn

Margie S. Keller
Admin Officer
Astronaut Office
281-244-8991

John Glenn's Return to Space: a Secondhand Account

In October of 1998, John Glenn returned to space aboard the space shuttle Discovery. It was on that mission that the first American to orbit the Earth made history again by becoming the oldest man to fly in space. He was a U.S. Senator from Ohio at the time. President Bill Clinton attended the launch as the first U.S. President to do so.

7. What is the difference in focus between the firsthand and secondhand account above?

Ⓐ The firsthand account and the secondhand account have the same focus.
Ⓑ The firsthand account is more accurate than the secondhand account.
Ⓒ The firsthand account focuses on providing information to President Bill Clinton, while the secondhand account focuses on details about John Glenn.
Ⓓ The firsthand account is an actual letter and the second is as well.

8. How are the two accounts similar?

Ⓐ They both give information about President Clinton being the first U.S. President to personally see a launch.
Ⓑ They both include information about the date of the historic mission.
Ⓒ They both detail the important research being conducted on the mission.
Ⓓ The firsthand account is an article and the second is an actual letter.

9. How are the two accounts different?

Ⓐ The firsthand account is a letter and tells a little bit about Glenn's personal experience, while the secondhand account is an informational paragraph and was most likely written by some one who did not know John Glenn.
Ⓑ The firsthand account discusses John Glenn's return to space in 1998, while the secondhand account discusses his first orbit around Earth in 1962.
Ⓒ The firsthand account is written in complete sentences, while the secondhand account is written in short, note-like form.
Ⓓ The firsthand account is an article and the second is an actual letter.

10. What is the difference between a firsthand account and secondhand account of an event or occurrence? Circle the correct answer choice.

Ⓐ Firsthand accounts are written by people who witness an event first, while secondhand accounts are written by people who witness the event second.
Ⓑ Firsthand accounts are written by people who witnessed the event, while secondhand accounts are written by people who learned details of the event from other sources.
Ⓒ Firsthand accounts are true, while secondhand accounts are usually made up.
Ⓓ Firsthand accounts are primary documents and secondhand accounts are not.

Question 11 is based on the paragraph below.

In the United States today, we are starting to see more and more of a problem with children who are overweight. Doctors and even the President's wife are trying to do something about it. They are recommending healthier foods and that children get daily exercise. They recommend that children go outside and do things instead of sitting in front of the tv. They have suggested that children get at least an hour of exercise a day by doing things like jumping rope or cycling, or anything else that makes their heart beat faster. This kind of exercise is known as aerobic exercise. They also recommend that children do exercises that strengthen the bones and muscles. There are lots of ways children can do this. Running is one example.

11. Which style of narration is used in the above text? Explain.

Chapter 3

Lesson 7: Using Text Features to Gather Information

Definitions:

Visually: shown as something that can be seen; a picture or movie.
Orally: spoken
Quantitatively: shown as a measure or an amount.
e.g.: for example

The following is an example of how to use this standard when it is assigned to you.

Example:
The computer technology teacher in the Deep Canyon school district did a survey of all students in grades 3 through 6 to find out the percentage of time students spend using computer software for three kinds of applications. He included students in the survey no matter what equipment they used to perform these applications, whether they used laptop, desktops, tablets or smartphones.

The results of the survey are shown in the table below.

Percentage of Time Students In The Deep Canyon School District Spend Using Computing Software				
Grade	School Work %	Social Media (Ex. Facebook, Twitter, You Tube, Email) %	Computer based Games %	%
3	15	70	5	100
4	30	60	10	100
5	40	50	10	100
6	50	35	15	100

The students were asked to answer the following questions using the information in the table:
1. The students in which grade spent the most time doing school work using computer software?
2. Did time spent using computer software for social media increase, stay the same, or decrease from grade 3 to grade 6?
3. The students in which grade spent the most time playing computer-based games?

Your assignment:

Your teacher has asked you to interpret (explain) the information in the table and explain how the information in the table helped you answer the three questions (interpreting text and explaining how a graph or table or other display helped you understand the text are required by the standard).

Here is an example of what you might write to finish this assignment.

The table shows the percentage of time spent by students in each of four grades using their computers for three different purposes. It was easy to look at the table to figure out the answers to the questions. If the information in the table had been written as text, it would have taken more time to figure out the answer, since I would have had to read each sentence and memorize or write down the percentages. For question 1, it was easy to look at the table and quickly see that the Grade 6 row had the highest percentage of time spent doing school work. For question 2, it was easy to look down each column and see that the percentages were decreasing from Grades 3 to 6. For question 3, it was easy to look at the Grade 6 row and see what the largest percentage was.

Publishers Note: In the example, we used a table to show the survey information. We could have used a chart or graph or diagram or any other display method mentioned in the standard to show the information, but the assignment would have been the same – that is, to interpret (explain) the meaning of the information in the table and then to explain how the information in the table helped you answer the questions that were assigned.

You can scan the QR code given below or use the url to access additional EdSearch resources including videos and mobile apps related to *Using Text Features to Gather Information*.

ed)Search	*Using Text Features to Gather Information*	
	URL	QR Code
	http://www.lumoslearning.com/a/ri47	

Question 1-3 are based on the passage below.

There are four types of tissues that are created as cells join together and work as a group. Each type of tissue has a unique structure and does a specific job. Muscle tissue is made up of long, narrow muscle cells. Muscle tissue makes the body parts move by tightening and relaxing. Connective tissue is what holds up the body and connects its parts together. The bone is made up of connective tissue. Nerve tissue is made up of long nerve cells that go through the body and carry messages. Epithelial tissue is made of wide, flat epithelial cells. This tissue lines the surfaces inside the body and forms the outer layer of the skin. Groups of tissue join together to form the organs in the body such as the heart, liver, lungs, brain, and kidneys just to name a few. Then these organs work together to form the body systems. Each system works together, and with the other systems of the body.

Muscle Tissue	Connective Tissue	Nerve Tissue	Epithelial Tissue
- long, narrow cells - contracts and relaxes causing movement	- holds up the body - connects body parts together	- long cells - carries messages throughout the body	- wide, flat cells - lines inside surfaces - forms outer skin layer

1. How does the chart help the reader understand the functions of each of the four types of tissues?

Ⓐ It adds details not mentioned in the text so the reader can gather more information.
Ⓑ It elaborates on details mentioned in the text.
Ⓒ It changes some of the details mentioned in the text.
Ⓓ It clarifies the details mentioned in the text by categorizing them by tissue type.

2. Which types of tissue have similarly shaped cells?

Ⓐ epithelial tissue and connective tissue
Ⓑ muscle tissue and connective tissue
Ⓒ connective tissue and nerve tissue
Ⓓ muscle tissue and nerve tissue

3. To help the reader visualize what each tissue looks like, what would be the BEST visual aid to include with this text?

Ⓐ A drawing of the heart, liver, lungs, brain, and kidneys
Ⓑ A microscopic views of each type of tissue
Ⓒ A diagram of a nerve cell
Ⓓ A chart providing information about each type of tissue

Question 4 is based on the passage below.

Most people think of koalas as koala bears, but they are not bears. They are marsupials and are in the same family as the wombat. Koalas live in a special place called a eucalyptus forest. They can be found in eastern and southeastern Australia. Adult koalas are one of only three animals that can live on a diet of eucalyptus leaves. These leaves contain 50% water. The eucalyptus leaves are mostly the main source of water for koalas.

The koala is a marsupial which means the baby crawls into a pocket, called a pouch, on the mother's tummy as soon as it is born. Baby koalas are called "joeys." When they are born, they cannot see, have no hair, and are less than one inch long. They stay in their mother's pouch for the next six months. First the mother feeds them milk. Then she feeds them a food called "pap" in addition to milk. Joeys continue to drink the mother's milk until they are a year old. The young koala will remain with its mother until another joey is born and comes into the pouch.

4. **Which picture or illustration would not help the reader understand the above text and should not be included?**

   Ⓐ a picture of an adult koala
   Ⓑ a picture of a newborn 'joey'
   Ⓒ a picture of a polar bear
   Ⓓ a map showing areas where koalas are found naturally

Question 5 is based on the paragraph below.

The digestive system is made up of the esophagus, stomach, liver, gall bladder, pancreas, large and small intestines, appendix, and rectum. Digestion actually begins in the mouth when food is chewed and mixed with saliva. Muscles in the esophagus push food into the stomach. Once there, it mixes with digestive juices. While in the stomach, food is broken down into nutrients, good for you, and turned into a thick liquid. The food then moves into the small intestine where more digestive juices complete breaking it down. It is in the small intestine that nutrients are taken into the blood and carried throughout the body. Anything left over that your body cannot use goes to the large intestine. The body takes water from the leftovers. The rest is passed out of your body.

5. **What visual aid should be included with the above text to enhance student understanding?**

   Ⓐ a diagram of the digestive system
   Ⓑ a diagram of the mouth
   Ⓒ a diagram of food
   Ⓓ a diagram of stomach tissue

Question 6 is based on the passage below.

Sacagawea

Sacagawea is a famous Native American woman from the Shoshone tribe. She became famous when she helped two male explorers named Lewis and Clark, find their way through the unknown west. When she was 12 years old, she was kidnapped by an enemy of the Shoshone tribe called the Hidatsa. Legend has it, that the chief of the Hidatsa tribe sold Sacagawea into slavery.

In 1804, she became a translator and guide for a group of explorers led by Lewis and Clark. She helped them find their way from near the Dakotas to the Pacific Ocean. She became a famous Native American woman in US history for being brave and helping these explorers discover unknown territory.

6. Which of the pictures below best represents what is being explained in the text?

Ⓓ None of the above

Question 7 is based on the passage below.

The blue whale is quite an amazing creature. It is a mammal that lives its entire life in the ocean. The size of its body is also amazing. This whale can grow up to 98 feet long and weigh as much as 200 tons. It is the largest known animal to have ever existed. Its body is long and elegantly tapered, unlike other whales which have a rounder, stockier build. The way that they are built, along with their extreme size, gives them a unique look. It also gives them the ability to move gracefully at greater speeds. Normally they travel around 12 mph, but they slow to 3.1 mph when feeding. They can even reach speeds up to 31 mph for short periods of time! Although they are extremely large animals, they eat small shrimp-like creatures called krill. Since the krill are so small, the blue whale eats about four tons daily as they swim deep in the ocean.

Blue whales do not live in tight-knit groups called pods like other whales. They live and travel alone or with one other whale. While traveling through the ocean, they come to the top to breathe air into their lungs through blowholes. They come from under the ocean, spitting water out of their blowholes. Then they roll and re-enter the water with a grand splash of their large tails. They make loud, deep, and rumbling low-frequency sounds that travel great distances. This allows them to communicate with other whales as far as 100 miles away. Their cries can be felt as much as heard. This resonating call makes them the loudest animal on Earth. If you ever have the opportunity to see or hear a blue whale, it will be an experience you will not soon forget.

7. What would be an important illustration or picture to include with this article?

Ⓐ a picture of the ocean
Ⓑ a picture of a pod of whales
Ⓒ a picture of an adult blue whale
Ⓓ a picture of a whaling ship

Question 8 is based on the passage below.

The following excerpt is from the November 12, 1892, edition of "Golden Days" magazine. It explains how condensed milk was made: The process very simple, the fresh milk is put into a great copper tank with a steam jacket. It is heated and sugar is added. The mixture is then moved into a vacuum tank, where evaporation is produced by heat.

The vacuum tank will hold approximately nine thousand quarts. It has a glass window at the top, through which the operator in charge monitors it. He can tell by the appearance of the milk when to shut off the steam. This must be done at just the right moment or else the batch will be spoiled.

Next, the condensed milk is drawn into forty-quart cans, set in very cold spring water to revolve rapidly by a mechanism so that the contents may cool evenly.

Ice is put into the milk to bring it down to the proper temperature if it is not cold enough. Finally the market sized tin cans are filled with the milk by a machine, which automatically pours exactly sixteen ounces of milk. There is a worker placing the cans beneath the spout while another worker removes them once they are filled.

8. **Which text feature would be most helpful for the reader to understand the process of making condensed milk?**

   Ⓐ a numbered list of steps with illustrations for each step
   Ⓑ a timeline of the events in the process
   Ⓒ a map of where evaporated milk was made in 1892
   Ⓓ a picture of an evaporated milk can

Question 9 is based on the details below.

BETWEEN WOOD AND FIELD. Arrange the wall tents with flys and set up with stakes.

THE TENT "GREEN." These are conical wall tents that accommodate eight cots. They are not easy to put up and give little head room.

Well-built floors keep out the damp ground, and make the supports level and steady.

9. **These photographs and captions are most likely included in which of the following texts?**

   Ⓐ a recipe book for outdoorsmen
   Ⓑ a guide to city life
   Ⓒ a guide to Girl Scout camps
   Ⓓ a fishing guide

Question 10 is based on the details below.

  Caterpillar feeds on a milkweed leaf as it prepares to begin its transition

  Caterpillar attached to leaf as it changes to the chrysalis phase

  The transition stage

  The chrysalis

10. What would these photographs and captions be most helpful in explaining?

   Ⓐ all about plants
   Ⓑ a very hungry caterpillar
   Ⓒ how a caterpillar begins its transformation into a butterfly
   Ⓓ how a caterpillar goes to sleep each night

Question 11 is based on the passage below.

Do you like frogs? Do you know what a spring peeper is?

Spring peepers are tiny little tree frogs that live in wooded areas near ponds. Although these frogs are tiny, only about an inch big, they make a very loud sound. They are found mostly in the center or Eastern part of the United States. So, when the weather begins to get warmer after winter, these little frogs start to sing. Their "peep", which is why they are called spring peepers, can be heard for miles around. They live near ponds so they can lay their eggs in the water.

When the weather starts getting colder again, the spring peepers start to go into hiding. They hibernate under logs or any other place they can find in the forest to protect them from the cold. For example, sometimes they hide under fallen leaves or even in a small hole in the ground.

11. Which picture below best illustrates what the text is about.

Ⓐ

Ⓑ

Ⓒ

Ⓓ None of the above

Question 12 is based on the passage below.

Geologic Maps

As we all know, there are maps of many kinds. Most of us are familiar with maps that show us location of places, such as the map of the United States. However, other maps show other thing. A geological map show where rocks and faults are at, as well as their location in an area. Then the map has various colors to show different information. It also includes many symbols. The geological map helps us to understand the earth beneath us, so we can understand the world around us better.

Notice the shaded areas on this map taken from the US Geological Survey website. Each area is colored to match the type of geological unit (volume of a certain kind of rock of a given age range). For example, one area might be colored bright orange to show a sandstone of one age while another might be pale brown to show another sandstone of a different age.

The geologists name and define the geological units they find. They determine everything they do based on their findings of rocks and the ages of the rocks. These continue to change as more investigations are completed. The science of geology can be quite interesting.

12. While reading about geological maps compare the information to the information on the map of United States

Write a sentence in the box below explaining the differences in the types of maps.

Chapter 3

Lesson 8: Finding the Evidence

Example: You have been assigned to read the following article, and then explain how the author uses reasons and evidence to support the opinions he/she states.

Scientists tell us that changes in our climate are happening. Average temperatures around the world are getting higher. The planet's average surface temperature has risen about 2.0 degrees Fahrenheit since the late 19th century. The warmest year on record was 2016; eight months were the warmest on record. The number of warm days in a year has increased while the number of cold days has decreased. This is called global warming.

Because of the rise in temperature, the ice cap in Greenland lost 281 Gigatons of ice from 2002 through 2016. Here and in Antarctica melting ice caps are causing sea levels to rise 8" in the last 100 years; glaciers are shrinking; ocean water temperatures are rising. Carbon dioxide levels in the air have risen from an average of 300 ppm (parts per million) to 400 ppm, the highest levels ever. Carbon dioxide forms a blanket above the earth that traps heat, an additional contributor to global warming.

Studies by scientists point out that global warming is having bad effects on humans, animals and plants. Carbon dioxide reduces air quality and it is not healthy for humans and animals to breathe. Water is essential for living creatures; without enough water, they die. Global warming decreases the amount of water on the planet. Some creatures cannot adapt quickly to changes in climates and will die, and those that migrate can be forced to change their migration patterns.

Why is this happening? Ninety seven percent of global scientists think this is happening because of things we humans are doing. Our use of fuels from fossils, such as oil and coal, are major causes, and our manufacturing activities are another cause.

Your assignment: To explain how the author used reasons and evidence to support his/her conclusions in the article.

The following is an example of what you might write.

The author says that global warming is happening. The author shows data proving that global temperatures have been rising, that a major ice cap is melting and that carbon dioxide levels in the atmosphere have increased, all of which are results of global warming.

The author says that science studies show that global warming is having bad effects on humans, animals and plants. The author supports this statement by presenting these effects, such as a reduction (decrease) in air quality, reduction in water supplies, inability (not able to do something) of some creatures to adapt to changes in climate and disruption (change) of migration patterns.

You can scan the QR code given below or use the url to access additional EdSearch resources including videos and mobile apps related to *Finding the Evidence*.

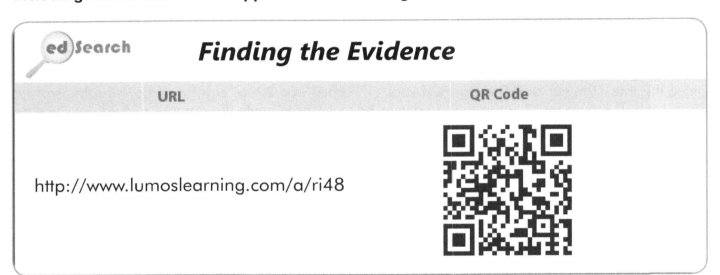

URL	QR Code
http://www.lumoslearning.com/a/ri48	

Question 1 and 2 are based on the passage below.

The blue whale is quite an amazing creature. It is a mammal that lives its entire life in the ocean. The size of its body is also amazing. This whale can grow up to 98 feet long and weigh as much as 200 tons. It is the largest known animal to have ever existed. Its body is long and elegantly tapered, unlike other whales which have a rounder, stockier build. The way that they are built, along with their extreme size, gives them a unique look. It also gives them the ability to move gracefully at greater speeds. Normally they travel around 12 mph, but they slow to 3.1 mph when feeding. They can even reach speeds up to 31 mph for short periods of time! Although they are extremely large animals, they eat small shrimp-like creatures called krill. Since the krill are so small, the blue whale eats about four tons daily as they swim deep in the ocean.

Blue whales do not live in tight-knit groups called pods like other whales. They live and travel alone or with one other whale. While traveling through the ocean, they come to the top to breathe air into their lungs through blowholes. They come from under the ocean, spitting water out of their blowholes. Then they roll and re-enter the water with a grand splash of their large tails. They make loud, deep, and rumbling low-frequency sounds that travel great distances. This allows them to communicate with other whales as far as 100 miles away. Their cries can be felt as much as heard. This resonating call makes them the loudest animal on Earth. If you ever have the opportunity to see or hear a blue whale, it will be an experience you will not soon forget.

1. **Which statement did the writer of this passage use to support his opinion that the size of a blue whale's body is amazing?**

   Ⓐ The blue whale is quite an extraordinary creature.
   Ⓑ Its body is long and elegantly tapered, unlike other whales which have a rounder, stockier body.
   Ⓒ This whale can grow up to 98 feet long and weigh as much as 200 tons, making it the largest known animal to have ever existed.
   Ⓓ Their build, along with their extreme size, gives them a unique appearance and the ability to move gracefully and at greater speeds than one might imagine.

2. **What evidence does the author provide in the second paragraph that supports the fact that whales communicate with one another?**

   Ⓐ Blue whales live and travel alone or with one other whale.
   Ⓑ They emerge from the ocean, spewing water out of their blowhole, roll over, and re-enter the water with a grand splash of their tail.
   Ⓒ They make loud, deep, and rumbling low-frequency sounds that travel great distances, which allow them to communicate with other whales as much as 100 miles away.
   Ⓓ Their cries can be felt as much as heard.

Question 3 and 4 are based on the letter below.

2362 West Main Street
Jojo, TX 98456

June 16, 2017

Dear Mr. Seymour:

I ordered a Magic Racing Top from your company. The toy was delivered to me today in a package that was badly damaged. I took a picture of the box before I opened it, which I am sending to you as proof of the damage. The toy inside was broken due to the damage of the package during shipping.

This toy was to be a gift for my friend's birthday. There is not enough time before his party to wait for a replacement toy; therefore, I no longer need the toy. I would like you to refund my money. Please send me a prepaid shipping label if you would like me to return the broken toy. Thank you for handling this matter for me. I look forward to hearing from you and hope we can satisfactorily resolve this problem.

Sincerely,
Tim West

3. **What evidence does the writer of this letter offer to support his claim that the package arrived damaged?**

   Ⓐ The toy was broken.
   Ⓑ He wanted a replacement or a refund.
   Ⓒ He is sending a picture of the damaged package.
   Ⓓ He wants to satisfactorily resolve the problem.

4. **The author does not want a replacement toy. What reason does he give for not wanting a replacement?**

   Ⓐ The package was damaged during shipping.
   Ⓑ The toy was a gift, and there is not enough time to ship a replacement.
   Ⓒ The toy is broken.
   Ⓓ He requests a prepaid shipping label to return the toy.

Question 5 is based on the passage below.

Digestive System

The digestive system is made up of the esophagus, stomach, liver, gall bladder, pancreas, large and small intestines, appendix, and rectum. Digestion actually begins in the mouth when food is chewed and mixed with saliva. Muscles in the esophagus push food into the stomach. Once there, it mixes with digestive juices. While in the stomach, food is broken down into nutrients, good for you, and turned into a thick liquid. The food then moves into the small intestine where more digestive juices complete breaking it down. It is in the small intestine that nutrients are taken into the blood and carried throughout the body. Anything left over that your body cannot use goes to the large intestine. The body takes water from the leftovers. The rest is passed out of your body.

5. **What evidence does the writer provide to support the fact that everything eaten is not used by the body for nutrients?**

    Ⓐ Digestion actually begins in the mouth when food is chewed and mixed with saliva.
    Ⓑ The food then moves into the small intestine where more digestive juices complete breaking it down.
    Ⓒ It is in the small intestine that nutrients are taken into the blood and carried throughout the body.
    Ⓓ Anything left over that the body cannot use goes to the large intestine. The body takes water from those leftovers. The rest is passed out of the body.

Question 6 and 7 are based on the paragraph below.

Smoking is a cheesy (icky) habit. It not only damages your health, but it also affects the way an individual looks and smells. People who smoke have dreadful breath that's comparable to a dirty ashtray, but it is not only their breath that smells awful. Their clothes and hair smell smoky, and if this isn't bad enough, smoking can cause their teeth to turn yellow.

6. **Above is a section from a persuasive essay written to encourage people not to smoke. What evidence does the writer provide that supports the claim that smoking affects the way you look?**

    Ⓐ Smoking is a cheesy (icky) habit.
    Ⓑ People who smoke have dreadful breath.
    Ⓒ Their clothes and hair smell smoky.
    Ⓓ Smoking can cause their teeth to turn yellow.

7. **Above is a section from a persuasive essay written to encourage people not to smoke. Which statement does NOT provide evidence that supports the claim that smoking causes you smell bad?**

Ⓐ People who smoke have dreadful breath thats comparable to a dirty ashtray.
Ⓑ Eating onions also may cause you to have bad breath.
Ⓒ It is not only people's breath that smells bad.
Ⓓ Their clothes and hair also smell like smoke.

Question 8 is based on the paragraph below.

Drinking alcohol and driving is a dangerous combination. This is because alcohol affects the nervous system. Alcohol can make an individual act silly and laugh at situations that are not funny. Alcohol slows down the brain. This can cause the driver to have a slowed reaction time and to have difficulty thinking accurately. It causes a motorist to not be able to make quick, clear decisions about traffic and road conditions. Alcohol's effect on the brain can cause a lack of coordination. This can lead to a driver to weaving in many directions on the road. It can cause a driver to have trouble applying the brakes when needed. Any one of these reactions can easily cause an accident that can be harmful to themselves and others.

8. **Above is a section from a persuasive essay written to encourage people not to drink. What statement does NOT provide evidence supporting the writer's claim that drinking alcohol and driving is dangerous?**

Ⓐ Alcohol can make an individual act silly and laugh at situations that are not funny.
Ⓑ Alcohol slows down the brain.
Ⓒ Alcohol's effect on the brain causes lack of coordination.
Ⓓ This can lead a driver weaving in many directions on the road or have trouble applying the brakes when needed.

Question 9 is based on the paragraph below.

Dr. Johnson thinks that everyone should take responsibility for preserving the toad species. By not mowing certain areas of our lawns, special areas of wild grass can be kept for toads. This practice may help to preserve the species. According to Dr. Johnson, dangerous chemicals found in pesticides and fertilizers are the reason that the toads are disappearing. The chemicals affect the food chain and kill the insects that toads eat. Dr. Johnson believes that the toads can be saved if we keep a space in our yards and stop using chemical fertilizers.

9. **What would be an appropriate title for the above text?**

Ⓐ Please Stop Mowing Your Lawn
Ⓑ Don't Let Toads Disappear
Ⓒ Please Stop Using Fertilizers
Ⓓ Dr. Johnson and the Toad

Question 10 is based on the paragraph below.

In the United States today, we are starting to see more and more of a problem with children who are overweight. Doctors and other health care professionals are trying to do something about it. They are recommending healthier foods and encouraging children get daily vigorous exercise. They also recommend that children go outside and play instead of sitting in front of the tv. They have suggested that children get at least an hour of exercise a day by participating in activities like jumping rope, cycling, or basketball, movement that makes the heart beat faster. This kind of exercise is known as aerobic exercise. Something else they recommend is for children to do exercises that strengthen the bones and muscles. There are a lot of ways that children can do this. One way is running.

10. What is the main idea of the above text? Circle the correct answer choice.

Ⓐ Doctors want you to move.
Ⓑ It is very important for kids to exercise daily.
Ⓒ Jumping and other activities help make bones strong.
Ⓓ Any physical exercise can help make the heart beat stronger.

Question 11 is based on the paragraph below.

Rosa Parks is famous for her actions during the Civil Rights movement. Although she initially dropped out of high school, she went back later to earn her high school diploma when she was around 20 years old. At that time, not many people in Montgomery, Alabama finished school. Thanks to her diploma, she was able to get a job at Maxwell Field, an air force base not far from her home. During the time Rosa worked on the military base, President Roosevelt decided that military bases could not be segregated. This meant that workers of different race could be together which wasn't the way it was outside the base. Segregation laws separated people of different races in all public places. So, on the bus that Rosa had to take home, she had to ride in the back.

11. Which details above help to explain segregation? Circle the correct answer choice.

Ⓐ Rosa Parks was one of the few people in Montgomery who had her high school diploma.
Ⓑ She worked at Maxwell Field.
Ⓒ Segregation laws said that Rosa had to ride in the back of the city buses.
Ⓓ Rosa boarded the city bus, paid her fare, and moved to the back of the bus.

Chapter 3

Lesson 9: Integrating Information

This standard includes the word "integrate," which means bring together or combine. The standard is requiring you to combine into one text the information on a subject from two different texts, in a way that does not lose important information from either text.

Here are two different texts on the subject of planning a live theater show.

Your assignment: Your teacher has asked you to read these two texts and write a third text that integrates (combines) the most important information from the two texts.

Text 1: Every year my grade is allowed to put on a show for all the kids in our school. I am so excited! I want to be in the show and I hope I will be chosen at the auditions. I wonder what kind of show it will be. Are you going to be in a show this year at your school? There are so many things to think about. Here are some suggestions for you to think about.

First, what kind of show will it be? A comedy, where the actors say and do goofy things to make the audience laugh? Or a drama, where everything is serious? Could it have singing and dancing - a musical?

I would like to be in a musical, because I like to sing and dance. If it is a musical, what do I need to perform in it? Special dance shoes, sheet music and a costume. Will I have the time to go to rehearsals? Yes because basketball will be over and softball will not have started. Well, I think that is all there is to think about for now. And, my best friends, who do not want to memorize lines or songs or dance steps, can still help by working backstage with props, scenery, the curtain, sound or lighting. Oh and I can't wait to see my name in the playbill!

Text 2: Every year my drama students are allowed to put on a show. I have to decide what kind of show my students are best at performing: an original variety show, or an existing comedy or tragedy? With singing and dancing or only with spoken dialogue (conversations)? Because time is limited, it has to be an existing show. Because so many have had dance and singing lessons, and audiences enjoy comedy, I think a musical comedy will be best. Next, I have to decide which musical comedy to choose. I want it to have a large cast, so many students can participate onstage or backstage. And an orchestra, which will allow even more students to participate. I will need scenery, which I will have to build, and props which I will have to buy or borrow. And costumes which I will have to make or buy or borrow. Sheet music for each singer and for the orchestra. And microphones and lighting, and the students who will run the audio and lights and move the curtains and scenery. I have to schedule auditions and rehearsals. And I need to design the playbill and be sure I include everyone! Lots to do – time to get started.

Integrated (combined) text:

Here is an example of what you might write.

If students are performing a show, there are lots of things they and their teachers have to do. First is choosing the show, usually done by a teacher. Choosing the show means deciding on the kind of show – an original variety or an existing comedy or tragedy, with singing and dancing or not, with a large cast or a small one, with musicians or not. Then planning auditions, to decide who is going to be in the show. They must order scripts and get costumes for the actors. They must get music for the singers and for the musicians (if music is needed). They must plan when to have rehearsals and performances. They have to decide how to decorate the stage and where to get the decorations (scenery) and what props and costumes are needed and where to get them. Also they need to decide who will move the props and scenery on the stage, and who will operate the curtains and lights and audio systems. Also, someone needs to design the playbill and list everyone involved with the show. Some of these jobs may be done by teachers, students or both.

Publishers Note: You might choose to use a list with bullet points to show the jobs that have to be done. For example:
- *Choosing the show: deciding on the kind of show – an original variety or an existing comedy or tragedy, with singing and dancing or not, with a large cast or a small one, with musicians or not.*
- *Planning auditions*

You can scan the QR code given below or use the url to access additional EdSearch resources including videos and mobile apps related to *Integrating Information*.

ed)Search **Integrating Information**

URL	QR Code
http://www.lumoslearning.com/a/ri49	

Question 1-3 are based on the passage below.

On the Trail: an Outdoor Book for Girls by Adelia Beard and Lina Beard

For any journey, by rail or by boat, one has a general idea of the direction to be taken, the character of the land or water to be crossed, and of what one will find at the end. So it should be in striking the trail. Learn all you can about the path you are to follow. Whether it is plain or obscure, wet or dry; where it leads; and its length, measured more by time than by actual miles. A smooth, even trail of five miles will not consume the time and strength that must be expended upon a trail of half that length which leads over uneven ground, varied by bogs and obstructed by rocks and fallen trees, or a trail that is all up-hill climbing.

How to Camp Out by John M. Gould

Think over and decide whether you will walk, go horseback, sail, camp out in one place, or what you will do; then learn what you can of the route you propose to go over, or the ground where you intend to camp for the season. If you think of moving through or camping in places unknown to you, it is important to learn whether you can buy provisions and get lodgings along your route. See some one, if you can, who has been where you think of going, [Pg 10]and put down in a note-book all he tells you that is important.

1. **Which sentence below integrates information from the above texts?**

   Ⓐ Hiking over logs or fallen trees is harder than hiking an even, clear trail.
   Ⓑ You should talk to someone who has been where you plan to go so you can get information and tips that will be helpful in planning your camping trip.
   Ⓒ Hiking over uneven land will take longer than going the same distance over flat land.
   Ⓓ When planning a camping trip, it is important to plan by considering both the type of the trail you will travel and whether you will walk or ride on horseback.

2. **Which paragraph below combines information from the above texts?**

   Ⓐ Camping is terribly difficult, and only true experts should try to camp overnight.
   Ⓑ If you plan to camp somewhere you've never been, you should learn everything you can about the trail. Find out what the land is like and where you can buy supplies along the way.
   Ⓒ Only boys can go on long camping trips across bogs or uneven land.
   Ⓓ You should always take a notebook on your camping trips to write about your trip and draw pictures of plants and animals you see.

3. Which pair of sentences shows similar information found in both texts?

Ⓐ "Learn all you can about the path you are to follow."
"Learn what you can of the route that you propose to go over."

Ⓑ "So it should be in striking the trail."
"Think over and decide whether you will walk, go horseback, sail, camp out in one place, or what you will do…"

Ⓒ "A smooth, even trail of five miles will not consume the time and strength that must be expended upon a trail of half that length which leads over uneven ground…"
"… It is important to learn whether you can buy provisions and get lodgings along your route."

Ⓓ All of the above

Question 4 and 5 are based on the passage below.

The Amazing Peacock

Did you know that the term, "peacock" only refers to the male of its species? A female peafowl is actually called a "peahen." Peacocks are native to India and other parts of Southeast Asia and are known for their brilliantly colored feathers. Their bodies can be thirty-five to fifty inches, while their beautiful tails can be as long as five feet! People admire peacocks for their beautiful feathers, but the tails also serve a purpose. The peacocks' tails help peahens choose their mates!

The Peafowl and It's Magnificent Tail

Peafowls are glorious animals and have long been admired by humans for their beautiful and brightly colored tail feathers. Their tails do not reach their full length until the peacock is four or five years old. When this happens, the peacock will strut day after day in hopes of attracting a mate. Peafowl are actually a kind of pheasant. Some are natives of India, while others come from Sri Lanka, Myanmar (Burma), or Java. Peafowl are some of the largest flying birds around!

4. Which paragraph below integrates information from both texts above?

Ⓐ The peafowl, more commonly known as the peacock, has beautiful tail feathers. Those feathers can grow to be around five feet long, but their growth usually does not peak until the peacock is four or five years old.
Ⓑ Peacocks are wonderful creatures. They come from India, and their bodies can grow to be thirty-five to fifty inches long.
Ⓒ Peacocks like to strut around all day with their beautiful feathers spread wide for all to see. This is what helps them to find a mate.
Ⓓ None of the above

5. Which sentence below combines information from both texts above?

(A) Peacocks have been admired by humans for over a thousand years because their tail feathers are so beautiful.

(B) "Peafowl" actually refers to both the male and female of its species, while "peacock" is the correct term for the male only.

(C) Peacocks are enormous.

(D) With bodies as big as thirty-five to fifty inches and tails as long as five feet, peacocks are some of the largest flying birds you will ever see.

Question 6-8 are based on the passage below.

Sacagawea

Sacagawea is a famous Native American woman from the Shoshone tribe. She became famous when she helped two male explorers named Lewis and Clark, find their way through the unknown west. When she was 12 years old, she was kidnapped by an enemy of the Shoshone tribe called the Hidatsa. Legend has it, that the chief of the Hidatsa tribe sold Sacagawea into slavery.

In 1804, she became a translator and guide for a group of explorers led by Lewis and Clark. She helped them find their way from near the Dakotas to the Pacific Ocean. She became a famous Native American woman in US history for being brave and helping these explorers discover unknown territory.

Lewis and Clark

Sacagawea, also spelled *Sacajawea*, is best known for her role in helping Meriwether Lewis and William Clark during their journey to explore the American West. They set out on their journey on May 14, 1804. They left from near Wood River, Illinois; it was during winter in South Dakota when they met Sacagawea. They reached the Pacific Ocean on the coast of Oregon in November 1805.

The journey was unique. The new frontier was full of unknown native people and the land was dangerous. Without the help of someone who knew the land, Lewis and Clark may not have made it to the Pacific.

Sacagawea was the young Shoshone wife of a French-Canadian fur trapper named Toussaint Charbonneau. Together, she and her husband served as interpreters, guides, and negotiators for Lewis and Clark. Their friendship with Clark was so strong that when they returned, they moved to his hometown of St. Louis. Clark became the guardian of her children after her death.

6. Which of the following sentences integrates information from both texts above?

Ⓐ Despite being kidnapped and sold into slavery at the age of 12, Sacagawea went on to guide and befriend Meriwether Lewis and William Clark on their journey of exploration from South Dakota to the Pacific Ocean in Oregon.

Ⓑ Sacagawea is a famous and brave Shoshone Indian who helped guide Lewis and Clark on their journey to find new territory.

Ⓒ Sacagawea developed such a strong bond with William Clark that after the expedition she moved to his city and even left her children in his care when she died.

Ⓓ Sacagawea was kidnapped by the Hidatsa in 1804.

7. Which of the following sentences combines information from both texts above?

Ⓐ Sacagawea was a Shoshone princess who very slyly took charge of one of the most famous explorations in American History.

Ⓑ Sacagawea did serve as interpreter and guide, but it was merely her presence that showed William's and Clark's peaceful intentions when the expedition encountered new tribes.

Ⓒ At twelve, Sacagawea was kidnapped and sold to a French-Canadian man; but she eventually married the fur trapper, Toussaint Charbonneau, and together they became part of an expedition that will live on in history.

Ⓓ Sacagawea was kidnapped by the Hidatsa in 1804.

8. Which of the following sentences combines information from both texts above?

Ⓐ Sacagawea was a member of the Shoshone tribe of Native Americans.

Ⓑ Sacagawea was brave because she was kidnapped as a child, went on a treacherous and historic journey across the American West, and also ventured to live in a new city.

Ⓒ Sacagawea could not have aided the Lewis and Clark expedition without the help of her husband, who was an experienced fur trapper.

Ⓓ Sacagawea was kidnapped by the Hidatsa in 1804.

Question 9 and 10 are based on the passage below.

One Theory on Dinosaur Extinction

Have you ever thought about what happened to the dinosaurs that once roamed the Earth? Well, scientists have developed several ideas throughout the years. One idea is that a giant meteorite crashed into our planet and caused a huge dust cloud to cover the Earth. The dust cloud was so enormous that it kept the Sun's rays from reaching Earth. This caused all of the plants to die. With nothing to eat, the herbivores died. The large carnivores also died, leaving the planet without dinosaurs.

Dinosaur Die-out: Competing Theories

There are many theories about how dinosaurs came to be extinct. Scientists do not all agree about what may have happened. The most recent idea says that a giant meteorite crashed into the earth. It kicked up enough dust and dirt that the Sun's rays did not reach Earth for a very long time. This prevented plants from making their own food via photosynthesis. Plant-eaters and then, meat-eaters died due to a lack of food.

The other leading idea says that dinosaurs died out when the Earth went through a time of volcanoes erupting. Like the meteorite idea, it is thought that the volcanoes spewed enough ash into the air that the Sun's rays were blocked. This also caused plant and animal life to die.

9. Which of the following paragraphs integrates information from both of the above texts? Circle the correct answer choice.

Ⓐ Dinosaurs are thought to have become extinct 65 million years ago, but some scientists theorize that they are still roaming remote parts of the Amazon Rainforest.

Ⓑ Dinosaurs became extinct because of widespread volcanic eruptions that blocked sunlight from reaching Earth. When this happened, plants died, beginning a disruption of the food chain that dinosaurs didn't survive.

Ⓒ One theory suggests a meteorite caused dinosaur extinction, while another claims widespread volcanic eruptions caused the animals to die. Both theories, however, center around the idea that plants did not get needed sunlight, and plant-eating and meat-eating animals died as a result.

Ⓓ None of the above

10. Which of the following sentences integrates information from both of the above texts? Circle the correct answer choice.

Ⓐ Several theories exist about how dinosaurs became extinct; but the two main theories are that either a meteorite crashing into Earth or a series of massive volcanic eruptions caused the animals to die out.

Ⓑ Dinosaurs may have become extinct because a giant meteorite crashed into the Earth somewhere near the Gulf of Mexico, but scientists are not sure.

Ⓒ If producers are unable to get sunlight, photosynthesis can't take place. This means plant-eating animals do not have food, thus meaning that meat-eating animals will not have food either.

Ⓓ All of the above

End of Reading: Informational Text

Answer Key and Detailed Explanations

Chapter 3: Reading: Informational Text

Lesson 1: It's All in the Details

Question No.	Answer	Detailed Explanations
1	D	The fourth answer choice is correct. The author says the ostrich, "cannot fly," and that, "it can travel faster by running." Traveling faster is an advantage for the ostrich.
2	D	The fourth answer choice is correct. By saying, "one of their favorite companions," the author implies the ostrich has many companions. The ostrich is not shy and solitary if it has many companions.
3	A	"Solitary" means alone. The first answer choice is correct because the statement contrasts the blue whale's behavior with the behavior of other whales that live in pods.
4	D	The fourth answer choice is correct because it mentions the advantage of getting friends to join. While the third answer choice does mention getting friends to join, it does not mention any benefit that would encourage the audience to recruit their friends.
5	A	The first choice is correct. While the text does make a convincing case for the theory that a meteorite crashed into the Earth, causing dinosaurs to die out, the author implies that there are other theories by saying, "<u>One</u> idea"
6	D	The second answer choice is correct. Paragraph 2 includes details like, "when the weather begins to get warmer after winter, these little frogs start to sing," and their song, "can be heard for miles around." Paragraph 3 also helps support the point by including details about how spring peepers "hide under fallen leaves or even in a small hole in the ground," when cold weather comes. Singing would make the peeper easy to find, while hiding would make it difficult to see.
7	C	The third answer choice is correct. The author does not include northwestern Australia as one of the areas koalas call home.
8	B	The author writes that, "muscle tissue makes body parts move by tightening and relaxing."
9	D	The passage directly states epithelial tissue forms the outer layer of the skin.
10	C	The third choice is correct. Although the letter is polite, Tim West was displeased with his experience. Only dissatisfied customers ask for refunds.

Lesson 2: The Main Idea

Question No.	Answer	Detailed Explanations
1	D	The fourth choice is the best title, because it is the main idea of the passage.
2	B	The second choice is correct, because it is what the passage is mostly about.
3	A	The first choice is correct because it is the main idea of the passage.
4	B	The second choice is correct, because the passage is about Beatrice not having good drinking water in the beginning and having it in the end.
5	C	Dumping large amounts of trash from factories and houses affects the soil according to the passage.
6	B	The second choice is correct because the passage states that shells are made by marine creatures to serve as their homes.
7	B	The second choice is correct because the passage was about Sacagawea and the amazing things she did. Though the other titles are accurate, they only refer to parts of her story.
8	A	The first choice is correct because it includes what the passage was about and the most important information. Although B is a correct statement, it is not covered in the passage.
9	A	The first choice is correct because the whole passage is about the uniqueness of a certain breed of dog.
10	C	Option C is the correct answer. Although each statement comes directly from the passage, only option C supports the main idea. As the sun was blocked from the dust, it killed off all plant life, leaving nothing for the dinosaurs to survive on.

Lesson 3: Using Details to Explain the Text

Question No.	Answer	Detailed Explanations
1	C	The third answer choice is correct. The text reads, "Digestion actually begins in the mouth when food is chewed and mixed with saliva."
2	D	The fourth choice is correct. The text reads, "nutrients are absorbed into the blood and carried throughout the body."
3	C	The third choice is correct. The text shows, "they surface to breathe air into their lungs through blowholes. They emerge from the ocean, spewing water out of their blowhole, roll, and re-enter the water with a grand splash of their large tail." Choice A is false, while choice B has the order of events incorrect.
4	A	The first choice is correct. The text reads, "They make loud, deep, and rumbling low frequency sounds that travel great distances, which allow them to communicate with other whales as far as 100 miles away."
5	D	The fourth choice is correct. It explains the basic idea of physical change as described in the text.
6	B	The second choice is correct. It explains the basic idea of chemical change as described in the text.
7	C	The third choice is correct. The text points out, "The difference between them is that physical changes are temporary or only last for a little while, and chemical changes are permanent, which means they last forever."
8	B	Because they were traveling unknown territory, they needed the help of a person who knew about the people that they would encounter and the land that they would navigate.
9	A	The first choice is correct. The text reads, "..the Sun's rays did not reach Earth for a very long time, preventing plants from producing their own food via photosynthesis. Plant-eaters died from lack of food, and then meat-eaters followed."
10	A	The first choice is correct. The text reads, "There are many theories about how dinosaurs came to be extinct." Then it goes on to describe two such theories: a meteorite collision and widespread volcanic eruptions.

Lesson 4: What Does it Mean?

Question No.	Answer	Detailed Explanations
1	B	Resonating means loud, because the passage says that their resonating sound makes them the loudest animal on earth.
2	B	An herbivore is an animal that eats only plants. The passage gives us a clue when it describes that the plants dying caused the herbivores to die.
3	D	Carnivores are animals that eat meat.
4	B	Personification is a type of figurative language that gives human qualities to a nonhuman object. Rain doesn't dance. Humans dance.
5	C	Vigorous means energetic and forceful. Exercise would be pointless if it wasn't energetic.
6	C	The word repaid is a context clue that helps us figure out what re-imbursed means.
7	D	Boycott means to refuse to buy something. In this case, the people would refuse to go to a store.
8	B	The second sentence shows the exact definition of copra.
9	C	Favorable means positive. The clue is that people enjoyed it.
10	A	Onomatopoeia is a word that makes a sound. Boom is the sound the bomb made, and hiss is the sound the snake made.

Lesson 5: How is it Written?

Question No.	Answer	Detailed Explanations
1	D	Descriptive text structures give characteristics of a particular topic in no particular order.
2	B	Compare/contrast passages tell how subjects are alike and different.
3	D	The text structure is sequence, because the steps are given in the order that they occurred.
4	A	The structure is compare/contrast, because it tells how chemical and physical changes are different.
5	C	The text structure is sequence, because it gives the events in the order and time that they occurred.
6	B	This is informative writing, because it gives true, factual information about a topic.
7	D	The text structure is chronological, because it gives the events in the order that they occurred.
8	D	This is persuasive writing, because it gives an opinion and tries to get others to agree.
9	C	This is comparative, because it tells about how two places are alike and different.
10	C	This would be narrative writing, because it tells about a personal experience from a first-person point of view.

Lesson 6: Comparing Different Versions of the Same Event

Question No.	Answer	Detailed Explanations
1	D	The fourth choice is correct. The first hand account is by the baton twirler and is limited to her personal experiences and observations. The second hand account covers the observations about the entire parade by the reporter.
2	D	The fourth choice is correct. There is information in both texts about the weather, the marching band, the baton twirlers, and the crowd. The other answer choices only appear in one of the two accounts.
3	A	The first choice is correct. We learn in the firsthand account that the narrator is embarrassed by the events during the parade, while the secondhand account omits emotions and includes mostly facts about the parade.
4	C	The third choice is correct. The firsthand account describes how bunches of people walked down the street on their way to the inauguration, and the secondhand account gives details about the inauguration on that same day.
5	D	The fourth choice is correct. The other answer choices are not accurate.
6	A	The first choice is correct. It could be argued that the details in both accounts are important, and the third and fourth choices are false.
7	C	The third choice is correct. The firsthand account is a letter from John Glenn himself to then President Bill Clinton. The secondhand account gives information about John Glenn's 1998 return mission to space.
8	A	The first choice is correct. It is the only information to appear in both documents.
9	A	The first choice is correct. It explains how the two texts are different.
10	B	The second choice is correct. Firsthand accounts represent people's personal experiences, while secondhand accounts are told or written by those who gather the information about the event from another source.
11		Third person point of view is when the story is being told by a person who is not a character in the story.

Lesson 7: Using Text Features to Gather Information

Question No.	Answer	Detailed Explanations
1	D	The fourth answer choice is correct. The chart makes the details clear by categorizing them according to tissue type. It does not add information or elaborate, but rather makes the information more concise. It does not change details.
2	D	The fourth answer choice is correct. The chart makes it easy to see that both muscle tissue and nerve tissue have long cells.
3	B	Microscopic views of each tissue type would show the reader exactly what each type looks like and how they are different.
4	C	A picture of a polar bear would not be helpful, because this passage is about koalas. Koalas are not bears.
5	A	A diagram of the digestive system would be helpful so that the reader could see what the different organs look like and where they are located in relationship to each other.
6	A	The picture of a Native American female is appropriate since the passage is about Sacagawea.
7	C	A picture of an adult blue whale would be useful, because the passage describes what they look like and how large they are.
8	A	The first choice is correct. The steps of a process would be most easily understood with the help of a numbered and illustrated list of steps. A timeline is meant to cover a longer time span, and a map would not help the reader understand the steps in a process.
9	C	The third choice is correct. Camping is the only topic listed that would require knowledge of tents like the ones pictured.
10	C	The third answer choice is correct. The photographs show the different stages of a caterpillar going into its chrysalis in preparation to become a butterfly. The captions use words like, "change" and "transition" to make the information clear.
11	A	The passage is about frogs, and there is a frog in the photo.
12		A map of The United States shows different places such as important states, cities, towns, etc., but a geological map shows rivers, mountains, types of rocks, etc.,

Lesson 8: Finding the Evidence

Question No.	Answer	Detailed Explanations
1	C	The third choice is correct. It gives specific details about the size and weight of the blue whale's body.
2	C	The third choice tells specifically how the whales communicate.
3	C	The third choice is correct. The picture is evidence that the package arrived damaged..
4	B	The second choice is correct. In the letter, the boy states that there is not enough time before his friend's birthday for the company to send a replacement toy.
5	D	The fourth choice tells what happens to the unabsorbed nutrients.
6	D	An individual having yellow teeth is a specific example of how smoking affects the way one looks.
7	B	Choice 2 describes how onions can make the breath smell bad, not cigarettes.
8	A	Choice 1 has nothing to do with driving.
9	B	Don't Let Toads Disappear is an appropriate title, because the purpose of the text is to encourage people to do things to prevent toads from vanishing.
10	B	The main idea is for kids to exercise. The entire passage is about exploring this concept.
11	C	The third choice explained one of the specific effects of segregation.

Lesson 9: Integrating Information

Question No.	Answer	Detailed Explanations
1	D	The fourth answer choice is correct. The first three choices include only information from one of the texts. The fourth choice integrates information from both texts.
2	B	The second choice is correct. Information from the other three choices are not found in the texts.
3	A	The first choice is correct. This is the only choice with a pair of sentences from each text that means essentially the same thing. When doing research, one should look for similar information found in multiple texts, as this adds to its validity.
4	A	The first choice is correct. It integrates information from both texts about the growth and length of a peacock's feathers.
5	D	The fourth choice is correct. It is the only answer choice that includes information from both texts.
6	A	Only the first choice includes information from both texts. Choice 2 only uses information from the first passage, while choice 3 only uses information from the second passage.
7	C	The third choice is correct. The first choice is untrue, and the second choice includes information not mentioned in either text.
8	B	The second choice is correct. It uses examples from both texts to justify bravery as a character trait of Sacagawea. The first choice is a statement of fact, rather than an integration of facts from multiple texts. The third choice is an opinion not represented in either text.
9	C	The third choice is correct. The first choice is untrue, and the second choice asserts the volcano theory as fact, disregarding any discussion of a meteorite.
10	A	The first choice is correct. It integrates information from both texts. The second choice gives additional information on only one theory, and the third choice further explains how blocked sunlight could result in dinosaur extinction.

Chapter 4 - Language

The objective of the Language standards is to ensure that the student is able to accurately use grade appropriate general academic and domain specific words and phrases related to Grade 4.

To support each student to master the necessary skills, we encourage the student to go through the resources available online on EdSearch to gain an in depth understanding of these concepts. EdSearch page for each lesson can be accessed with the help of the url or the QR code provided.

Chapter 4

Lesson 1: Pronouns

You can scan the QR code given below or use the url to access additional EdSearch resources including videos and mobile apps related to *Pronouns*.

ed Search	**Pronouns**

URL	QR Code
http://www.lumoslearning.com/a/l41	

1. Choose the correct pronoun to complete the sentence.

Bobby and I have practice every day. The 7th graders practice first and their practice always runs long. I live closer but Bobby is on my team, so ___ walk to the games together.

 Ⓐ I
 Ⓑ we
 Ⓒ us
 Ⓓ they

2. Choose the correct pronoun to complete the sentence.

My father asked me to bring ____ book inside.

 Ⓐ he
 Ⓑ him
 Ⓒ his
 Ⓓ us

3. Choose the correct pronoun to complete the sentence.

I would like you to meet Jamie. _____ is my best friend.

 Ⓐ He
 Ⓑ Him
 Ⓒ Its
 Ⓓ Their

4. Choose the correct pronoun to complete the sentence.

My dogs love to play with _____ squeaky toys.

 Ⓐ his
 Ⓑ its
 Ⓒ their
 Ⓓ them

5. Choose the correct pronoun to complete the sentence.

The little girl put _____ doll in the toy box before going to bed.

    Ⓐ she
    Ⓑ its
    Ⓒ their
    Ⓓ her

6. Choose the correct pronoun to complete the sentence.

The dancers practice every night in order to learn _____ dance steps.

    Ⓐ its
    Ⓑ them
    Ⓒ their
    Ⓓ our

7. Choose the appropriate pronoun.

Kelly and I have been going to dances for two years now, but her little sister wants to come with us this time. This is _____ first time at a school dance.

    Ⓐ her
    Ⓑ my
    Ⓒ she
    Ⓓ it

8. Complete the sentence with the appropriate pronoun.

_____ went hiking in the mountains together.

    Ⓐ His
    Ⓑ Her
    Ⓒ They
    Ⓓ Them

9. Choose the correct pronoun.

I baked fancy Christmas cupcakes for my teacher. She is my favorite teacher and I couldn't wait until Monday to give them to _____.

Ⓐ she
Ⓑ him
Ⓒ he
Ⓓ her

10. Choose the correct pronoun.

Alice and Jennifer like going ice skating. _____ are going to the ice skating rink this afternoon.

Ⓐ Their
Ⓑ They
Ⓒ Them
Ⓓ Her

11. Choose the appropriate pronoun. Fill in the blank by choosing the correct answer from the options given below

_____ have been going to school together since first grade.

Ⓐ Them
Ⓑ He
Ⓒ Him
Ⓓ They

12. Choose the pronoun that fits in the blank above. Fill in the blank by choosing the correct answer from the options given below

Please bring the remote control to _____.

Ⓐ me
Ⓑ I
Ⓒ they
Ⓓ we

Chapter 4

Lesson 2: Progressive Verb Tense

You can scan the QR code given below or use the url to access additional EdSearch resources including videos and mobile apps related to *Progressive Verb Tense*.

Progressive Verb Tense

URL	QR Code
http://www.lumoslearning.com/a/l41	

1. Choose the correct progressive verb tense.

Efrain, accompanied by his parents, _____ to Europe this summer.

    Ⓐ are traveling
    Ⓑ will be traveling
    Ⓒ was traveling
    Ⓓ is traveling

2. Choose the correct verb to complete the sentence.

Darrel and I _____ the football game with friends this Friday night.

    Ⓐ is attending
    Ⓑ am attending
    Ⓒ was attending
    Ⓓ will attend

3. Choose the sentence that has the proper progressive verb tense.

    Ⓐ Minnie, Jill, and Sandra are singing the birthday song to Ann right now.
    Ⓑ Bob, Jim, and Harry have played baseball next summer.
    Ⓒ One of my five hamsters might get out of the cage tomorrow night.
    Ⓓ Twenty-five dollars are too much to charge for that bracelet.

4. Choose the sentence that has proper verb tense.

    Ⓐ Everyone in my neighborhood, including the woman with nine dogs, were walking each night after dinner.
    Ⓑ Contestants from Europe, America, and Germany are competing in last year's contest.
    Ⓒ Neither of the girls is planning to audition for the school play today.
    Ⓓ No one in my history class wishes that we had more homework each night.

5. Choose the correct one.

Jenny, one of my many friends, _____ to buy a new car this summer with money she earns during this school year at her baby-sitting job.

    Ⓐ will be saving
    Ⓑ is saving
    Ⓒ am saving
    Ⓓ be hoping

6. What could be the correct form of the sentence?

The cheerleader, who was cheering for her team, wore one of the team's new uniforms.

    Ⓐ The cheerleader, who was cheering for her team, were dressed in one of the team's new uniforms.
    Ⓑ The cheerleader, who was cheering for her team, was wearing one of the team's new uniforms.
    Ⓒ The cheerleader, who were cheering for her team, were wearing one of the team's new uniforms.
    Ⓓ The cheerleaders, who was cheering for her teams, will be wearing one of the teams new uniforms.

7. What could be the correct form of the sentence?

The trees that keeps waved in the wind on the side of the street show how forceful the wind is.

    Ⓐ The trees that waved in the wind on the side of the street show how forceful the wind is.
    Ⓑ The trees that will be waving in the wind on the side of the street show how forceful the wind is.
    Ⓒ The trees that keep waving in the wind on the side of the street show how forceful the wind is.
    Ⓓ The trees that waving in the wind on the side of the street shows how forceful the wind is.

8. Choose the correct sentence.

The world change so rapidly that we can hardly keep up.

    Ⓐ The world will be changing so rapidly that we can hardly keep up.
    Ⓑ The world change so rapidly that we can hardly keep up.
    Ⓒ The world is changing so rapidly that we can hardly keep up.
    Ⓓ The worlds change so rapidly that we can hardly keep up.

9. Choose the correct sentence.

She sitted at the table by the window when the waiter approached.

    Ⓐ She sitting at the table by the window when the waiter approached.
    Ⓑ She was sitting at the table by the window when the waiter approached.
    Ⓒ She is sitting at the table by the window when the waiter approached.
    Ⓓ Shes will be sitting at the table by the window when the waiter approached.

10. Which verb best completes the sentence?

Kenji and Briana _____ at recess when their parents pick them up for their doctor appointments.

   Ⓐ play
   Ⓑ will play
   Ⓒ will be playing
   Ⓓ were playing

Chapter 4

Lesson 3: What's the Verb?

You can scan the QR code given below or use the url to access additional EdSearch resources including videos and mobile apps related to *What's the Verb?*

ed Search

What's the Verb?

URL	QR Code
http://www.lumoslearning.com/a/l41	

1. "I picked it up on the beach last weekend."
   In the above sentence, find the simple predicate.

   Ⓐ picked it up
   Ⓑ I
   Ⓒ I picked it
   Ⓓ picked

2. Choose the correct word to fill in the blank.
   I heard a sound. Did you _____ a sound?

   Ⓐ hearing
   Ⓑ heard
   Ⓒ hear
   Ⓓ will hear

3. Mary sang in the school choir last year, but this year she _____ in the church choir.
   Choose the correct verb for the above sentence.

   Ⓐ sung
   Ⓑ had sang
   Ⓒ is singing
   Ⓓ has sung

4. At the game last week, Lauren hit the ball over the fence and scored the winning run.
   Choose the verbs from the sentence above.

   Ⓐ ball, fence
   Ⓑ hit, scored
   Ⓒ winning, run
   Ⓓ over, run

5. I _____ so nervous about standing in front of the class and reciting my poem today that
   my hands are shaking.
   Choose the correct verb for the sentence above.

   Ⓐ are
   Ⓑ is
   Ⓒ were
   Ⓓ am

6. My mother finished the work on my sister's tomato costume for the play. Choose the simple predicate from the sentence above.

Ⓐ play
Ⓑ finished
Ⓒ costume
Ⓓ work

7. Choose the sentence that uses a present tense verb.

Ⓐ I stood outside and watched the lunar eclipse with my family.
Ⓑ The farmer will be planting corn this year instead cotton and soybeans.
Ⓒ Randy and Paul are sitting in the bus at the end of the line.
Ⓓ You had to go to detention today because you forgot to do your homework.

8. My grandmother's love for flowers shows in her beautiful painting. Choose the verb in the sentence above.

Ⓐ shows
Ⓑ love
Ⓒ beautiful
Ⓓ painting

9. I saw a bear and her cubs as they walked through the forest. Did you _____ them? Choose the correct verb to complete the above sentence.

Ⓐ seeing
Ⓑ seen
Ⓒ saw
Ⓓ see

10. Choose the sentence that is written in past tense.

Ⓐ The sea gulls swooped down suddenly and captured the unsuspecting fish.
Ⓑ My mother says that everyone will be in a hurry to finish their shopping today.
Ⓒ Although he wants to buy a computer, Bill plans to buy a new cell phone instead.
Ⓓ I do not know the answer to that question, but I will find the answer before our next class.

11. **The kids at my school have all mysteriously disappeared!**

   What is the entire verb phrase in this sentence? Circle the correct answer choice.

   (A) have disappeared
   (B) have all
   (C) have all disappeared
   (D) have mysteriously

12. **This morning I cleaned my room.**

   Identify the simple predicate in the sentence above. Circle the correct answer choice.

   (A) This
   (B) morning
   (C) cleaned
   (D) room

Chapter 4

Lesson 4: Modal Auxiliary Verbs

You can scan the QR code given below or use the url to access additional EdSearch resources including videos and mobile apps related to *Modal Auxiliary Verbs*.

ed Search

Modal Auxiliary Verbs

URL	QR Code
http://www.lumoslearning.com/a/l41	

1. Which sentences contain an auxiliary verb?

(1) Rae and her mother need to find a birthday gift for Rae's father, Joseph. (2) They discussed shopping online, walking to the store in their neighborhood, or going to the mall to find the gift. (3) Because Rae's mother suffers from arthritis, I don't think they will walk to the store to buy the gift. (4) They may decide it's most efficient to buy the gift online.

Ⓐ sentence 1
Ⓑ sentences 2 and 3
Ⓒ sentence 4
Ⓓ sentences 3 and 4

2. What is the purpose of the modal auxiliary verb, "may," in the sentence?

Oliver may go to school tomorrow if his fever has dissipated.

Ⓐ It is being used to express doubt.
Ⓑ It is being used to talk about a future event with uncertainty.
Ⓒ It is being used to talk about something that will definitely happen.
Ⓓ It is being used to talk about something that definitely will not happen.

3. Replace "can" with the correct verb in the sentence.

Liam can have taken the test before he went on vacation, but he did not inform his teacher about the trip in advance.

Ⓐ will
Ⓑ must
Ⓒ can't
Ⓓ could

4. What is the auxiliary modal verb in the sentence?

Dana had to leave the party when her mother called to inform her of an emergency at home.

Ⓐ called to
Ⓑ at
Ⓒ had to
Ⓓ will

5. Choose the sentence that contains a modal auxiliary verb.

Ⓐ You shouldn't have handled your disagreement with physical violence.
Ⓑ I want to have a birthday party.
Ⓒ Everyone needs to look up.
Ⓓ That is the most beautiful painting I have ever seen.

6. Choose the sentence that contains a modal auxiliary verb.

Ⓐ You are a very good reader.
Ⓑ Sara is having a great time on her Hawaiian vacation.
Ⓒ I am not a big fan of Justin Beiber.
Ⓓ You could be a really good student if you applied yourself to your studies.

7. Choose the sentence that contains a modal auxiliary verb.

Ⓐ Jerome has potential to be an excellent science fiction writer.
Ⓑ Margaret is the most beautiful dancer on the stage.
Ⓒ I shall never think another bad thought again.
Ⓓ Jenny is eating a sandwich for dinner.

8. (1)If I could dine with any person, living or dead, I would choose Maya Angelou. (2)She endured hardships in her life but went on to become one of the most influential literary figures of the 20th century. (3)I will ask her what inspired her most.

"Will" is not the best verb choice in the 3rd sentence.

What word should the speaker have used instead to express possibility rather than certainty?

Ⓐ can
Ⓑ may
Ⓒ shall
Ⓓ would

9. Why did Marvin's mother respond this way?

"Can you hand me that apple?" Marvin asked his mother.
"Yes," she answered. But she didn't move a muscle.

Ⓐ She had an extremely long and tiring day at work. Marvin's mother did not want to hand him the apple.
Ⓑ Marvin's mother recognizes she can hand him the apple and knows there is a better way for him to ask using the word "will".
Ⓒ Marvin's mother does not approve of apples.
Ⓓ She thinks Marvin should have to get his own apple.

10. Choose the sentence that correctly uses a modal auxiliary verb.

Ⓐ I might have to see a doctor if this headache does not go away.
Ⓑ I shall all the items on the menu.
Ⓒ She musted remembered to lock the front door before leaving for work each day.
Ⓓ Her might need to go to the school for a conference tomorrow.

Chapter 4

Lesson 5: Adjectives and Adverbs

You can scan the QR code given below or use the url to access additional EdSearch resources including videos and mobile apps related to *Adjectives and Adverbs*.

Adjectives and Adverbs

URL	QR Code
http://www.lumoslearning.com/a/l41	

1. Identify the _adverb_ used in <u>sentence 2</u>.

(1) Mary went to visit her grandmother last weekend. (2) She likes to visit her grandmother frequently. (3) While visiting, they enjoy walking. (4) They strolled in the beautiful park and talked. (5) Mary and her grandmother enjoyed their visit.

- Ⓐ likes
- Ⓑ visit
- Ⓒ frequently
- Ⓓ her

2. Identify the _adjective_ used in <u>sentence 4</u>.

(1) Mary went to visit her grandmother last weekend. (2) She likes to visit her grandmother frequently. (3) While visiting, they enjoy walking. (4) They strolled in the beautiful park and talked. (5) Mary and her grandmother enjoyed their visit.

- Ⓐ strolled
- Ⓑ beautiful
- Ⓒ park
- Ⓓ talked

3. Identify an _adjective_ in the below sentence.

Zelda and her family visited the Jackson Zoo last weekend although it was alarmingly cold and rainy.

- Ⓐ last
- Ⓑ although
- Ⓒ and
- Ⓓ cold

4. Identify the _adjective_ in the below sentence.

The fastest runner in our school practices frequently in order to increase his speed.

- Ⓐ fastest
- Ⓑ practices
- Ⓒ frequently
- Ⓓ increase

5. Choose the appropriate word for the sentence below.

I think that my daughter is the _____ girl in the world.

- Ⓐ beautifulest
- Ⓑ beautifuler
- Ⓒ most beautiful
- Ⓓ more beautiful

6. Choose the correct _comparative adjective_ to complete the below sentence.

The wind was much _____ than it was last weekend.

- Ⓐ cold
- Ⓑ coldest
- Ⓒ more cold
- Ⓓ colder

7. Choose the proper comparative adjective to complete the below sentence.

While standing at the intersection, I heard a loud noise and turned my head to see the _____ wreck imaginable.

- Ⓐ horrificest
- Ⓑ most horrificest
- Ⓒ more horrificest
- Ⓓ most horrific

8. What's the correct order of adverbs in the sentence below?

The huge tiger hungrily and stealthily walked in the black, spiky bush getting ready to pounce.

- Ⓐ huge, spiky
- Ⓑ hungrily and stealthily
- Ⓒ stealthily and hungrily
- Ⓓ black spiky

(1) Lindsay, Laine, and John were excited. (2) Each put their things in an overnight bag. (3) They were going to spend two nights with Aunt Margaret, and the next night with their Auntie Jo.

9. Part A

What is the adjective in sentence 1?

Ⓐ John
Ⓑ Lindsay
Ⓒ Laine
Ⓓ excited

(1) Lindsay, Laine, and John were excited. (2) They put their things in his or her overnight bag. (3) They were going to spend two nights with Aunt Margaret, and the next night with their Auntie Jo, who was their mom's sister.

9. Part B

What is one of the adjectives in sentence 3?

Ⓐ aunt
Ⓑ they
Ⓒ two
Ⓓ mom's

10. It was determined that James was the _____ runner on our track team.
Fill in the blank using the correct adjective from the options given below.

Ⓐ most fast
Ⓑ fastest
Ⓒ most fastest
Ⓓ faster

Chapter 4

Lesson 6: Prepositional Phrases

You can scan the QR code given below or use the url to access additional EdSearch resources including videos and mobile apps related to *Prepositional Phrases.*

ed Search   *Prepositional Phrases*

URL	QR Code
http://www.lumoslearning.com/a/l41	

1. Choose the sentence that contains a prepositional phrase.

Ⓐ The monkey was washing its paws.
Ⓑ The lion jumped into the pool of cool water.
Ⓒ That is the most beautiful dog I have ever seen.
Ⓓ When you decide, let me know.

2. Identify the prepositional phrase in the below sentence.

You will find the new notebooks underneath the journals.

Ⓐ will find
Ⓑ notebooks underneath
Ⓒ new notebooks
Ⓓ underneath the journals

3. Choose the sentence that contains a prepositional phrase.

Ⓐ Please put your paper down so that others won't see your answers.
Ⓑ Because he doesn't have enough money to buy ice cream, he must do without.
Ⓒ Do not leave for school without your lunch box.
Ⓓ Please don't forget to let the dog in.

4. Choose the sentence that contains a prepositional phrase.

Ⓐ When entering the room, Ana tripped on the rug and fell.
Ⓑ I want to see the Rocky Mountains.
Ⓒ Everyone needs to look up.
Ⓓ That is the most beautiful painting I have ever seen.

5. Identify the prepositional phrase in the below sentence.

Finding his money, Lee and Jose rushed to join their friends at the fair.

Ⓐ finding his money
Ⓑ rushed to join
Ⓒ their friends
Ⓓ at the fair

6. Identify the sentence that contains two prepositional phrases.

Ⓐ Terrance went into the room to get his book.
Ⓑ Terrance went into the room.
Ⓒ Terrance went into the room and sat in his favorite chair.
Ⓓ Terrance sat in his favorite chair to read.

7. Identify the prepositional phrase in the below sentence.

The puppy barked loudly and chased the kitten across the yard.

- (A) barked loudly
- (B) chased across
- (C) barked loudly and chased
- (D) across the yard

8. Identify the sentence that contains a prepositional phrase.

- (A) The intoxicating aroma filled the air.
- (B) The aroma coming from the kitchen was inviting.
- (C) I forgot to purchase a loaf of bread.
- (D) A lovely young woman watched as the band marched.

9. Identify the sentence that DOES NOT contain a prepositional phrase.

- (A) Are you going to let him answer the question?
- (B) The answer to the question was wrong.
- (C) The teacher put a huge red checkmark on my paper.
- (D) The questions on this test were very difficult.

10. Identify the prepositional phrase in the sentence below.

The fox chased the deer down the trail.

- (A) chased the deer
- (B) the fox
- (C) down the trail
- (D) the deer down

11. Which sentence does NOT contain a prepositional phrase? Circle the correct answer choice.

- (A) No, Mr. Johnson doesn't go to the library.
- (B) Jenny and Andy hiked through the valley.
- (C) They will not go to the beach because of the rain.
- (D) I sent all the packages.

12. **Which sentence does NOT contain a prepositional phrase? Circle the correct answer choice.**

Ⓐ I wish that my children wouldn't fight with each other.
Ⓑ My little dog likes to sit on the couch.
Ⓒ I will eat cereal for breakfast this morning.
Ⓓ It is very hot outside today.

Chapter 4

Lesson 7: Complete Sentences

You can scan the QR code given below or use the url to access additional EdSearch resources including videos and mobile apps related to *Complete Sentences*.

ed Search

Complete Sentences

URL	QR Code
http://www.lumoslearning.com/a/l41	

1. Which answer choice corrects this run-on sentence?

Jordan wants to go outside and play with her neighbor her mother said she had to clean up her room first.

    Ⓐ Jordan wants to go outside and play with her neighbor, but her mother said she had to clean up her room first.

    Ⓑ Jordan wants to go outside and play but her mother won't let her.

    Ⓒ Jordan wants, to go outside and play with her neighbor but her mother said she had to clean up her room first.

    Ⓓ Jordan wants to go outside. And play with her neighbor. But her mother said she had to clean up her room first.

2. Which answer choice corrects the run-on sentence below?

George Washington Carver is best known for his work with peanuts but he also taught his students about crop rotation that's when farmers plant different crops each year to avoid draining the soil of its nutrients.

    Ⓐ George Washington Carver is best known for his work with peanuts, but he also taught his students about crop rotation, that's when farmers plant different crops each year to avoid draining the soil of its nutrients

    Ⓑ George Washington Carver is best known for his work with peanuts, but he also taught his students about crop rotation. That's when farmers plant different crops each year to avoid draining the soil of its nutrients.

    Ⓒ George Washington Carver is best known for his work with peanuts. But he also taught his students about crop rotation. That's when farmers plant different crops each year to avoid draining the soil of its nutrients

    Ⓓ George Washington Carver is best known for his work with peanuts but he also taught his students about crop rotation that's when farmers plant different crops each year to avoid draining the soil of its nutrients

3. Which answer choice is a fragment, rather than a complete sentence?

    Ⓐ Be careful what you wish for.
    Ⓑ He should not run with scissors.
    Ⓒ If you can't say something nice.
    Ⓓ Don't say anything at all.

4. What would transform this fragment into a complete sentence?

Three ways to transfer heat.

 Ⓐ Replacing the period with a question mark at the end of the sentence
 Ⓑ Adding "convection, conduction, and radiation" to the end of the sentence.
 Ⓒ Adding "There are" to the beginning of the sentence.
 Ⓓ Nothing. The sentence is complete already.

5. Which sentence is a fragment, rather than a complete sentence?

(1)Producers make their own food from the sun during a process called photosynthesis. (2)The Greek root, "photo," means "light." (3)Means "to put together." (4)So "photosynthesis" means "to put together with light," which is exactly what plants do when they make their own food.

 Ⓐ Sentence 1
 Ⓑ Sentence 2
 Ⓒ Sentence 3
 Ⓓ Sentence 4

6. Choose the best edited version of the paragraph below. Pay attention to run-on sentences and fragments.

(1)Jawaad held his head high. (2)As he strode to the front of the classroom to present his research report. (3)The report compared the Norse god, Thor, to the Marvel Comic version of Thor. (4)He was proud of his work and thought the class would really enjoy it.

 Ⓐ Jawaad held his head high. As he strode to the front of the classroom to present his research report. The report compared the Norse god, Thor, to the Marvel Comic version of Thor. He was proud of the work and thought the class would really enjoy it.

 Ⓑ Jawaad held his head high. As he strode to the front of the classroom to present his research report, the report compared the Norse god, Thor, to the Marvel Comic version of Thor. He was proud of the work and thought the class would really enjoy it.

 Ⓒ Jawaad held his head high. As he strode to the front of the classroom to present his research report. The report compared the Norse god, Thor, to the Marvel Comic version of Thor he was proud of the work and thought the class would really enjoy it.

 Ⓓ Jawaad held his head high as he strode to the front of the classroom to present his research report. The report compared the Norse god, Thor, to the Marvel Comic version of Thor. He was proud of the work and thought the class would really enjoy it.

7. Choose the run-on sentence.

- (A) Felix has a mischievous spirit he is somehow quite well-behaved.
- (B) Margaret is the most beautiful dancer on the stage.
- (C) The sky was the limit for a bright, energetic, young prodigy like Ben.
- (D) None of the above

8. Identify the run-on sentence.

(1)If I could dine with any person, living or dead, I would choose Maya Angelou. (2)She endured hardships in her life but went on to become one of the most influential literary figures of the 20th century. (3)I would ask her what inspired her most.

- (A) Sentence 1
- (B) Sentence 2
- (C) Sentence 3
- (D) None of the above

9. What would transform the fragment into a complete sentence?

A really great pair of shoes.

- (A) A really great pair of shoes, two ironed shirts, and two pairs of dress pants.
- (B) A really great pair of shoes should be both stylish and comfortable.
- (C) Doesn't need a really great pair of shoes.
- (D) My friend's really great pair of shoes.

10. Choose the complete sentence.

- (A) While she is a very sweet puppy, I can't justify adopting her.
- (B) While she is a very sweet puppy.
- (C) Because my apartment is too small.
- (D) I can't justify adopting this puppy my apartment is too small.

Chapter 4

Lesson 8: Frequently Confused Words

You can scan the QR code given below or use the url to access additional EdSearch resources including videos and mobile apps related to *Frequently Confused Words.*

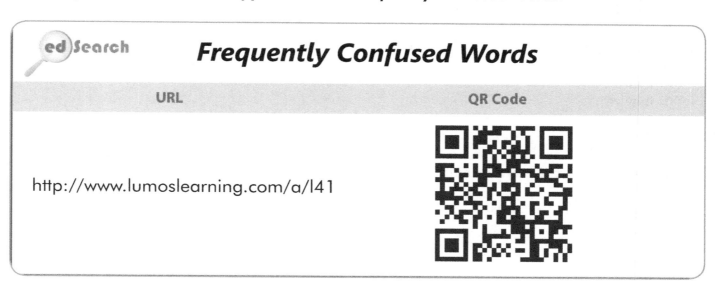

ed Search **Frequently Confused Words**

URL	QR Code
http://www.lumoslearning.com/a/l41	

1. Choose the correct word to complete the sentence.

Divya and her family celebrate Diwali, a traditional festival in _____ culture.

    Ⓐ their
    Ⓑ they're
    Ⓒ there
    Ⓓ the're

2. Choose the correct word to complete the sentence.

Place your projects over _____ until it's time to present.

    Ⓐ their
    Ⓑ they're
    Ⓒ there
    Ⓓ the're

3. Choose the correct word to complete the sentence.

Gretchen and Laura are thankful _____ able to peer edit each other's writing.

    Ⓐ their
    Ⓑ they're.
    Ⓒ there
    Ⓓ the're

4. Choose the best edited version of the sentence.

We're going too my grandmother's house for Thanksgiving, but we'll be driving back home on Friday.

    Ⓐ We're going two my grandmother's house for Thanksgiving, but we'll be driving back home on Friday.
    Ⓑ Were going too my grandmother's house for Thanksgiving, but we'll be driving back home on Friday.
    Ⓒ We're going to my grandmother's house for Thanksgiving, but we'll be driving back home on Friday.
    Ⓓ The sentence is correct already.

5. What error did the writer make?

I assumed the mall would be crowded today. Were are all the people?

    Ⓐ She wrote a run-on sentence.
    Ⓑ She spelled "assumed" incorrectly.
    Ⓒ She used "were" instead of "where."
    Ⓓ She wrote a fragment.

6. Which word best completes the sentence?

We don't have any milk or bread, so _____ going to the grocery store right this instant.

    Ⓐ were
    Ⓑ we're
    Ⓒ where
    Ⓓ there

7. What error did the writer make?

I can't take another breathe until I know how this book will end.

    Ⓐ She should have used the word, "breath," rather than "breathe."
    Ⓑ She should never hold her breath because she could faint.
    Ⓒ She should have used "took," rather than "take."
    Ⓓ She should have used "an other" instead of "another."

8. Choose the correct word to complete the sentence.

Amal _____ his exam with flying colors. He knew it was because he studied so hard.

    Ⓐ pessed
    Ⓑ pest
    Ⓒ past
    Ⓓ passed

9. Choose the correct word to complete the sentence.

I have to _____ that science does not come easily for me. If I want to do well I will have to work at it.

- Ⓐ except
- Ⓑ accept
- Ⓒ expect
- Ⓓ exccept

10. Choose the correct sentence.

- Ⓐ We base our school rules around the common principal that everyone should be treated with respect.
- Ⓑ The principal called Evelyn to her office to reward her for perfect attendance.
- Ⓒ Jamar was extatic when he was chosen as a principle dancer in the ballet.
- Ⓓ Kelsey became the most principaled person at the school.

Chapter 4

Lesson 9: How is it Capitalized?

You can scan the QR code given below or use the url to access additional EdSearch resources including videos and mobile apps related to *How is it Capitalized?*

ed Search

How is it Capitalized?

URL	QR Code
http://www.lumoslearning.com/a/l42	

1. Identify the words that need to be capitalized in the below sentence.

Although spring and summer are my favorite seasons, our family gathering on thanksgiving makes november my favorite month.

- Ⓐ Spring, November
- Ⓑ Thanksgiving, November
- Ⓒ Summer, Thanksgiving
- Ⓓ Seasons, November

2.1. Correctly capitalize the underlined portion of the below address.

<u>dr. j. howard smith</u>
1141 east palm street
washington, la 98654

- Ⓐ Dr. J. Howard Smith
- Ⓑ DR. J. Howard Smith
- Ⓒ Dr. J. howard smith
- Ⓓ Dr. j. Howard Smith

2.2. Correctly capitalize the underlined portion of the below address.

dr. j. howard smith
<u>1141 east palm street</u>
washington, la 98654

- Ⓐ 1141 east Palm Street
- Ⓑ 1141 East palm Street
- Ⓒ 1141 east palm Street
- Ⓓ 1141 East Palm Street

3. Correctly capitalize the underlined portion of the below address.

dr. j. howard smith
1141 east palm street
<u>washington, la 98654</u>

- Ⓐ Washington, LA 98654
- Ⓑ Washington, La 98654
- Ⓒ washington, LA 98654
- Ⓓ washington, La 98654

4. Edit the below sentence for capitalization. Choose the sentence that is written correctly.

Next Semester, I plan to take English, History, Math, Spanish, and Music.

Ⓐ Next Semester, I plan to take English, History, Spanish, math and music.
Ⓑ Next semester, I plan to take English, History, Spanish, Math and Music.
Ⓒ Next semester, I plan to take english, history, spanish, Math and music.
Ⓓ Next semester, I plan to take English, history, Spanish, math and music.

5. Choose the title of the book that has correct capitalization.

In Mrs. Hart's English class, we are reading <u>the indian in the cupboard</u>.

Ⓐ <u>The Indian In The Cupboard</u>
Ⓑ <u>The Indian in the Cupboard</u>
Ⓒ <u>The indian in the Cupboard</u>
Ⓓ <u>the Indian in the Cupboard</u>

6. Choose the correctly capitalized version of the below sentence.

The entire family is excited and looking forward to our visit with aunt jenny, my uncle, my grandfather, and grandma.

Ⓐ The entire Family is excited and looking forward to our visit with Aunt jenny, my uncle, my grandfather, and Grandma.
Ⓑ The entire family is excited and looking forward to our visit with Aunt jenny, my uncle, my Grandfather, and Grandma.
Ⓒ The entire family is excited and looking forward to our visit with Aunt Jenny, my uncle, my grandfather, and Grandma.
Ⓓ The entire family is excited and looking forward to our visit with aunt Jenny, my Uncle, my Grandfather, and Grandma.

7. Choose correctly capitalized version of the below letter closing.

yours truly,
timmy newlin

    Ⓐ Yours Truly,
         Timmy Newlin

    Ⓑ yours truly,
         Timmy Newlin

    Ⓒ Yours truly,
         Timmy Newlin

    Ⓓ Yours truly,
         Timmy newlin

8. Which words should be capitalized?

the chicago river runs into the mississippi valley waterways.

    Ⓐ The, Chicago
    Ⓑ The, Chicago River
    Ⓒ The, Chicago River, Mississippi
    Ⓓ The, Chicago River, Mississippi Valley

9. Which word in the below sentence should be capitalized?

I love these lime green nike shoes that my grandma got me for my birthday.

    Ⓐ Grandma
    Ⓑ Birthday
    Ⓒ Nike
    Ⓓ Shoes

10. Which word in the sentence below should be capitalized? Circle the correct answer choice.

One of my favorite authors, Ernest hemingway, wrote some amazing books and short stories.

 Ⓐ authors
 Ⓑ hemingway
 Ⓒ favorite
 Ⓓ The sentence is correct.

11. Which word in the sentence below should be capitalized? Circle the correct answer choice.

Beau is having his birthday party at the Stone County City pool.

 Ⓐ Birthday
 Ⓑ Party
 Ⓒ Pool
 Ⓓ The sentence is correct.

Chapter 4

Lesson 10: What's the Punctuation?

You can scan the QR code given below or use the url to access additional EdSearch resources including videos and mobile apps related to *What's the Punctuation?*

 ed)Search

What's the Punctuation?

URL	QR Code
http://www.lumoslearning.com/a/l42	

1. Choose the sentence that is punctuated correctly. Circle the correct answer choice.

Ⓐ Before I go to bed each night I brush my teeth.
Ⓑ The rabbit scampered across the yard, and ran into the woods.
Ⓒ I don't like to watch scary movies but I like to read scary books.
Ⓓ Our teacher gave us time to study before she gave us the test.

2. Choose the sentence that correctly punctuates a quotation. Circle the correct answer choice.

Ⓐ "Did you remember to lock the door," asked Jenny?
Ⓑ "Did you remember to lock the door? asked Jenny."
Ⓒ Jenny asked "Did you remember to lock the door?"
Ⓓ Jenny asked, "Did you remember to lock the door?"

3. Choose the sentence that contains a punctuation error.

Ⓐ Cindy wants to go to the mall this afternoon, but her mother will not let her.
Ⓑ Wendy stayed up all night completing her science project, but forgot to take it with her.
Ⓒ Henry forgot to close the gate securely, so his dog escaped from the backyard.
Ⓓ Jimmy and John joined the Army; Billy and George joined the Navy.

4. What is the correct way to write the sentence below?

Do you know Shel Silverstein's poem The Boa Constrictor our teacher asked.

Ⓐ "Do you know Shel Silverstein's poem 'The Boa Constrictor'?" our teacher asked.
Ⓑ "Do you know Shel Silverstein's poem "The Boa Constrictor"? our teacher asked.
Ⓒ "Do you know Shel Silverstein's poem The Boa Constrictor"? our teacher asked.
Ⓓ "Do you know Shel Silverstein's poem The Boa Constrictor" she asked?

5. What is the correct way to write the sentence below?

Of all the poems in his latest book she said this is my favorite. It's really very funny she added.

Ⓐ "Of all the poems in his latest book" she said "this is my favorite." "It's really very funny she added."
Ⓑ "Of all the poems in his latest book," she said, "this is my favorite. It's really very funny," she added.
Ⓒ "Of all the poems in his latest book she said this is my favorite. It's really very funny she added."
Ⓓ "Of all the poems in his latest book," she said "this is my favorite. "It's really very funny" she added.

6. What is the correct way to write the sentence below?

Tom's English professor asked him what was wrong.

Ⓐ The sentence is correct.
Ⓑ Tom's English professor asked him "what was wrong?"
Ⓒ "Tom's English professor asked him what was wrong."
Ⓓ Tom's English professor, asked him, what was wrong.

7. Choose the sentence that correctly punctuates the above sentence.

Coco Chanel my best friends dog loves to play chase with me when I visit.

Ⓐ Coco Chanel, my best friends dog, loves to play chase with me when I visit
Ⓑ Coco Chanel, my best friend's dog, loves to play chase with me, when I visit.
Ⓒ Coco Chanel, my best friend's dog, loves to play chase with me when I visit.
Ⓓ Coco Chanel, my best friend's dog loves to play chase, with me when I visit.

8. Which sentence below is written correctly?

We are having broccoli and beets roast chicken and ice cream for dinner.

Ⓐ We are having broccoli, and beets, roast chicken, and ice cream for dinner.
Ⓑ We are having broccoli and beets, roast chicken, and ice cream for dinner.
Ⓒ We are having broccoli, and beets, roast, chicken, and ice cream for dinner.
Ⓓ We are having broccoli and beets, roast chicken and ice cream for dinner.

9. Which sentence below is written correctly?

A famous basketball player Kobe Bryant won many MVP awards.

Ⓐ A famous basketball player Kobe Bryant won many MVP awards.
Ⓑ A famous basketball player, Kobe Bryant won many MVP awards.
Ⓒ A famous basketball player, Kobe Bryant, won many MVP awards.
Ⓓ A, famous basketball player, Kobe Bryant, won many MVP awards.

10. Which sentence below has the correct end punctuation?

Ⓐ Their cat is black!
Ⓑ Help, a clown is chasing me!
Ⓒ Are you sure that goes there!
Ⓓ I wish I knew what time it was!

Chapter 4

Lesson 11: Conjunctions and Interjections

You can scan the QR code given below or use the url to access additional EdSearch resources including videos and mobile apps related to *Conjunctions and Interjections*

ed Search

Conjunctions and Interjections

URL	QR Code
http://www.lumoslearning.com/a/l42	

(1) Mary went to visit her grandmother last weekend. (2) She likes to visit her grandmother frequently. (3) While visiting, they enjoy walking. (4) They strolled in the beautiful park and talked. (5) Mary and her grandmother enjoyed their visit.

1. Which sentences contain a conjunction?

A. sentences 1 and 2
B. sentences 2 and 3
C. sentences 3 and 4
D. sentences 4 and 5

2. Identify the conjunction in the below sentence.

Billy does not like to play basketball, nor does he enjoy watching it on TV.

A. not
B. nor
C. does
D. to

3. Identify the subordinating conjunction in the below sentence.

As soon as I finish my homework, I am going to watch my favorite TV show.

A. soon
B. as soon as
C. to
D. to watch

4.1. Identify the <u>coordinating conjunction</u> in the below sentence.

Zelda and her family visited the Jackson Zoo last weekend although it was cold and rainy.

A. last
B. although
C. and
D. cold

4.2. Identify the <u>subordinating conjunction</u> in the above sentence.

Zelda and her family visited the Jackson Zoo last weekend although it was cold and rainy.

A. last
B. although
C. and
D. cold

5. Choose the compound sentence that uses the proper coordinating conjunction.

  Ⓐ My favorite food is pizza, or Jenny's favorite food is tacos.
  Ⓑ The junior high baseball game was exciting, nor the varsity game was even better.
  Ⓒ I forgot to do my math homework, but I am being sent to detention.
  Ⓓ I love horseback riding, so I am looking forward to the trail ride this weekend.

6.1. Identify the <u>interjection</u> in the below sentence.

No, you cannot go to the mall with your friends this weekend because we are going to visit Grandma and Grandpa.

  Ⓐ no
  Ⓑ to
  Ⓒ because
  Ⓓ and

6.2. Identify the <u>coordinating conjunction</u> in the below sentence.

No, you cannot go to the mall with your friends this weekend because we are going to visit Grandma and Grandpa.

  Ⓐ no
  Ⓑ to
  Ⓒ because
  Ⓓ and

7. Identify the subordinating conjunction in the below sentence.

No, you cannot go to the mall with your friends this weekend because we are going to visit Grandma and Grandpa.

  Ⓐ no
  Ⓑ to
  Ⓒ because
  Ⓓ and

8. Identify the interjection in the below sentence.

Wow! That was the most amazing trick I have ever seen.

  Ⓐ most
  Ⓑ amazing
  Ⓒ that
  Ⓓ wow

9. Go put on either your shoes and your boots.

Fix the sentence by replacing and with an appropriate conjunction.

Chapter 4

Lesson 12: How is it Spelled?

You can scan the QR code given below or use the url to access additional EdSearch resources including videos and mobile apps related to *How is it Spelled?*

ed Search	How is it Spelled?	
	URL	**QR Code**
	http://www.lumoslearning.com/a/l42	

1. Choose the correctly spelled word that best completes the sentence.

Vargas asked his partner, "Could you please _____ your question to make it easier to understand?"

- Ⓐ clearify
- Ⓑ Clerify
- Ⓒ carefully
- Ⓓ clarify

2. Find the misspelled word.

- Ⓐ ostrich
- Ⓑ vehicel
- Ⓒ wings
- Ⓓ horse

3. Which of the following words are spelled correctly?

- Ⓐ pollution
- Ⓑ polution
- Ⓒ plloution
- Ⓓ polltion

4. Choose the word that is incorrectly spelled in the below sentence.

Mom asked the mayor, "Do you beleive in ghosts?"

- Ⓐ asked
- Ⓑ mayor
- Ⓒ beleive
- Ⓓ ghosts

5. Choose the word that is correctly spelled.

- Ⓐ monkies
- Ⓑ strawberrys
- Ⓒ cherrys
- Ⓓ donkeys

6. Choose that word that is incorrectly spelled in the below sentence.

Nicky set the table for dinner, but she forgot to place knifes at each place setting.

- Ⓐ dinner
- Ⓑ knifes
- Ⓒ setting
- Ⓓ table

7. Choose the word that is NOT spelled correctly.

- Ⓐ collaterol
- Ⓑ enthusiasm
- Ⓒ infrequently
- Ⓓ vigorous

8. Choose the sentence with the misspelled word.

- Ⓐ Rosemary skipped across the room to give her grandfather a hug.
- Ⓑ I bought a beautiful new aquarium for my goldfish while at the flea market.
- Ⓒ After tripping in the cafeteria and spilling her tray, Mary ran from the room crying.
- Ⓓ When I opened the box, I realized that the attachment I wanted was sold seperately and not included in the package.

9. Choose the sentence that contains a misspelled word.

- Ⓐ Our class just completed a study on the lifecycle of butterflies.
- Ⓑ The delivery man stacked the packages and boxxes in his truck.
- Ⓒ The turtle jumped from its log, creating quite a splash.
- Ⓓ When firefighters were able to contain the flames, the crowd cheered.

10. Which word below is spelled correctly?

- Ⓐ nerrate
- Ⓑ nihrayt
- Ⓒ narrete
- Ⓓ narrate

11. Unscramble the word IWLD

12. Unscramble the word FWEOLR

13. r ___ m ____ ____ n

Fill in the missing vowels to make a proper word.

Ⓐ romoin
Ⓑ rimain
Ⓒ remain
Ⓓ ramian

14. ____ v ____ n ____ ____

Fill in the missing vowels to make a proper word.

Ⓐ ivinae
Ⓑ avinie
Ⓒ avenue
Ⓓ evenie

Chapter 4

Lesson 13: Word Choice: Attending to Precision

You can scan the QR code given below or use the url to access additional EdSearch resources including videos and mobile apps related to *Word Choice: Attending to Precision*.

URL	QR Code
http://www.lumoslearning.com/a/l43	

1. Choose the word that best completes the sentence.

Alexander _____ into the living room to show off his new suit. He had a very high opinion of himself!

- Ⓐ walked
- Ⓑ strutted
- Ⓒ trudged
- Ⓓ waddled

2. Choose the word that best completes the sentence.

Collecting the garbage was _____ work, but Tom was happy to do it. The job wore on his body, especially during the hottest days of summer, but he knew he was providing an important public service to his community.

- Ⓐ uncomfortable
- Ⓑ grueling
- Ⓒ bad
- Ⓓ stupid

3. Choose the word that best completes sentence.

Dante was _____ about his award for most improved swimmer. He had never wanted anything more!

- Ⓐ peaceful
- Ⓑ happy
- Ⓒ elated
- Ⓓ disappointed

4. Choose the word that best completes the sentence.

The baby babbled sweetly, making it difficult for her mother to be upset about the _____ mess she had made when she threw spaghetti all over the kitchen.

- Ⓐ gigantic
- Ⓑ big
- Ⓒ wide
- Ⓓ deep

5. Choose the word that best completes the sentence.

The defendant's fingerprint at the scene of the crime was the most _____ evidence in the trial. The jury had no choice but to convict her.

- (A) worst
- (B) damaging
- (C) bad
- (D) wonderful

6. Choose the word that best completes the sentence.

Shelby was a _____. She was fiesty, and she did not let anyone push her around.

- (A) ham
- (B) scrooge
- (C) shrinking violet
- (D) fireball

7. Choose the word that best completes the sentence.

The girls _____ to the front of the crowd to get a glimpse of their favorite boy band.

- (A) walked
- (B) skipped
- (C) dove
- (D) clambered

8. Anne is paying attention to choosing precise words in her writing. Which sentence should she use in her personal narrative to describe the overflowing bathtub?

- (A) The water <u>dripping</u> over the edge reminded her of a waterfall.
- (B) The water <u>spraying</u> over the edge reminded her of a waterfall.
- (C) The water <u>bubbling</u> over the edge reminded her of a waterfall.
- (D) The water <u>cascading</u> over the edge reminded her of a waterfall.

9. Riley is paying attention to choosing precise words in his writing. Which sentence should he use to help persuade the reader to recycle?

Ⓐ Recycling <u>cuts down on</u> the amount of waste that goes into landfills each year.
Ⓑ Recycling <u>helps us put a little bit less</u> waste into landfills each year.
Ⓒ Recycling <u>reduces</u> the amount of waste that goes into landfills each year.
Ⓓ Recycling <u>makes us put not as much</u> waste into landfills each year.

10. Choose the word that best completes the sentence.

Janet _____ with delight when she called her mother to say she had been accepted to her top choice college.

Ⓐ squealed
Ⓑ spoke
Ⓒ sneezed
Ⓓ growled

Chapter 4

Lesson 14: Punctuating for Effect!

You can scan the QR code given below or use the url to access additional EdSearch resources including videos and mobile apps related to *Punctuating for Effect!*

ed Search

Punctuating for Effect!

URL	QR Code
http://www.lumoslearning.com/a/l43	

1. Choose the punctuation that means Jermain's mother is speaking to him.

Jermaine mother said you have to clean your room.

- (A) Jermaine mother said you have to clean your room.
- (B) "Jermaine, Mother said you have to clean your room."
- (C) Jermaine Mother said, "You have to clean your room."
- (D) "Jermaine," Mother said, "you have to clean your room."

2. Choose the punctuation that means a third character is shouting at Jermaine to tell him his mother said to clean his room.

Jermaine mother said you have to clean your room.

- (A) "Jermaine," Mother said, "you have to clean your room!"
- (B) "Jermaine, Mother said you have to clean your room!"
- (C) "Jermaine," Mother said, "you have to clean your room?"
- (D) "Jermaine, Mother said you have to clean your room."

3. Choose the most appropriate end punctuation.

Dante was elated about his award for most improved swimmer. He had never wanted anything more

- (A) .
- (B) ?
- (C) !
- (D) $

4. Choose the sentence that is punctuated correctly.

- (A) The tiger crept carefully through the jungle?
- (B) The tiger crept carefully through the jungle!
- (C) The tiger crept carefully through the jungle
- (D) The tiger crept carefully through the jungle.

5. Choose the appropriate end punctuation for sentence 1.

James was furious when Gemma squirted ketchup all over his new white shirt(1) Sheesh (2) What did Gemma expect to happen (3)

- (A) .
- (B) !
- (C) ?
- (D) *

6. Choose the appropriate end punctuation for sentence 2.

James was furious when Gemma squirted ketchup all over his new white shirt(1) Sheesh (2) What did Gemma expect to happen (3)

Ⓐ .
Ⓑ !
Ⓒ ?
Ⓓ *

7. Choose the appropriate end punctuation for sentence 3.

James was furious when Gemma squirted ketchup all over his new white shirt(1) Sheesh (2) What did Gemma expect to happen (3)

Ⓐ .
Ⓑ !
Ⓒ ?
Ⓓ *

8. Which punctuation best follows "Wow"?

Wow( ) I can't believe I am going to compete in the national chess competition for my age group!

Ⓐ .
Ⓑ !
Ⓒ ?
Ⓓ &

9. Which of the following sentences is NOT punctuated correctly?

Ⓐ Gee whiz!
Ⓑ I can't believe my good fortune!
Ⓒ Why does water evaporate faster when the sun is out!
Ⓓ Clean your room this instant!

10. Which of the following sentences is punctuated correctly?

Ⓐ She startled me when she jumped out of the bushes!
Ⓑ I'm so hungry I'm afraid I won't make it to lunch?
Ⓒ Our teacher is an amazing #storyteller
Ⓓ This is my favorite time of year, "Jenny said."

Chapter 4

Lesson 15: Finding the Meaning

You can scan the QR code given below or use the url to access additional EdSearch resources including videos and mobile apps related to *Finding the Meaning*.

ed Search	**Finding the Meaning**	
URL		QR Code
http://www.lumoslearning.com/a/l43		

1. What does the word _extracted_ mean in the below sentence?

The milk is extracted from the coconut, which is used to prepare a variety of dishes and sweets.

- (A) To put in
- (B) To take out of something
- (C) To make
- (D) To throw out

2. Using context clues from the below sentence, the word _despondent_ means: Circle the correct answer choice.

The poor woman was despondent after losing everything she owned in the fire.

- (A) excited
- (B) questioning
- (C) disheartened
- (D) radiant

3. Based on the below sentence, console means: Circle the correct answer choice.

My father tried to console me after my dog died, but nothing he did made me feel better.

- (A) entertain
- (B) comfort
- (C) talk to
- (D) explain

4. The sleepy kittens crawled into bed with their mother. They quickly nestled cozily beside her and went to sleep.

The word _nestled_ means:

- (A) purred softly
- (B) lay down
- (C) leaned against
- (D) snuggled up to

5. Based on the below sentence, the best meaning for the word _gawked_ is:

Larry gawked in wide-eyed astonishment at the woman wearing the glass hat with fish swimming in it.

Ⓐ glanced at
Ⓑ stared intensely
Ⓒ laughed at
Ⓓ yelled at

6. The word _cease_ means:

If the talking does not cease immediately, you will have 50 additional math problems for homework.

Ⓐ become less noisy
Ⓑ continue
Ⓒ decrease
Ⓓ stop

7. The word _weary_ means:

The young men rode their bikes 60 miles to the fair. They did not stop for a break the entire trip. Once they arrived, they were too weary to walk around and enjoy the rides, so they simply lounged on the bleachers and watched the quilt judging contest.

Ⓐ excited
Ⓑ tired
Ⓒ energized
Ⓓ enthusiastic

8. The word _lounged_ means:

The young men rode their bikes 60 miles to the fair. They did not stop for a break the entire trip. Once they arrived, they were too weary to walk around and enjoy the ride, so they simply lounged on the bleachers and watched the quilt judging contest.

Ⓐ watched
Ⓑ sat rigidly
Ⓒ stood
Ⓓ relaxed

9. **Based on the context clues in the below sentence, the best meaning of the word** _plummeted_ **is:**

At the football game Friday night, Bill broke his leg when he plummeted to the ground from the top of the bleachers.

    Ⓐ floated
    Ⓑ drifted
    Ⓒ slipped
    Ⓓ plunged

10. **According to the sentence below, the word** _frigid_ **means:**

The weather man is predicting several days of frigid temperatures in the mountains. After watching the weather report, I decided to pack thermal shirts and pants, wool sweaters, gloves, and my warmest coat for the camping trip this weekend.

    Ⓐ rising
    Ⓑ freezing
    Ⓒ warm
    Ⓓ chilly

Chapter 4

Lesson 16: Same Word Different Meanings

You can scan the QR code given below or use the url to access additional EdSearch resources including videos and mobile apps related to *Same Word Different Meanings*.

 Search

Same Word Different Meanings

URL	QR Code
http://www.lumoslearning.com/a/l44	

1. **Choose the correct meaning for the word 'ornaments' in the following sentence. The shells are also made into cups and ornaments.**

   Ⓐ a statue
   Ⓑ cap
   Ⓒ books
   Ⓓ jewelry worn by women

Question 2 is based on the poem below.

> I found a shell, a curly one;
> Lying on the sand.
> I picked it up and took it home,
> Held tightly in my hand.
>
> Mommy looked at it and then,
> She held it to my ear,
> And from the shell there came a song
> Soft and sweet and clear.
>
> I was surprised, I listened hard,
> And it was really true:
> If you can find a nice big shell,
> You'll hear the singing too.
>
> --- Unknown

2. **In the poem find the word that means 'hard outer covering'.**

   Ⓐ song
   Ⓑ sweet
   Ⓒ shell
   Ⓓ soft

(1) Jim was given the Most Valuable Player award at the banquet last night. (2) Everyone agreed that he was the best batter on the team this year. (3) Because he won the award, Mindy wanted to give him a surprise party. (4) She invited all of his friends and even baked him a cake. (5) In the end, the surprise was on Mindy because she had put salt in the batter instead of sugar.

3. **The meaning of the word 'batter' in sentence 2 is:**

   Ⓐ a mixture for baking
   Ⓑ to damage
   Ⓒ user of a baseball bat
   Ⓓ to hit repeatedly

4. The meaning of the word *'batter'* in sentence 5 is:

- Ⓐ a mixture for baking
- Ⓑ to damage
- Ⓒ user of a baseball bat
- Ⓓ to hit repeatedly

Question 5-7 are based on the details below.

(1) Kelly and her sister picked strawberries today. (2) When they arrived home, they decided to make strawberry jam. (3) They had picked so many strawberries that they wouldn't all fit in the pot they had chosen. (4) Kelly got a large spoon and began to jam the strawberries into the pot. (5) Once they were cooked, she then put them into the blender. (6) Her mother warned her not to put too much into the blender because it would cause it to jam. (7) To prevent this from happening, Kelly blended the berries in small batches. (8) Once the berries were blended, they realized how late it was. (9) They asked their mother if she would finish for them so that they could go to the jam session their favorite band was having. (10) She agreed, and they happily left to join their friends.

5. Choose the meaning of the word *'jam'* in sentence 2.

- Ⓐ to pack tightly
- Ⓑ a fruit spread like jelly
- Ⓒ become stuck
- Ⓓ an informal gathering of musicians

6. Choose the meaning of the word *'jam'* in sentence 4.

- Ⓐ to pack tightly
- Ⓑ a fruit spread like jelly
- Ⓒ become stuck
- Ⓓ an informal gathering of musicians

7. Choose the meaning of the word *'jam'* in sentence 6.

- Ⓐ to pack tightly
- Ⓑ a fruit spread like jelly
- Ⓒ become stuck
- Ⓓ an informal gathering of musicians

8. (1) I cannot stand to waste my time waiting in line. (2) It hurts my back to stand for so long.
   In sentence 1, the word stand means:

   Ⓐ tolerate or endure
   Ⓑ to undergo
   Ⓒ a small rack or table
   Ⓓ to maintain an upright position on your feet

9. (1) I cannot stand to waste my time waiting in line. (2) It hurts my back to stand for so long.
   In sentence 2, the word stand means:

   Ⓐ tolerate or endure
   Ⓑ to undergo
   Ⓒ a small rack or table
   Ⓓ to maintain an upright position on your feet

10. **The Cub Scout was taught to create a loop as part of the knot-making process.**

    Choose the sentence that uses the word loop in the same way. Circle the correct answer choice.

    Ⓐ Tory was taught to create a <u>loop</u> in order to tie her shoes.
    Ⓑ On my website, I created a segment <u>loop</u>.
    Ⓒ The producer created a <u>loop</u> to be broadcast during the newsreel.

11. **My mother went to the bank to deposit her pay check.**

    Choose the sentence that uses the word bank in the same way. Circle the correct answer choice.

    Ⓐ My dad drove to the bank and withdrew some cash.
    Ⓑ We went fishing at the bank of the river.
    Ⓒ I can bank my passing grades and retake the tests I didn't pass.
    Ⓓ I am always right, and you can bank on that!

Chapter 4

Lesson 17: Context Clues

You can scan the QR code given below or use the url to access additional EdSearch resources including videos and mobile apps related to *Context Clues*.

ed Search	**Context Clues**	
URL		**QR Code**
http://www.lumoslearning.com/a/l44		

1. What is the meaning of the word, "sentiment" in the paragraph below?

Franklin D. Roosevelt gave his first inaugural address in 1933, during the midst of the Great Depression. He famously said, "The only thing we have to fear is… fear itself." His <u>sentiment</u> helped assuage the fears of many Americans, giving them hope for better days ahead.

- Ⓐ a person who often cries
- Ⓑ a view or attitude toward a situation or event
- Ⓒ a nice piece of jewelry
- Ⓓ blame

2. What is the meaning of the word, "assuage" in the paragraph below?

Franklin D. Roosevelt gave his first inaugural address in 1933, during the midst of the Great Depression. He famously said, "The only thing we have to fear is… fear itself." This sentiment helped <u>assuage</u> the fears of many Americans, giving them hope for better days ahead.

- Ⓐ to make worse
- Ⓑ to ease
- Ⓒ to heighten
- Ⓓ to strengthen

3. What is the meaning of the word, "affluent" in the paragraph below?

The restaurant catered to an <u>affluent</u> crowd. The food was very expensive, the tablecloths were crisp and white, and patrons were expected to dress nicely.

- Ⓐ practical
- Ⓑ wealthy
- Ⓒ honest
- Ⓓ poor

4. What is the meaning of the word, "patrons" in the paragraph below?

The restaurant catered to an affluent crowd. The food was very expensive, the tablecloths were crisp and white, and <u>patrons</u> were expected to dress nicely in order to eat there.

- Ⓐ doctors
- Ⓑ waiters
- Ⓒ cooks
- Ⓓ customers

5. In the paragraph below, what is the meaning of the word, "miser"?

In Charles Dickens's classic tale, Ebenezer Scrooge is a <u>miser</u>-- someone who wishes to spend as little money as possible. As a result, his life is devoid of any meaningful relationships with other people. He does not have any true friends to speak of.

- Ⓐ someone who gives gifts often
- Ⓑ someone who wishes to spend as little money as possible
- Ⓒ someone who thinks of others before themselves
- Ⓓ someone who is very old

6. In the paragraph below, what is the meaning of the word, "devoid"?

In Charles Dickens's classic tale, Ebenezer Scrooge is a miser-- someone who wishes to spend as little money as possible. As a result, his life is <u>devoid</u> of any meaningful relationships with other people. He does not have any true friends to speak of.

- Ⓐ blooming
- Ⓑ decorated
- Ⓒ filled with
- Ⓓ entirely lacks

7. What is the meaning of the word, "corridor" in the paragraph below?

The hospital <u>corridor</u> was long and cold. Door after door opened into room after room of patients in various stages of rest and recovery. Hazel was earnest in her desire to bring some degree of joy to each of them. That's what clowns are for, after all!

- Ⓐ bed
- Ⓑ room
- Ⓒ desk
- Ⓓ hallway

8. What is the meaning of the word, "earnest" in the paragraph below?

The hospital corridor was long and cold. Door after door opened into room after room of patients in various stages of rest and recovery. Hazel was <u>earnest</u> in her desire to bring some degree of joy to each of them. That's what clowns are for, after all!

- Ⓐ willing
- Ⓑ excited
- Ⓒ negligent
- Ⓓ serious

9. In the paragraph below, what is the meaning of the word, "invest?"

Marcus decided to <u>invest</u> in Mel and Deena's lemonade stand. He gave them twenty dollars to buy fresh lemons, cups, and sugar. In return Mel and Deena will reimburse him with money they earn selling the lemonade plus ten percent of each cup they sell.

Ⓐ to really enjoy lemonade
Ⓑ to cheer someone one by clapping and shouting
Ⓒ to give someone money for fun
Ⓓ to give someone money with hopes of making money

10. In the paragraph below, what is the meaning of the word, "reimburse."

Marcus decided to invest in Mel and Deena's lemonade stand. He gave them twenty dollars to buy fresh lemons, cups, and sugar. In return Mel and Deena will <u>reimburse</u> him with money they earn selling the lemonade plus ten percent of each cup they sell.

Ⓐ repay
Ⓑ hit
Ⓒ shower
Ⓓ take

Lesson 18: The Meaning of Words

You can scan the QR code given below or use the url to access additional EdSearch resources including videos and mobile apps related to *The Meaning of Words*.

ed Search

The Meaning of Words

URL	QR Code
http://www.lumoslearning.com/a/l44	

1. Mindy was surprised to discover how disorganized the students had left the books. What is the meaning of the word <u>disorganized</u>?

   Ⓐ organized
   Ⓑ not organized
   Ⓒ neat
   Ⓓ torn

2. Which of the following words contains a prefix that means <u>again</u>?

   Ⓐ preview
   Ⓑ international
   Ⓒ rewind
   Ⓓ disagree

3. Which of the following words refers to half of the globe?

   Ⓐ longitude
   Ⓑ hemisphere
   Ⓒ parallel
   Ⓓ latitude

4. The prefix 'sub' in submarine means:

   Ⓐ back or again
   Ⓑ above or extra
   Ⓒ under or below
   Ⓓ across or over

5. The prefix 'hyper' in hyperactive means:

   Ⓐ within, into
   Ⓑ over or excessive
   Ⓒ lacking or without
   Ⓓ out of or former

6. If biology is the study of life, which answer choice explains the meaning of the word *geology*?

   Ⓐ appreciation for the earth
   Ⓑ a science class
   Ⓒ the study of the earth
   Ⓓ the study of life

7. Choose a word with the prefix below to replace the words _came back_.

Once upon a time, Jane and Jill were best friends. One day, Jane decided that she wanted to travel the world and asked Jill if she could borrow some money. When Jane came back from her vacation she went to see Jill immediately.

    Ⓐ unfair
    Ⓑ returned
    Ⓒ disappear
    Ⓓ replay

8. Choose a word with the prefix below to replace the words _pay back_.

Jill wanted Jane to pay back the money.

    Ⓐ repay
    Ⓑ unpay
    Ⓒ redo
    Ⓓ undo

9. Choose a word below that is appropriate for the sentence.

The frog _____ grabbed the insect.

    Ⓐ quick
    Ⓑ quickful
    Ⓒ quickly
    Ⓓ quicker

10. The prefix 're' in returned means:

    Ⓐ under or below
    Ⓑ before
    Ⓒ back or again
    Ⓓ above or extra

11. What is the root word of understandable? Write your answer in the box below.

12. In the word 'bewailed', the prefix is _____.

Chapter 4

Lesson 19: For Your Reference

You can scan the QR code given below or use the url to access additional EdSearch resources including videos and mobile apps related to *For Your Reference.*

ed Search

For Your Reference

URL	QR Code
http://www.lumoslearning.com/a/l44	

1. Where would one look to find the definition of a key word when reading a science textbook?

  Ⓐ the glossary
  Ⓑ the thesaurus
  Ⓒ the dictionary
  Ⓓ the table of contents

2. What part of speech is the word, "component," in the thesaurus entry below?

Component. — n. component; component part, integral part, integrant part; element, constituent, ingredient, leaven; part and parcel; contents; appurtenance; feature

  Ⓐ adjective
  Ⓑ verb
  Ⓒ adverb
  Ⓓ noun

3. How many definitions of "silently" are there in the dictionary entry below?

> **Si.lently,** adv.   [f. SILENT a. + - LY ².]
> **(1)In a silent manner; without speaking, in Silence; without noise or commotion, noiselessly, Quietly; without mention or notice.**
> **1570-6** LAMBARDE *Peramb. Kent* (1826) 157, I could not silently slip over such impieties. 1590 SHAKS. *Mids*. N. III.
> i. 206 Type vp my louers tongue, bring him silently. 1617 MORYSON *Itin.* 1. 246 The Turkey company in London was at this time..silently enjoying the safety and profit of this trafficke.
> **(2)Gradually, imperceptibly. Obs.⁻¹**
> **1668** CULPEPPER & COLE *Barthol. Anat.* I. xiii. 30 It goes by little and little straight forward, and is silently terminated towards the spleen.

  Ⓐ 3
  Ⓑ 4
  Ⓒ 1
  Ⓓ 2

4. According to the thesaurus entry below, what is a synonym for the word, "veteran?"

Veteran.— n. veteran, old man, seer, patriarch, graybeard; grandfather, grandsire; grandam; gaffer, gammer; crone; pantaloon; sexagenarian, octogenarian, nonagenarian, centenarian; old stager.

- Ⓐ veterinarian
- Ⓑ graybeard
- Ⓒ young man
- Ⓓ None of the above

5. What is the definition of "skeletal?"

Skeletal (ske.l/tal), a. [f. SKELET-ON sb. + -AL.] Of or belonging to, forming of formed by, forming part of, or resembling, a skeleton.
Skeletal muscle, a muscle attached to and controlling a part of a skeleton.
1854 OWEN in *Orr's Cire. Sci., Org. Nat. I.* 168 The skeletal framework.. does not go beyond the fibrous stage.
1872 HUMPHRY *Myology* 8 The skeletal formations in the sternal region of the visceral wall.

- Ⓐ A bodily system made of muscle and bones, the most important system in the body.
- Ⓑ Made of bones
- Ⓒ The skeletal region of the visceral wall
- Ⓓ Of or belonging to, forming or formed by, forming part of, or resembling, a skeleton

6. Which of the following is NOT a synonym for "edge?"

Edge. — n. edge, verge, brink, brow, brim, margin, border, confine, skirt, rim, flange, side, mouth; jaws, chops, chaps, fauces; lip, muzzle. threshold, door, porch; portal &c. (opening) 260; coast, shore. frame, fringe, flounce, frill, list, trimming, edging, skirting, hem, selvedge, welt, furbelow, valance, gimp. adj. border, marginal, skirting; labial, labiated, marginated.

- Ⓐ brink
- Ⓑ flank
- Ⓒ verge
- Ⓓ rim

7. Where might one see a sitar?

> **Sitar** (si.tar). *Anglo-Ind*. Also sitarre. [Urdu سـتار sitar.] A form of guitar, properly
> having three strings, used in India.
> **1845** STOCQUELER *Hdbk. Brit*. India (1854) 26 A trio of sitars, or rude violins.
> **1859** J. LANG *Wand. India* 152 Two or three of the company..played alternately
> on the sitarre (native guitar or violin).
>
> **Si.tarch.** *rare-°*. [ad. Gr. oiTapxns or oiTapxos, f. oiTos corn, food.]
> **1656** BLOUNT *Glossogr.*, Sitark, he that hath the Office to provide Corn, and
> Victuals sufficient.
> **1676** COLICS, *Starck*, a Pourveyor.

Ⓐ a hospital
Ⓑ a construction site
Ⓒ an international music festival
Ⓓ at the doctor's office.

8. Which of the following is not a meaning of the word, "skyscape?"

> **Sky.scape. [f. SKY sb.¹ after *landscape*, *seascape*.]** A view of the sky ; also in
> painting, etc., a representation of part of the sky.
> **1817** SOUTHEY *Let.* in *Life* (1850) IV. 283 It was the unbroken horizon which
> impressed me,..and the skyscapes which it afforded.
> **1861** C.J. ANDERSON Okavango x. 137
> The beautiful and striking skyscapes and atmospheric coruscations attendant on
> these storms.
> **1878** GROSART
> *More's Poems* Introd. p. xii, The great ancient Painters, whose backgrounds of
> portraits..rather than land-scape, or sea-scape, or sky-scape proper, assure us
> [etc.]

Ⓐ escaping by way of the sky
Ⓑ a view of the sky
Ⓒ a representation of part of the sky in painting, etc.
Ⓓ B & C

9. Which of the following synonyms for "notch" is a verb?

Notch. — n. notch, dent, nick, cut; indent, indentation; dimple. embrasure, battlement, machicolation; saw, tooth, crenelle, scallop, scollop, vandyke; depression; jag. v. notch, nick, cut, dent, indent, jag, scarify, scotch, crimp, scallop, scollop, crenulate, vandyke. adj. notched &c. v.; crenate, crenated; dentate, dentated; denticulate, denticulated; toothed, palmated, serrated.

Ⓐ nick
Ⓑ embrasure
Ⓒ toothed
Ⓓ palmated

10. Which of the following is NOT a definition of the word, "slog?"

Slog (slog), v. colloq. [Of obscure origin. Cf. SLUG v.[4]]
1. *trans*. To hit or strike hard ; to drive with blows. Also *fig*., to assail violently.
1853 ' C.BEDE *Verdant Green* xi. 106 His whole person [had been] put in chancery, stung, bruised, fibbed,..slogged, and otherwise ill-treated.
1884 'R. BOLDREWOOD' *Melb.*
Memories iv. 32 We slogged the tired cattle round the fence.
1891 *Spectator* to Oct. 487/1 They love snubbing their friends and 'slogging' their enemies.
b. *Cricket*. To obtain (runs) by hard hitting.
1897 H. W. BLEAKLEY *Short innings* iii. 49 Mr. Dolly slogged sixes and fours until he had made about eighty.
2. *intr*. To walk heavily or doggedly.
1872 CALVERLEY *Fly Leaves* (1903) 119 Then abiit..off slogs boy. **1876** Mid-Yorks. *Gloss., Slog*, to walk with burdened feet, as through snow, or puddle. **1907** Westm.
Gaz. 2 Oct. 2/1 Overtaking the guns, we 'slogged' on with them for a mile or more.
3. To deal heavy blows, to work hard (at something), to labour away, etc.
1888 *Daily News* 22 May 5/2, I slogged at it, day in and day out.
1894 HESLOP *Northumberland Gloss.* s.v., They slogged away at the anchor shank.

Ⓐ to hit or strike hard
Ⓑ to walk heavily or doggedly
Ⓒ to deal heavy blows, to work hard
Ⓓ to jump high and score

Lesson 20: Similes and Metaphors

You can scan the QR code given below or use the url to access additional EdSearch resources including videos and mobile apps related to *Similes and Metaphors*.

ed Search	Similes and Metaphors	
URL		**QR Code**
http://www.lumoslearning.com/a/l45		

1. What does the metaphor in the first sentence mean?

The sky was an angry, purple monster. It roared fiercely as the thunder crashed and the rain poured down.

Ⓐ The sky had clouds in the shape of a monster.
Ⓑ The sky was stormy.
Ⓒ Monsters invaded the town.
Ⓓ None of the above

2. What purpose does the author's simile serve in the paragraph?

In the days after Dad was laid off almost everyone was gloomy. Sam didn't smile, <u>Mom hovered over everyone like a cloud full of rain</u>. It was Sasha who was the ray of sunshine when she declared, "It's alright. Hugs are free!"

Ⓐ It describes the setting after Dad was laid off.
Ⓑ It makes the point that mom was gloomy and likely to cry.
Ⓒ It shows that Sasha was a happy, upbeat presence in the house.
Ⓓ It reminds us that hugs are free.

3. By comparing Kevin to a brick wall, what is the speaker trying to say about Kevin?

The starting goalie was out with an injury, so Kevin was finally getting his chance to prove his worth. He knew he could do it. He was ready. Kevin was a brick wall.

Ⓐ He would not allow the opponent to score he'd block the goal posts.
Ⓑ He was hard-headed.
Ⓒ He built a wall in front of his soccer goal.
Ⓓ He threw bricks at his opponent.

4. What purpose does the author's metaphor serve in the paragraph?

In the days after Dad was laid off almost everyone was gloomy. Sam didn't smile, Mom hovered over everyone like a cloud full of rain. <u>It was Sasha who was the ray of sunshine when she declared, "It's alright. Hugs are free!"</u>

Ⓐ It describes the setting after Dad was laid off.
Ⓑ It makes the point that mom was gloomy and likely to cry.
Ⓒ It shows that Sasha was a happy, upbeat presence in the house.
Ⓓ It reminds us that hugs are free.

5. What does the simile in the below paragraph mean?

<u>Their family was like a patchwork quilt</u> of diversity. Each adopted child added something beautiful to the whole.

Ⓐ Like a patchwork quilt, the family was old and ragged. It was probably time to throw it out.
Ⓑ Their family had old-fashioned traditions, like a patchwork quilt from generations past.
Ⓒ Like a patchwork quilt, the children were adopted by parents who loved them very much.
Ⓓ Like a patchwork quilt that has bits of different fabric stitched together, the family had children of different ethnic origins living together as siblings. The overall effect was beautiful.

6. Why does the speaker compare ballerinas to swans?

The ballerinas were like swans gliding over the stage.

Ⓐ to show that they were white
Ⓑ to show that they squawked like birds
Ⓒ to show that they can swim
Ⓓ to show that they are graceful and elegant

7. Which similes below would be helpful in describing a terrified look on someone's face?

Ⓐ Her eyes drooped like wilted flowers, and her hands hung limp like wet spaghetti noodles.
Ⓑ Her eyes were as sharp as arrows, and her fists clenched tight like hammers waiting to strike.
Ⓒ Her eyes were soft like a morning dew, and her hands lay still as resting cherubs.
Ⓓ Her eyes were as big as sewer lids, and her hands trembled like tiny earthquakes.

8. Which metaphor below would be helpful in describing a presentation that went awry?

Ⓐ In that moment Alfonso was a lion tamer, and the crowd was a well-trained pride eating from the palm of his hand.
Ⓑ In that moment Alfonso was the conductor of a train that was steady on its rails and going full steam ahead.
Ⓒ In that moment Alfonso was a bright flame, and the people gathered like moths around him.
Ⓓ In that moment Alfonso was the captain of an ill-fated voyage, and he was going down with his ship.

9. **Which simile below would help describe a child's joy in being reunited with a mother returning from a military tour of duty in another country?**

Ⓐ   Hannah's face lit up like fireworks on the Fourth of July when she glimpsed her mother rounding the corner. It was really her!

Ⓑ   Hannah closed up like a locked bedroom door when she saw her mother for the first time.

Ⓒ   Hannah pounded her fist on the counter like it was a judge's ruinous gavel when she saw her mother rounding the corner.

Ⓓ   Hannah's eyes turned down, and her face turned red as a beet when she glimpsed her mother for the first time.

10. **Which metaphor below would be helpful in describing a huge crowd of people at a festival?**

Ⓐ   The people marched through the streets with purpose, like an army marching toward battle.

Ⓑ   The streets were a barren desert, and the music echoed off of empty storefronts.

Ⓒ   A sea of delighted people swept over the sidewalks and into the street as they passed from attraction to attraction.

Ⓓ   I was on an emotional roller coaster on the day of the festival.

Chapter 4

Lesson 21: Idiomatic Expressions and Proverbs

You can scan the QR code given below or use the url to access additional EdSearch resources including videos and mobile apps related to *Idiomatic Expressions and Proverbs*.

Search **Idiomatic Expressions and Proverbs**

URL	QR Code
http://www.lumoslearning.com/a/l45	

1. What is meant by the idiom _hit the ceiling_ in the below sentence?

If Wendy's dad found out that she took her cell phone to school, he would hit the ceiling.

Ⓐ Wendy's dad will jump high.
Ⓑ Wendy's dad will be very angry.
Ⓒ Wendy's dad will laugh loudly.
Ⓓ Wendy's dad will congratulate her.

2. What is meant by the idiom swallow your pride?

I think that you need to swallow your pride and apologize to your teacher for talking in class.

Ⓐ to swallow hard
Ⓑ to deny doing something
Ⓒ to forget about being embarrassed
Ⓓ to pretend you are sorry

3. What does the idiom 'walking on air' mean?

Mindy was walking on air after she went backstage and met Adam Levine.

Ⓐ Mindy was floating through the air.
Ⓑ Mindy was dreaming.
Ⓒ Mindy was in a state of bliss.
Ⓓ Mindy was disappointed.

4. What is the meaning of '_play it by ear_' in the below sentence?

I am not sure how long I will stay at the dance. I'm going to play it by ear.

Ⓐ Play a musical instrument without sheet music.
Ⓑ As you see how things go decide rather than making plans.
Ⓒ Listen for someone to tell you what to do.
Ⓓ Think carefully before making a decision.

5. What does the idiom 'like <u>a chicken with its head cut off</u>' mean?

After winning a million dollars, Kelly was running around like a chicken with its head cut off.

Ⓐ to act in a calm manner
Ⓑ to be bleeding profusely
Ⓒ to run around clucking and flapping your arms
Ⓓ to act in a frenzied manner

6. What does 'down in the dumps' mean in the sentence?

Jackie was not very happy. Not only did she lose her favorite necklace, but she also learned that her best friend was going to sleep-away camp for the whole summer while she had to go to summer school. Jackie really felt down in the dumps.

Ⓐ sad
Ⓑ bringing the garbage to the end of the driveway
Ⓒ excited
Ⓓ flabbergasted

7. What does a 'little white lie' mean in the sentence?

Amy's aunt spent months knitting a scarf for Amy. When Amy received the present and looked at it, she really didn't like the colors. She couldn't let her aunt know that she was disappointed after all of her aunt's hard work, so she told a little white lie instead.

Ⓐ huge made up story
Ⓑ truth
Ⓒ lie that is told to avoid hurting someone's feelings
Ⓓ the lie was painted white

8. What does 'cut corners' mean in the sentence?

The renovations the Johnsons were making on the house were getting too expensive. The Johnsons wanted the very best, but they didn't have enough money to pay for it. Their architect came to speak with them. "You have some great ideas, but we're going to need to cut corners. We may have to change some of the original plans to save money; otherwise we won't be able to finish the house."

Ⓐ cut the edges of the play's program
Ⓑ clip some coupons
Ⓒ use money wisely and try to save by spending only what is necessary
Ⓓ mow the lawn

9. What does the idiom 'Half a loaf is better than none' mean?

Ⓐ You can't judge a person's character by how he or she looks.
Ⓑ You usually do better than others if you get there ahead of others.
Ⓒ This means having something is better than not having anything at all.
Ⓓ Mind your own business and let others mind theirs.

10. What does the idiom 'Beauty is only skin deep' mean? Circle the correct answer choice.

   Ⓐ If something unfortunate happens, it usually won't happen again.
   Ⓑ Take care of a small problem before it becomes a big one.
   Ⓒ A picture can explain things better than words.
   Ⓓ You can't judge a person's character by how he or she looks.

11. Which sentence contains an idiom? Circle the correct answer choice.

   Ⓐ It's raining cats and dogs outside!
   Ⓑ It's thundering loudly outside.
   Ⓒ It rained 6 inches last week.
   Ⓓ Wear a raincoat and boots, because it's raining really hard outside.

Chapter 4

Lesson 22: Synonyms and Antonyms

You can scan the QR code given below or use the url to access additional EdSearch resources including videos and mobile apps related to *Synonyms and Antonyms.*

 Synonyms and Antonyms

URL	QR Code
http://www.lumoslearning.com/a/l45	

1. **Choose the correct set of synonyms for "small."**

   Ⓐ enormous, giant
   Ⓑ minute, gargantuan
   Ⓒ small, unseen
   Ⓓ miniature, minute

2. **Choose the correct set of *synonyms*.**

   Ⓐ unrealistic, believable
   Ⓑ noteworthy, important
   Ⓒ noteworthy, insignificant
   Ⓓ unfair, just

3. **Choose the correct set of *antonyms*.**

   Ⓐ radiant, dull
   Ⓑ rescue, save
   Ⓒ chortle, laugh
   Ⓓ sparkle, shine

4. **Choose the synonym for "happy."**

   Ⓐ miserable
   Ⓑ ecstatic
   Ⓒ subdued
   Ⓓ wretched

5. **Choose the correct set of antonyms for "pretty."**

   Ⓐ repulsive, unattractive
   Ⓑ lovely, handsome
   Ⓒ enticing, glamour
   Ⓓ appealing, grotesque

6. **What is a synonym for the word, "chaos?"**

   Ⓐ huge
   Ⓑ agree
   Ⓒ disorder
   Ⓓ famous

7. Find the correct set of synonyms below.

Ⓐ fat and aged
Ⓑ tend and thick
Ⓒ fat and thick
Ⓓ aged and tend

8. Find the correct set of antonyms below.

Ⓐ peculiar and general
Ⓑ peculiar and common
Ⓒ general and included
Ⓓ general and common

9. What would be a good antonym for the word, "recall?"

Ⓐ contend
Ⓑ assert
Ⓒ forget
Ⓓ urge

10. What is an antonym for the word, "active?"

Ⓐ lazy
Ⓑ energetic
Ⓒ healthy
Ⓓ running

11. Match the Synonyms for the following words

Rush.　　**Error.**　　**Present**

Mistake	
Hurry	
Gift	

12. Pick the Synonyms for the word Peek from the list below and write it in the box given below.

Stare, Glance, Ogle, glimpse, look, watch

Chapter 4

Lesson 23: Academic and Domain Specific 4th Grade Words

You can scan the QR code given below or use the url to access additional EdSearch resources including videos and mobile apps related to *Academic and Domain Specific 4th Grade Words.*

 Academic and Domain Specific 4th Grade Words

URL	QR Code
http://www.lumoslearning.com/a/l46	

1. Choose the word that best completes the sentence.

When Jeremy arrived home his mom _____ him about the dance until he could think of no more details to give her.

   Ⓐ yelled at
   Ⓑ quizzed
   Ⓒ praised
   Ⓓ waddled

2. Choose the word that best completes the sentence.

The woodlands of the Mid Atlantic region are filled with all sorts of interesting _____.

   Ⓐ movies
   Ⓑ wildlife
   Ⓒ colleges
   Ⓓ mortar

3. Choose the word that best completes sentence.

The _____ John Muir helped preserve our country's natural beauty by helping to establish Yosemite National Park.

   Ⓐ antagoinist
   Ⓑ pianist
   Ⓒ conservationist
   Ⓓ statistician

4. Choose the word that best completes the sentence.

Sarah was _____ at the news that the giant oak she had worked to protect was going to be removed in order to build a parking lot.

   Ⓐ crestfallen
   Ⓑ starstruck
   Ⓒ jovial
   Ⓓ greedy

5. Choose the word that best completes the sentence.

When an animal is _____ the government will sometimes place restrictions on hunting it.

Ⓐ rabid
Ⓑ threatening
Ⓒ special
Ⓓ endangered

6. Choose the word that best completes the sentence.

"Mommmmm, do I haaaaaave to?" Lester _____ as his mother sat across the table with her eyes trained on his Brussels sprouts.

Ⓐ said
Ⓑ called
Ⓒ shrieked
Ⓓ whined

7. Choose the word that best completes the sentence.

"Wha-wha-what was th-that?" Dera _____ as she climbed the creaky stairs in the old house.

Ⓐ commanded
Ⓑ announced
Ⓒ stammered
Ⓓ laughed

8. My _____ is that the celery's stalk turned blue because it absorbed the colored water in the vase.

Ⓐ idea
Ⓑ intuition
Ⓒ guess
Ⓓ hypothesis

9. Monica _____ Peter's reasoning by referring to an example in the text that did not support the idea he suggested.

Ⓐ agreed
Ⓑ dissed
Ⓒ critiqued
Ⓓ slammed

10. Choose the word that best completes the sentence.

When putting forth an idea about what a character is thinking, it is best to use _____ from the text.

    Ⓐ characters
    Ⓑ evidence
    Ⓒ chapters
    Ⓓ nonfiction

End of Language

Answer Key and Detailed Explanations

Chapter 4: Language

Lesson 1: Pronouns

Question No.	Answer	Detailed Explanations
1	B	'We' refers to Bobby and the author. While 'us' could also refer to both Bobby and the author, it is not the correct pronoun for this set of sentences.
2	C	His is a possessive pronoun referring to something belonging to the father.
3	A	'He' refers to Jamie which makes it the correct pronoun in this sentence.
4	C	'Their' is a possessive pronoun. It refers to the dogs' possession. Since there is more than one dog, a plural pronoun must be used.
5	D	'Her' is a possessive pronoun. It refers to the girl's possession so it is the correct pronoun to use.
6	C	'Their' is a possessive pronoun and 'their' refers to the dancers.
7	A	'Her' is a possessive pronoun. Because the sentence set refers to the sister's first dance, a possessive pronoun is the correct choice.
8	C	'They' is the subject of the sentence. Since the sentence has the word together, we know more than one person is involved.
9	D	'Her' is the correct choice. Although him' would also work in the sentence correctly, the second sentence refers to the teacher as a female, so 'her' is most correct.
10	B	'They' refers correctly to Alice and Jennifer. Although A and C also refer to more than one person, 'they' is most accurate.
11	D	Since the sentence contains the word together, we know that more than one person is involved.
12	A	To is a preposition. Me is the correct pronoun when used as the object of a preposition.

Lesson 2: Progressive Verb Tense

Question No.	Answer	Detailed Explanations
1	B	Efrain is the subject of the sentence. Since he will be traveling to Europe in the future, the future progressive tense is correct.
2	D	Darrel and I are the subjects of the sentence. Since there is a plural subject, 'will attend' is the correct verb.
3	A	Since Minnie, Jill, and Sandra are singing presently, use the present progressive tense.
4	C	This is something the girls are not planning to do now; use the present progressive tense.
5	B	Jenny is working now to earn money; so she is saving in the present progressive tense.
6	B	The cheerleading was ongoing in the past; so use the past progressive tense.
7	C	The trees are presently engaged in the ongoing action of waving in the wind. Our evidence for this is the verb *show* later in the sentence. Therefore, the present progressive must be used.
8	C	Change in the sentence is ongoing and is happening now, so we use the present progressive tense.
9	B	She was engaged in the ongoing act of sitting when the waiter approached, so we use the past progressive tense.
10	C	Kenji and Briana's parents will pick them up in the future, so future progressive tense is appropriate.

Lesson 3: What's the Verb?

Question No.	Answer	Detailed Explanations
1	D	The simple predicate is the verb. Picked is an action verb.
2	C	You is a singular subject, so hear is the correct verb for the sentence.
3	C	She is a singular subject, so is singing is the correct future tense verb to complete the sentence.
4	B	Hit and scored are both action verbs.
5	D	I is a singular subject, so am is the correct present tense verb to complete the sentence.
6	B	The simple predicate is the verb. Finished is the action verb in the sentence.
7	C	Present tense means it's happening right now.
8	A	Shows is the verb in the sentence.
9	D	You is a singular subject, so see is the correct present tense verb to complete the sentence.
10	A	Past tense means it has already happened. Swooped is the past tense verb.
11	A	Have is the helping verb, and disappeared is the main verb. Mysteriously is an adverb and is not included in the verb phrase.
12	C	The simple predicate is the verb. In this sentence, it is cleaned.

Lesson 4: Modal Auxiliary Verbs

Question No.	Answer	Detailed Explanations
1	D	"Will" in sentence 3 and "may" in sentence 4 are both modal auxiliary verbs. These modal auxiliaries are connected to ideas of doubt or probability of future events.
2	B	Modal auxiliaries can be used for each of these purposes; but in this case it is uncertain whether or not Oliver's fever will go away.
3	D	"Could" is the correct answer choice. It is being used to express a past possibility.
4	C	"Had" is the modal auxiliary verb. It is being used to affirm that Dana had no choice about leaving the party.
5	A	"Shouldn't" is the modal auxiliary verb. It is being used to give advice.
6	D	"Could" is the modal auxiliary verb. It is being used in this sentence to express possibility.
7	C	"Shall" is a form of "will" and is the modal auxiliary verb. It is being used to express a decision or promise the speaker has made.
8	D	"Would" is a better choice, because it is not certain that the speaker will ever interview Maya Angelou.
9	B	By asking if she "can" hand him the apple, Marvin is really asking if she is capable. He should use the auxiliary modal verb "will" instead if he wants her to actually do the action.
10	A	"Might" is used correctly in the first choice to express uncertainty about a future event. Choice B lacks a verb after "shall." Choice C should read, "She must remember…"

Lesson 5: Adjectives and Adverbs

Question No.	Answer	Detailed Explanations
1	C	Frequently is the adverb modifying 'visits'. It answers the question when.
2	B	Beautiful modifies park. It answers the question what kind.
3	D	Cold is an adjective in the sentence. It is modifying 'it'.
4	A	Fastest is the superlative adjective that modifies runner.
5	C	Most beautiful is the correct superlative adjective that modifies girl.
6	D	Colder is a comparative adjective.
7	D	Most horrific is the correct superlative adjective that completes the sentence.
8	B	Hungrily and stealthily are the adverbs that modify the verb walked and are in the correct order.
9 Part A	D	Excited is the adjective that modifies Lindsay, Laine, and John.
9 Part B	C	Two is the adjective that modifies nights.
10	B	Fastest is the superlative adjective that completes the sentence.

Lesson 6: Prepositional Phrases

Question No.	Answer	Detailed Explanations
1	B	"Into the pool" and "of cool water" are both prepositional phrases.
2	D	"Underneath" is the preposition. Journals is the object of the preposition.
3	C	"For school" and "without your lunchbox" are both prepositional phrases.
4	A	"On the rug" is the prepositional phrase.
5	D	"At the fair" is the prepositional phrase.
6	C	"Into the room" and "in his favorite chair" are both prepositional phrases.
7	D	"Across" is the preposition, and "yard" is the object of the preposition.
8	B	"From the kitchen" is the prepositional phrase.
9	A	There is not a prepositional phrase in this sentence.
10	C	"Down" is the preposition, and "trail" is the object of the preposition.
11	D	There is no prepositional phrase in the fourth choice.
12	D	There is no prepositional phrase in the fourth choice.

Lesson 7: Complete Sentences

Question No.	Answer	Detailed Explanations
1	A	The first answer choice makes the run-on sentence into a compound sentence by adding a comma and the coordinating conjunction, "but." This is appropriate because both parts of the sentence have a subject and predicate.
2	B	The second choice is correct. This resolves the run-on sentence by creating a compound sentence followed by a second complete sentence with a subject and predicate.
3	C	The third answer choice is correct. All of the other sentences have subjects and predicates, but the third choice is a dependent clause.
4	C	The third answer choice is correct. As is, the sentence doesn't have a verb. The subject is "ways." Adding "There are," gives this sentence a verb and makes it complete.
5	C	The third answer choice is correct. This sentence lacks a subject, most likely "Synthesis."
6	D	The fourth answer choice is correct. The editor noticed that the 2nd "sentence" in the paragraph was actually a dependent clause, not a complete sentence. He solved the problem by combining it with the first sentence.
7	A	The first answer choice is correct. This choice contains two complete sentences that are not joined by a comma and coordinating conjunction.
8	D	The fourth answer choice is correct. It is tempting to say the second sentence is a run-on, but it is one complete sentence with a compound predicate.
9	B	The second choice is correct. "A really great pair of shoes," is the complete subject and, "should be both stylish and comfortable," is the complete predicate.
10	A	The first answer choice is correct. It consists of a dependent clause and an independent clause separated by a comma. Choices B and C are fragments, and Choice D is a run-on sentence.

Lesson 8: Frequently Confused Words

Question No.	Answer	Detailed Explanations
1	A	The first answer choice is correct. "Their" shows ownership.
2	C	The third choice is correct. "There" refers to a place.
3	B	The second answer choice is correct. The contraction, "they're" means "they are."
4	C	The third choice is correct. The word "to" should replace "too" because it is being used as a preposition before "my grandmother's house." "Too" is incorrect because it means "also," which would not make sense in this sentence.
5	C	The third answer choice is correct. The word "were" is a verb that does not make sense in the sentence, but "where" references a place.
6	B	The second choice is correct. The contraction, "we're," means "we are."
7	A	The first answer choice is correct. The word "breathe" is a verb, but "breath" is a noun.
8	D	The fourth answer choice is correct. The word "passed" is the verb meaning he successfully took his test. The word "past" refers to time.
9	B	The second choice is correct. The word "accept" means "to take," while "except" means "to leave out."
10	B	The second choice is correct. The principal is the leader of a school. A principle is a commonly held truth.

Lesson 9: How is it Capitalized?

Question No.	Answer	Detailed Explanations
1	B	Holidays and months should be capitalized. The names of seasons should not.
2.1	A	Titles, initials, and names of people should all be capitalized.
2.2	D	Street names are capitalized.
3	A	Names of cities and abbreviations for states are capitalized.
4	B	The word "semester" is not a proper noun and is not capitalized. Names of school classes that are proper adjectives (related to a proper noun such as a country) are capitalized.
5	B	The first word of a title and all important words in a title are capitalized.
6	C	Titles, people's names, family terms when followed by a person's name, and family terms used as a person's name are all capitalized.
7	C	The first word of a closing of a letter is capitalized. A person's first and last name are capitalized.
8	D	The first word of a sentence is capitalized. Names of rivers and landmarks are capitalized.
9	C	The brand names of products are capitalized.
10	B	People's names should be capitalized.
11	C	Names of places should be capitalized.

Lesson 10: What's the Punctuation?

Question No.	Answer	Detailed Explanations
1	D	The fourth choice is the only sentence that is punctuated correctly.
2	D	Use commas and quotation marks to highlight direct speech.
3	B	Commas are used before the coordinating conjunction in a compound sentence. The comma in the sentence is not needed. It is not a compound sentence because it has only one subject.
4	A	Use commas and other punctuation to highlight direct speech.
5	B	Use quotation marks and a comma to indicate direct speech.
6	A	There are no errors in the sentence. The writer is merely explaining what the teacher asked, not quoting him directly.
7	C	"My best friend's dog" should be separated by commas, because it is an appositive that gives more information. There should be an apostrophe in friend's, because it is showing possession.
8	B	Commas are used correctly with items in a series in this sentence.
9	C	Kobe Bryant should be separated by commas, because it is extra information.
10	B	An exclamation point at the end of the sentence is correct, because the sentence shows strong feeling or emotion.

Lesson 11: Conjunctions and Interjections

Question No.	Answer	Detailed Explanations
1	D	And is the conjunction used in both sentences.
2	B	Nor is the conjunction used to connect the two sentences.
3	B	As soon as is the subordinating conjunction. It introduces the sentence.
4.1	C	And is the coordinating conjunction that connects ideas in the sentence.
4.2	B	Although is the subordinating conjunction that serves as a transition word in the sentence.
5	D	So is the appropriate conjunction, because the sentence expresses a cause/effect relationship.
6.1	A	No is the interjection that expresses excitement or emotion in the sentence.
6.2	D	And is the coordinating conjunction that connects ideas in the sentence.
7	C	Because is the subordinating conjunction. It connects the two simple sentences to form a compound sentence.
8	D	'Wow' is the interjection that expresses excitement or emotion.
9	or	Or is the conjunction that connects the ideas.

Lesson 12: How is it Spelled?

Question No.	Answer	Detailed Explanations
1	D	*Clarify* is the correctly spelled word that best fits the sentence. *Carefully* is also spelled correctly, but it does not make sense in the sentence.
2	B	*Vehicle* is the correct spelling.
3	A	*Pollution* is the correct spelling.
4	C	*Believe* is the correct spelling.
5	D	*Monkeys, strawberries,* and *cherries* are the correct spellings of the other choices.
6	B	*Knives* is the correct spelling for the plural form of knife.
7	A	*Collateral* is the correct spelling.
8	D	*Separately* is the correct spelling.
9	B	*Boxes* is the correct spelling.
10	D	*Narrate* is the correctly spelled word.
11	WILD	Wild is the correctly spelled word.
12	FLOWER	Flower is the correctly spelled word.
13	C	Remain is the correctly spelled word.
14	C	Avenue is the correctly spelled word.

Lesson 13: Word Choice: Attending to Precision

Question No.	Answer	Detailed Explanations
1	B	"Strutted" makes the most sense in the sentence. Although all of the choices are verbs that could describe how a person enters a room, "strutted" emphasizes walking with a sense of pride.
2	B	"Grueling" means extremely tiring and demanding. While the job may be described as "uncomfortable," "grueling" describes the work more emphatically, based the context of the second sentence.
3	C	"Elated" is the most precise word choice. The second sentence gives context indicating that Dante was excited about his award.
4	A	"Gigantic" makes the most sense in this sentence. While "big" could also describe the mess, it is not as expressive. "Gigantic" gives the reader an idea of how big the mess was.
5	B	"Damaging" is the best answer choice because it indicates that this evidence hurt the defendant's case, leading to her conviction.
6	D	"Fireball" makes the most sense in the sentence. A "ham" is someone who likes to entertain people by being funny; a "scrooge" is miserly, and a "shrinking violet" is bashful. A "fireball" is feisty.
7	D	"Clambered" is the most precise word for the sentence. To clamber means to climb, move, or get in or out of something in an awkward or laborious way. This is how a frenzied girl might move through a crowd of people to see the musicians.
8	D	The fourth answer choice is most precise. Waterfalls are more likely to be described as "cascading" than any of the other less precise answer choices.
9	C	"Reduces" is a more precise word to help explain that recycling eliminates some landfill waste.
10	A	"Squealing" is a noise a very excited person might make, and Janet was excited by the news she was sharing.

Lesson 14: Punctuating for Effect!

Question No.	Answer	Detailed Explanations
1	D	The fourth answer choice is correct. In the first choice there aren't any quotation marks to indicate speech; the second choice implies a third person is speaking; and the third choice would need an apostrophe "s" after "Jermaine" (with a lower case "m") in order to be correct.
2	B	The second answer choice is correct. It is the only choice that implies another character is speaking, and it has an exclamation point at the end to indicate excitement or shouting.
3	C	An exclamation point is the correct way to end this sentence. Dante is very excited about his award.
4	D	The fourth answer choice is correct. This is neither a question, nor an exclamatory sentence. The third answer choice is without punctuation.
5	A	The first answer choice is correct. A period is an appropriate end punctuation for a declarative sentence or statement.
6	B	The second choice is correct. An exclamation point is appropriate when punctuating an interjection, which "Sheesh!" is in the second sentence.
7	C	The third choice is correct. The third sentence asks a question.
8	B	The second choice is correct. An exclamation point is appropriate end punctuation for the interjection, "Wow!", which expresses surprise and excitement.
9	C	The third choice is correct. It is incorrect to end a question with an exclamation point. The other answer choices use the exclamation point to imply excitement or add emphasis to the sentence.
10	A	The first choice is correct. The exclamation point implies excitement in the sentence.

Lesson 15: Finding the Meaning

Question No.	Answer	Detailed Explanations
1	B	Extracted means took out. The milk is taken out of the coconut.
2	C	After losing everything in a fire, a person would be really sad and upset. Disheartened means very upset.
3	B	We know that it means comfort, because dad did it after the girl's dog died.
4	D	We know the kittens are in bed against their mother, so it means "snuggled up to."
5	B	"In wide-eyed astonishment" is the clue that lets us know it means astonished, and "stared intensely" most closely matches phrase "gawked at".
6	D	Cease means to stop.
7	B	We know that weary means tired, because the man biked for a very long time.
8	D	We know they rested on the bleachers, so lounged means relaxed.
9	D	He went from the top of the bleachers to the ground, so plummeted means plunged.
10	B	Since the writer is packing cold weather clothes, frigid is defined as freezing.

Lesson 16: Same Word Different Meanings

Question No.	Answer	Detailed Explanations
1	D	Ornaments mean types of jewelry in this sentence.
2	C	A shell is a hard, outer covering.
3	C	The word team gives us a clue of the meaning of batter.
4	A	Salt and sugar are clues to the meaning of the word batter.
5	B	Strawberry is a clue to the meaning of the word jam.
6	A	"Large spoon" and pot are clues to the meaning of the word jam.
7	C	It was something she didn't want to happen to the blender. That helps us figure out the meaning of the word jam.
8	A	"Waste my time" is a clue to the meaning of stand.
9	D	"Hurts my back" is a clue to the word stand.
10	A	Loop means the rope was in a circular position.
11	A	Bank is a place to manage money.

Lesson 17: Context Clues

Question No.	Answer	Detailed Explanations
1	B	"Sentiment," is a view or attitude toward a situation or event, in this case the suffering of Americans during the Great Depression. Roosevelt's view was that the biggest obstacle to progress was fear. The other answer choices do not make sense in the paragraph.
2	B	"Assuage," means "to ease." The words Roosevelt shared in his speech helped to ease people's fear. The second sentence says, "giving them hope." This provides context that assuage is a positive word and that Roosevelt made them feel better, not worse.
3	B	"Affluent" means wealthy or having a lot of money. Context clues are that the food was expensive and patrons had to dress nicely.
4	D	"Patrons" are customers. The context clue is that they had to, "dress nicely in order to eat there." The customers of a restaurant are the people who eat there, unlike the cooks or the waiters. "Doctors" is unrelated to the clues in the paragraph.
5	B	A "miser" is someone who wishes to spend as little money as possible. The definition is included in the sentence.
6	D	"Devoid" means lacking or without. The clue is that, "he does not have any true friends to speak of."
7	D	A "corridor" is a hallway. Context clues describe the corridor as "long" and as having "door after door." Long hallways in hospitals are lined with doors.
8	D	In this paragraph, "earnest" refers to Hazel's state of mind. She was serious about making patients smile.
9	D	"Invest" means to give someone money with the intention of making money. Marcus was expecting Mel and Deena to repay him the ten dollars plus ten percent of each cup that was sold.
10	A	"Reimburse" means to repay. Marcus expected Mel and Deena to repay him the money that he lent them to buy supplies for their lemonade stand. The clue in the text is "plus ten percent of each cup they sell."

Lesson 18: The Meaning of Words

Question No.	Answer	Detailed Explanations
1	B	"Dis-" is a prefix meaning *not or opposite of.*
2	C	"Re-" is a prefix that means *again.*
3	B	"Hemi" is a prefix that means *half*, so *hemisphere* refers to half of the earth.
4	C	The prefix "sub" means *below*
5	B	The prefix "hyper" means *excessive.*
6	C	Adding the suffix -ology (which means "study of")to the root word geo creates the new word geology, which means the study of the earth
7	B	Returned means the same thing as "came back."
8	A	Repay means the same thing as "pay back."
9	C	Quickly is the adverb that modifies the verb grabbed.
10	C	The prefix "re-" means again.
11	Under-stand	Understand is the root word, because it can stand alone.
12	be	"Be-" is a prefix added to the word "wailed."

Lesson 19: For Your Reference

Question No.	Answer	Detailed Explanations
1	A	The first choice is correct. Textbook glossaries contain definitions of key words in the textbook.
2	D	The fourth choice is correct. The "n." at the beginning of the entry tells the reader that the word is a noun.
3	D	There are 2 definitions in the entry for "silently." They are numbered in bold, with the most common definition listed first.
4	B	The second choice is correct. The entry word in a thesaurus is followed by the part of speech and a list of synonyms. Antonyms are also frequently listed after that.
5	D	The fourth choice is correct. The definition appears after the pronunciation.
6	B	The second choice is correct. It is the only word not listed as a synonym.
7	C	The third choice is correct. Because the sitar is a) an instrument, and b) used in India, an international music festival is the most likely place to see one.
8	A	The first choice is correct. It is the only definition not found in the entry above.
9	A	The word "nick" is the only synonym above listed after the "v." The word "Embrasure" is a noun, while "toothed" is an adjective.
10	D	The answer choice D is correct. Each of the three definitions in the answer choices are accurate, "None of the above" would NOT be a definition of slog because all of the choices are real.

Lesson 20: Similes and Metaphors

Question No.	Answer	Detailed Explanations
1	B	The second answer choice is correct. The metaphor compares the sky to an angry monster. They are both purple, the thunder sounds like roaring. The stormy sky is like a monster, it is fierce and threatening.
2	B	The simile describes Mom as being like a rain cloud. Rain clouds are dark and gloomy, which matches Mom's mood.
3	A	Brick walls are strong and do not allow objects to pass through them. By comparing Kevin to a brick wall, he is saying Kevin will block his opponent from scoring a goal.
4	C	The metaphor compares Sasha to a ray of sunshine. Sunshine is considered happy like Sasha because she looked at the bright side of the situation.
5	D	The fourth answer choice is correct. It best explains the meaning of the simile. The other answer choices are not supported by the context in the paragraph.
6	D	Ballerinas are dancers, and swans are birds. The speaker uses the simile to compare their movement, which are graceful and elegant. The word, "gliding," supports this comparison.
7	D	The fourth answer choice is correct. When someone is terrified, their eyes often widen and their hands might tremble. The first answer choice seems to describe someone sad or hopeless, the second is determined and powerful, and the third is peaceful and kind.
8	D	The fourth answer choice is correct. This is the only metaphor that does not describe Alfonso as in-control, steady, or charismatic. Instead it him describes as the captain of a sinking ship.
9	A	The first answer choice is correct. It is the only choice that paints a joyous picture of the reunion between a daughter and her mother.
10	C	The third answer choice is correct. It is the only choice that is a) a metaphor, b) describes the crowd, and c) describes the way a crowd would behave at a festival—a jovial, happy occasion.

Lesson 21: Idiomatic Expressions and Proverbs

Question No.	Answer	Detailed Explanations
1	B	'Hit the ceiling' means to get very angry.
2	C	'Swallow your pride' means to ignore your pride and do something anyway.
3	C	'Walking on air' means really happy.
4	B	'Play it by ear' means figure out things as you go along.
5	D	Like 'a chicken with its head cut off' means running around wildly.
6	A	'Down in the dumps' means really sad and depressed.
7	C	'A little white lie' means a lie that is not meant to hurt anyone.
8	C	'Cut corners' means to take shortcuts.
9	C	'Half a loaf is better than none' means to appreciate what you have instead of wanting more.
10	D	'Beauty is only skin deep' means that true beauty is based on personality.
11	A	"It's raining cats and dogs" means that it is really raining a lot and hard outside.

Lesson 22: Synonyms and Antonyms

Question No.	Answer	Detailed Explanations
1	D	"Miniature" and "minute" are synonyms of "small." Synonyms are words that have the same meaning.
2	B	"Noteworthy" and "important" are synonyms, or words that have the same meaning.
3	A	"Radiant" and "dull" are antonyms, or words that have the opposite.
4	B	"Ecstatic" and "happy" are synonyms, or words that have the same meaning.
5	A	"Repulsive" and "unattractive" are antonyms for "pretty." Antonyms are words that have opposite meanings.
6	C	"Chaos" and "disorder" are synonyms, or words that have the same meaning.
7	C	"Fat" and "thick" are synonyms, or words that mean the same.
8	B	"Peculiar" and "common" are antonyms, or words that have opposite meanings.
9	C	"Recall" and "forget" are antonyms, or words that mean the opposite of each other.
10	A	"Active" and "lazy" are antonyms, or words that mean the opposite of each other.
11	-	Mistake - Error Hurry - Rush Gift - Present
12	Glance, glimpse, look, watch	Synonyms are words which have the same meaning as the given word. Glance, glimpse, look, watch mean the same as Peek. Hence, these are the synonyms. Stare and Ogle mean the opposite which are opposites.

Lesson 23: Academic and Domain Specific 4th Grade Words

Question No.	Answer	Detailed Explanations
1	B	The word "quizzed" makes the most sense in the sentence. It means she questioned him for details about the dance.
2	B	The word "wildlife," meaning plants and animals, is the best choice. None of the other answer choices make sense.
3	C	The word "conservationist," meaning someone who works to preserve wildlife, is the best choice here. The other choices doesn't make sense in the sentence.
4	A	The word "crestfallen," meaning disappointed, is the best choice to describe Sarah's emotion. The other choices do not make sense.
5	D	The word "endangered," meaning in danger of becoming extinct, is the best choice. The other choices do not make sense in the sentence.
6	D	Although "said," "called," and "shrieked," are all verbs that could convey how a person spoke to another person, "whined" emphasizes the best fit in this sentence.
7	C	The word "stammered," meaning stuttered, is the best word for the sentence.
8	D	The word "hypothesis" is the best fit for the sentence. Scientists make hypotheses based on the evidence that they have in order to explain an event.
9	C	The word "critiqued," meaning evaluated or criticized, is the best fit for the sentence. The word "agreed," does not make sense, and the other two choices are not fit to use in an academic context.
10	B	The word "evidence" is the best choice for the sentence. The other words are related to reading but do not make sense in the sentence.

GMAS FAQs

What will GMAS Assessment Look Like?

In many ways, the GMAS assessments will be unlike anything many students have ever seen. The tests will be conducted online, requiring students complete tasks to assess a deeper understanding of the Georgia standards. The students will take the Summative Assessment at the end of the year.

The time for the ELA Summative assessment for each grade is given below:

Estimated Time on Task in Minutes			
Grade	Section 1	Section 2	Section 3
3	80	75	75
4	80	75	75
5	80	75	75
6	80	75	75
7	80	75	75
8	80	75	75

How is this Lumos tedBook aligned to GMAS Guidelines?

The practice tests provided in the Lumos Program were created to reflect the depth and rigor of the GMAS assessments based on the information published by the test administrator. However, the content and format of the GMAS assessment that is officially administered to the students could be different compared to these practice tests. You can get more information about this test by visiting https://www.gadoe.org/Curriculum-Instruction-and-Assessment/Assessment/Pages/EOG-Study-Resource-Guides.aspx

What item types are included in the Online GMAS Test?

Because the assessment is online, the test will consist of a combination of new types of questions:

1. Selected Response or Multiple choice questions
2. Multi select or two part questions
3. Short Constructed response
4. Extended Constructed response
5. Drag and Drop
6. Hot text

For more information on 2022-23 Assessment year, visit
http://www.lumoslearning.com/a/gmas-2022-faqs
OR Scan the **QR Code**

Why Practice with Repeated Reading Passages?

Throughout the Lumos Learning Common Core Practice workbooks, students and educators will notice many passages repeat. This is done intentionally. The goal of these workbooks is to help students practice skills necessary to be successful in class and on standardized tests. One of the most critical components to that success is the ability to read and comprehend passages. To that end, reading fluency must be strengthened. According to Hasbrouck and Tindal (2006), "Helping our students become fluent readers is absolutely critical for proficient and motivated reading" (p. 642). And, Nichols et al. indicate, (2009), "fluency is a gateway to comprehension that enables students to move from being word decoders to passage comprehenders" (p. 11).

Lumos Learning recognizes there is no one-size-fits-all approach to build fluency in readers; however, the repeated reading of passages, where students read the same passages at least two or more times, is one of the most widely recognized strategies to improve fluency (Nichols et al., 2009). Repeated reading allows students the opportunity to read passages with familiar words several times until the passage becomes familiar and they no longer have to decode word by word. As students reread, the decoding barrier falls away allowing for an increase in reading comprehension.

The goal of the Lumos Learning workbooks is to increase student achievement and preparation for any standardized test. Using some passages multiple times in a book offers struggling readers an opportunity to do just that.

References
Hasbrouck, J., and Tindal, G. (2006). Oral reading fluency norms: A valuable assessment tool for reading teachers. Reading Teacher, 59(7), 636644. doi:10.1598/RT.59.7.3. Nichols, W., Rupley, W., and Rasinski, T. (2009). Fluency in learning to read for meaning: going beyond repeated readings. Literacy Research & Instruction, 48(1). doi:10.1080/19388070802161906.

Discover Engaging and Relevant Learning Resources

Lumos EdSearch is a safe search engine specifically designed for teachers and students. Using EdSearch, you can easily find thousands of standards-aligned learning resources such as questions, videos, lessons, worksheets and apps. Teachers can use EdSearch to create custom resource kits to perfectly match their lesson objective and assign them to one or more students in their classroom.

To access the EdSearch tool, use the search box after you log into Lumos StepUp or use the link provided below.

www.lumoslearning.com/a/edsearchb	

The Lumos Standards Coherence map provides information about previous level, next level and related standards. It helps educators and students visually explore learning standards. It's an effective tool to help students progress through the learning objectives. Teachers can use this tool to develop their own pacing charts and lesson plans. Educators can also use the coherence map to get deep insights into why a student is struggling in a specific learning objective.

Teachers can access the Coherence maps after logging into the StepUp Teacher Portal or use the link provided below.

www.lumoslearning.com/a/coherence-map	

Progress Chart

Standard		Lesson	Page No.	Practice		Mastered	Re-practice /Reteach
GMAS	CCSS			Date	Score		
ELAGSE4RL1	RL.4.1	Finding Detail in the Story	10				
ELAGSE4RL1	RL.4.1	Inferring	26				
ELAGSE4RL2	RL.4.2	Finding the Theme	35				
ELAGSE4RL2	RL.4.2	Summarizing the Text	44				
ELAGSE4RL3	RL.4.3	Describing Characters	57				
ELAGSE4RL3	RL.4.3	Describing the Setting	72				
ELAGSE4RL4	RL.4.4	Describing Events	88				
ELAGSE4RL4	RL.4.4	Figurative Language	104				
ELAGSE4RL5	RL.4.5	Text Structure	114				
ELAGSE4RL6	RL.4.6	Point of View	128				
ELAGSE4RL7	RL.4.7	Visual Connections	142				
ELAGSE4RL9	RL.4.9	Comparing and Contrasting	153				
ELAGSE4RI1	RI.4.1	It's All in the Details	191				
ELAGSE4RI2	RI.4.2	The Main Idea	199				
ELAGSE4RI3	RI.4.3	Using Details to Explain the Text	205				
ELAGSE4RI4	RI.4.4	What Does it Mean?	211				
ELAGSE4RI5	RI.4.5	How is it Written?	217				
ELAGSE4RI6	RI.4.6	Comparing Different Versions of the Same Event	223				
ELAGSE4RI7	RI.4.7	Using Text Features to Gather Information	231				
ELAGSE4RI8	RI.4.8	Finding the Evidence	241				
ELAGSE4RI9	RI.4.9	Integrating Information	248				

Standard		Lesson	Page No.	Practice		Mastered	Re-practice /Reteach
GMAS	CCSS			Date	Score		
ELAGSE4L1a	L.4.1.A	Pronouns	267				
ELAGSE4L1b	L.4.1.B	Progressive Verb Tense	271				
N/A	L.4.1.B	What's the Verb?	275				
ELAGSE4L1c	L.4.1.C	Modal Auxiliary Verbs	279				
ELAGSE4L1d	L.4.1.D	Adjectives and Adverbs	283				
ELAGSE4L1e	L.4.1.E	Prepositional Phrases	287				
ELAGSE4L1f	L.4.1.F	Complete Sentences	291				
ELAGSE4L1g	L.4.1.G	Frequently Confused Words	295				
ELAGSE4L2a	L.4.2.A	How is it Capitalized?	299				
ELAGSE4L2b/c	L.4.2.B/C	What's the Punctuation?	304				
N/A	L.4.2.C	Conjunctions and Interjections	307				
ELAGSE4L2d	L.4.2.D	How is it Spelled?	311				
ELAGSE4L3a	L.4.3.A	Word Choice: Attending to Precision	315				
ELAGSE4L3b	L.4.3.B	Punctuating for Effect!	319				
ELAGSE4L3c	L.4.3.C	Finding the Meaning	322				
N/A	L.4.4	Same Word Different Meanings	326				
ELAGSE4L4.a	L.4.4.A	Context Clues	330				
ELAGSE4L4.b	L.4.4.B	The Meaning of Words	334				
ELAGSE4L4.c	L.4.4.C	For Your Reference	338				
ELAGSE4L5.a	L.4.5.A	Similes and Metaphors	343				
ELAGSE4L5.b	L.4.5.B	Idiomatic Expressions and Proverbs	347				
ELAGSE4L5.c	L.4.5.C	Synonyms and Antonyms	351				
N/A	L.4.6	Academic and Domain Specific 4th Grade Words	355				

Lumos Learning
Developed by Expert Teachers

Grade 4

GEORGIA
Math
GMAS Practice

Updated for 2022-23

ONLINE

2 GMAS Practice Tests

7 Question Types

COVERS 30+ SKILLS

Available

• At Leading book stores

• Online www.LumosLearning.com